Y0-CDG-372

GOVERNORS STATE UNIVERSITY LIBRARY
3 1611 00240 7168

PANTOMIMES
For Stage and Study

BY

T. EARL PARDOE

Published By
BENJAMIN BLOM, INC.

First published New York, 1931
Reissued 1971 by
Benjamin Blom, Inc.
New York, N.Y. 10025

Library of Congress
Catalog Card Number 73-173118

Printed in the
United States of America

Dedicated to the memory of

LELAND T. POWERS

and

ROBERT B. MANTELL

ACTORS, TEACHERS, FRIENDS

and

ANNIE ADAMS KISKADDEN

WHO ENTRUSTED HER LAST DRAMATIC EFFORTS TO MY DIRECTION AND GAVE ME THE FIRST SUGGESTION FOR WRITING THIS BOOK.

PREFACE

THIS book has been written in response to the requests of many students and friends, both on and off the stage, and for the joy of recording some thoughts in defense of a noble art.

Pantomime, as a great art, is disappearing from the stage, in America and abroad. The indifference to carriage and action is one of the chief reasons for the decline of great acting. The application of "naturalness" has produced a slovenly personal appearance, and "realism" is usually the product of much ignorance and greater conceit.

Good acting is an intelligent application of natural laws over a period of many years, until technic is unconscious and emotion responds to control. It is presenting life in terms of art.

All great artists know and understand their media of workmanship. The dramatic artist of to-day knows least, of all the artists, about the materials of his art. The body, the voice, the words, with the stage, constitute the most animate of all art agencies. And the body is studied least, though it is the most complex. It is with this agent of expression that this book is primarily concerned.

Pantomime, for decades, had one synonym, Pierrot. All honor to Pierrot, Pierrette, Columbine, the Doctor, Pantaloon and their many friends! They have served their many and merry purposes, but now pantomime has come to mean more than buffoonery and clowning, or even disappointed love. It concerns the every action of the body which reveals a thought or gesture sequence in depicting the mind and its responses. Out of profound respect to Pierrot and his band of cohorts, there are no pantomimes in this volume which tell of his or their ambitions and antics. The great body of selections presented deal with modern life and its complexities.

The teaching of dramatic art has chiefly been done by "emotional" dictatorship. This is the main reason for many or most of the actor-students failing when applying for work in the professional groups. One cannot be taught to feel; one cannot be taught emotion. The form of emotion is teachable; the awareness of emotion must ever remain personal. Therein lies the province of the technic of the language of the body. A director is saved many hours in preparation for the final production if the actors can give form to their feelings so that the audience properly responds to the desired effect. This cannot be done merely by thinking. Acting is practiced action to portray the thoughts and emotions of a character from the stage of life.

I am indebted to Dr. F. S. Harris, Maude Scheerer, Mrs. A. Star Best, Mrs. Carol Hoyt Powers, Mary Woolley, Sue Anne Wilson and Jayne Hibbert Crawley for their advice and help. Mrs. Crawley supplied the last ten pantomimes in the General Pantomime chapter. Without the help, criticism, and patience of my wife, Kathryn, this book would not have reached completion. The librarians of Columbia University, Brigham Young University, Santa Monica, Glendale and Los Angeles have supplied invaluable aid and coöperation.

T. E. P.

Rossmoyne,
Glendale, California.

CONTENTS

CHAPTER I

ART AND THE HUMAN BODY

KNOWLEDGE of consciousness may come to an individual in many ways. The average person is aware of body and self only in terms of pleasure and pain, joy and sorrow. He seldom recognizes the real joy of body powers and abilities until he gets a situation that makes him tired or one that unduly exhilarates him. The process of becoming aware is one of the great phenomena of life. A babe will watch his fingers and toes by the hour, and all movements seem to create a new interest in their very animation. But just when it comes to the child that he has a finger and toe and that they are integral parts of him is an entirely different matter. He accepts his finger or toe until a sliver or blister calls attention to a condition which is not normal—normal in the sense of his previous indifference or awareness. Such a condition causes him to investigate and note the cause of the disturbance or consciousness. A child will usually run to his mother and ask to have the sliver removed. It is some time in life before he asks why the sliver is a menace, and why the blood flows from the wound, and what illness means. And in adulthood he is quite as satisfied with a superficial answer.

This consciousness of body power and health, this awareness of certain rules of conduct for greater freedom and adaptability is only now becoming a part of race education. For centuries, asking questions about the human body was considered a sacrilege. Thinking of body in terms of beauty and grace made the Grecian civilization of the golden days a conspicuous page in life's history. Interested inquiry into human conduct and resultant relationships is again in the ascendant and modern times are asking more of this knowledge of consciousness than at any time in man's existence. The Grecians knew the joy of rhythmic poise and action and made religion fit their concepts of this idealization.

When Christianity was introduced, the attention was fixed more upon the unseen and the moral issues of man's life and the human body was generally accepted as an agent of corruption and mystery. The few men who dared to state that the human body was divine until corrupted by civilization or ignorance are recorded in history for their radical ideas and atheistic points of view. Revolutionary were the findings of Harvey, and even more revolutionary were the principles of Rousseau. The Puritans forbade expression of certain natural responses in the grimness of their religious devotions. Their joyous, exuberant selves were inhibited and childish prattling was soon calmed to demure reserve, or cautious restraint. No national group had become aware that the mental and the physical man were capable of separate study and that each should harmonize in all its powers better to strengthen the worth and value of the other.

It was not until the middle of the nineteenth century that inquisitive man, the scientist, turned his attention to the mental man. Why should we accept mental activities with no knowledge of their sources, causes, and manipulations? Are race habits reflected in the individual? Is there such a thing as a diseased mind and a healthy body? Could the body act without a conscious knowledge of the mental self? What is the significance of the nervous system? To what extent is walking a conscious process when a person is carrying on an animated conversation? Does the vicious mind reflect itself upon the visage of the individual? Could a wicked thought live long in a mind without it being shown on the countenance? Do trade habits and responses reveal themselves in a general conduct of that particular group? Are different types of language due to different types of thinking? Is awkwardness of movement a physical response solely? Or does awkwardness reveal anything mental? How closely connected are the movements of the body with the processes of thinking and awareness? At what age does man start to lose childish naturalness and adopt codes of civilization and moral conduct? Does the body affect the mind as much as the mind affects the body?

In short, this modern period of study and application of the knowledge of relationships between the mind and the body has given man new powers in all art endeavors. Tools are but extended fingers and greater artistry is being born of these scientific understandings. Such arts which use the human body itself, are considerably strengthened by this new knowledge of mind and body interdependence. An artist must be conscious of the materials of his art. He cannot use materials without a working knowledge of their textures and relationships. The sculptor knows the grain of his marble; he is not concerned alone with the exterior of his statue. *Awareness is the chief motivation of art.*

It is not the purpose of this chapter to deal with all of the questions asked in the preceding paragraph, but we are concerned with such phases of art as deal with the human body as an expressive agent. Some of the questions must be dealt with before we can mutually understand any proposition for development. Before we discuss the materials of dramatic art, and pantomimic art in particular, it is necessary to define art.

Art, in its simplest terms, is the handiwork of man. Anything made by man is art. This definition is a good one, in that it clearly separates nature from art. A tree is, of course, a product of nature. But when I see a desk, a floor, a chair, or some paper, I see one of the many uses to which the tree has been put by the handiwork of man. It is by reshaping or differently using this material of nature that man expresses himself in terms of art. Art is man's expression; it is proof of the progress and adaptability of his awareness.

When man first took the piece of fallen tree and made a very crude seat out of it, by merely adjusting its shape for his use, he fulfilled the development of an idea. He was tired with the day's walk and looked about for some place to rest; he did not care to lie down, so he used this convenient piece of tree and sat down. He did not say he was sitting, at first, but it soon became necessary to use a symbol of thought that would express his desire to rest in this manner. When he moved camp, it occurred to him that that particular piece of wood or tree would be a convenient article for his further comfort. It became a part of his household belongings. When he first told his son to get his piece of tree, he had difficulty in making himself clear, as the adopted furniture was not in sight and the word-symbol, tree, was not explicit enough for the young boy to understand just what his father meant. So the two went to the desired object and the father pointed out to the son just what he meant.

Pantomime was first used in such designation, but the time came when the father could not go to the immediate proximity of the new household luxury, so he grunted a particular sound, different from any the son had ever heard, and, in the course of time, that sound became the word symbol designating what we now call, in English, a chair or stool.

In just such a manner, but far more intricate and laborious than this telling, the use of sounds came into existence to express human thoughts. Articles not near were designated by particular sounds of identification. The word-symbol, chair, when said in general sense today, may mean one of hundreds of designs or plans, as experience warrants. But there was a time when chair meant but one thing in a very definite sense.

Primitive man was very simple and frugal in his desires

and in his expressions. The significant point I wish to make here is that art is the embodiment of thought, in whatever manner it may be expressed. Whether we see chair as a word, a painting, a photograph, or an actuality, we think in terms of what it means to our consciousness. And the universality of such thinking would be that this expression meant an article for a certain kind of rest or bodily comfort. The object made by man out of the material of nature conveys definite thought relations to all other objects in man's domain. The thing made is art; not the thing conceived or planned or wanted. Art does not exist merely in the realm of thinking, it must be an actuality in physical material. It exists to express the embodiment of man's ideas or thoughts, and by that we recognize it as art.

So many people conceive of art only in terms of beauty. They are thinking of fine art. To clarify this situation, it is helpful for us to think of fine art as that art which is dominated by a sense or consciousness of beauty, cultural or æsthetic.

The practical art is one in which utility dominates. This phase is better understood because of its direct association with general livelihood and existence. A fine art may be practical just as the practical art is very often fine. Architecture is a good example of this duality of purpose. This art may, or may not, be a fine art. America is gradually awakening to the fact that architecture may be a fine art as well as one of utility merely. The automobile industry is now recognizing this duality of purpose, and the ugly lines of the car of a few years ago have been displaced by lines of beauty and individuality.

Utility and beauty are aiding each other. The fine arts are such arts as painting, music, sculpture, literature, drama, etching, embroidery, landscape gardening, etc., and the practical arts are such as blacksmithing, masonry, carpentry, mining, glazing, cooking, etc. It needs no further statement here to conclude that any art is the greater when it has served mankind in this dual purpose, beauty and utility, though I grant that I have met some who would deny the existence of beauty as of any benefit to man. For them, this book is not intended. Sometimes it would be difficult to determine when an object of art is more for utility than for æsthetic purposes. I am thinking now of the little rag doll that my baby girl cherished for nearly four years. Though we gave her other dolls, some of them beautiful, she gave her greatest affection to the little doll made of a white rag with eyes sewed in the rounded head. But there came a transition. A particular friend remarked that the doll with curls was the prettier. No longer would the rag doll suffice; her main interest now went to the most beautiful of her dolls. This became her home-doll as well as her company-doll. Our little girl had responded to a universal situation in art.

Appreciation of beauty comes with a growth of intelligence and a sense of the fitness of environments. A beginning of any new era in civilization has always dominated in utilitarian arts. As the complexities of racial development are augmented, the greater becomes the capacity for beauty as a part of national consciousness. Egypt, Greece, and Italy have all written chapters in this great "artologue." Nor do I defend the thesis of beauty being life's paramount issue, any more than I do that utility is the sum total of man's existence. I am concerned in the fact that art is the embodiment of thought and that civilizations are best reflected in their arts.

Another observation should be made at this point. Art is good art in proportion as *thought* dominates, and art is bad art in proportion as *material* dominates. I ask you to look at the picture on my wall. If the first and last impression of that picture were that it is nothing but a blotch of paint on canvas, then that would indeed be a very bad piece of art. The materials of which it was made dominated. But if you told me that it was a wonderful picture of a California mission or an Italian villa, then the thought of the artist would have been revealed to you without the intrusion of the materialistic in the picture. The paint did not exist to your mind in the appreciation of the thought depicted or embodied. If the material of any art is conspicuous and calls attention to itself, that art is, in just that proportion, bad art.

Any mannerisms of an actor which are not a part of the character revealed mitigate the real artistry of the selection or interpretation. The questions, of what is it made? or, how is it done? are vastly different propositions from what does it mean? We are interested chiefly in art for the thought it reveals, whether it be for utility or beauty. The manner in which art appeals to intelligence is another important proposition for our better understanding.

We have stated that the material of art is the material of nature. The carpenter uses wood, nails, glue, and other materials of nature; painting is the result of the application of oils from coal products and vegetable matters placed with brushes upon cloth fiber—all natural products; music is harmonic vibrations of the air in varying pitch as recorded by the ear; sculpture is form in marble or clay; all arts are the expression of thoughts in physical materials. To understand an art best, one must comprehend something of the nature of its component parts and relationships, and to what avenue of perception the respective parts appeal.

Painting appeals to our consciousness primarily through the eye. We are not concerned with the feeling of the paint, nor can we hear any vibratory rate from the different pigments. Paintings, sculptures, etchings, landscape gardens, cinemas, the printed page, all appeal to intelligence through the eye. But music appeals to our intelligence through the ear. The very difference of the materials of these arts are the chief causes for their being classed as different arts. Perfumery is one of the oldest arts of which we have record. And it appeals only to the olfactory sense for its significance. We do not see or hear perfume in art values; the person who cannot smell has little need for perfume. And when we think of some of the fine arts we realize they are important to us only in close proximity. Perfume in a dance hall several rods away has no value to the people in the restaurant as they watch the distant dancers. Music floats to us across the lake. But you can *see* the capitol building several miles in the distance. Seeing covers miles for us when the light conditions are favorable. Hearing takes in an expanding circular area, not so great in distance as sight. Sight comes to man in straight lines (this statement is true for our purpose), and hearing covers a circular area without regard to the retina and time of day. Smell is limited to a smaller area without sight or hearing. But the tactual sense and tasting are very personal senses. They act only in the immediate propinquity of the object affecting such senses. We must actually associate with articles to appreciate their temperature; just as certain kinds of cheese cannot be felt or smelt to approximate their real worth to some connoisseurs.

The associative values of these sense impressions are very important. It is difficult for the psychologist to state accurately whether a picture painted with consummate skill can make a greater effect upon an individual than a soothing melody or a comfortable chair. The differences in individual tastes, education, desires, and environment are so complex. One man would rather part with a great painting from his wall than give up his favorite chair; while for others, this would not be true.

There are some people who enjoy a banquet of the senses when they see a steak cooking. They hear the sizzling, which has become a well-defined sound to the consciousness; they see the succulent meat primed with all the necessary seasoning and proper cooking; they smell the aroma of delicious savor; the fork proves the tenderness of the desired article of delectation; and the consummate test of all the prophecies of hearing, seeing, smelling, and feeling is proved in the ultimate taste. A rhapsody of personal enjoyment! But what a different effect when the grandfather appears—he sees the steak and walks away with one major impression, dyspepsia.

The actual value of associate senses is, indeed, a difficult equation to decipher. We are quite certain that some positive conclusions are possible. An object seen, heard, and felt is more a part of our consciousness or awareness than if the article had been only seen or heard. There seems to have been a duality of association in our very creation. Sight and hearing have such definite relations in so many walks of life, as do touch, smell and taste.

We are not here concerned whether taste is a form of smell, or how many other senses we possess in the wholeness of man's system. The five senses suffice for our observations. Still life soon adjusts itself to our consciousness; it makes its appeal to awareness through sight. And the greater number of impressions throughout life come to consciousness through the eye, in a normal person. The art of reading has greatly swung the balance of knowledge-getting to the eye, almost to a preponderance of importance. But it is significant in animated life that we like to hear what we see and we wish to see what we hear. Boys will go blocks to see the band that they hear. A whirring airplane will call for a searching process with the eye. A crack of a bush will quickly call the eye of the hunter to the approximate place of location. Even though we hear a voice over the radio, there is a universal tendency to associate a face with it.

It is this association of the two major art-senses that has caused some of our greatest inventors to work on pictures that will talk; it is this relationship that compels the moving-picture houses to accompany all their pictures with music, music as appropriate as possible. And now, special music is being arranged for all the better films. It is possible to state with a certain degree of accuracy that an harmonious appeal to the intelligence through more than one of the senses simultaneously produces a greater effect than when the intelligence is made aware in only one sense. It is better to see and hear than merely to see or hear. And this is an important observation when we come to the study of dramatic art and pantomime.

Man consciously endeavors to satisfy his curiosity and knowledge by more than one appeal to the senses and tries to obtain information simultaneously through several channels. He communicates with his fellow beings primarily in two major ways, movements of the body (gesture) and speech. Speech is a twofold operation, involving tone and words.

We may state simply, that *the material of dramatic art is the body, the voice, and words.*[1] The study of these three materials brings out some very interesting data and calls for considerable thought on the part of the student. It is obvious that the language of the body, gesture, reaches the intelligence of the audience through the eye; that the language of tone reaches the intelligence of the audience through the ear, as does the language of words, when spoken. The question which confronts us is, which of the three materials used in man's expression has the greater importance and which is the first to develop? Also, is it possible for one of the languages to detract or annul the purpose of the other? And this is further provocative of the question, which is the more important to man, sight or sound? Some of these can be answered sufficiently to our purpose.

Of the three languages used by man in his conversational and stage deportment I am not going to conclude that one has more importance than the other, but I shall make certain deductions which can be used by each student as his own judgment warrants. All three are very necessary for the full strength of man's expressive powers. Pantomime is useless in the dark and voice in the dark can-

[1] We are not concerned with *stage* or *platform* at this point.

not long be used to create any lasting impression. Such a play as Kennedy's "The Terrible Meek" is an experiment of that type. Excellent in itself and a good play to read from the book, but never popular in production. Certain crook plays have utilized a suspensive darkness to good effect, but you will observe that the producer has always accompanied this darkness with almost a vocal silence.

Underlighting has killed many a play, as has underspeaking. Words are absolutely necessary to convey thoughts which have distant cognition. We cannot speak of London when in New York except in terms of words. For the purely personal, sight and tone suffice, but for the distant, words are paramount. So let us conclude that all three languages are important to man and all have their respective strengths. But when we use all three simultaneously, then we have raised another question.

This fact we must note from the beginning, that pantomime and tone languages are inherent, and words are invented. The first two are instinctive and early develop, but the language of words is acquired and is learned from adults. Words are made and the vocabulary is changing with the times, while the responses to sight in body movement and to the ear in tonal evaluations, have remained constant, as far as history reveals. The language of the body is the most universal and the language of tone is next in universality. These two statements could be augmented considerably, but each student may carry on his own investigation as the subject best interests him. We read in Genesis of a confusion of tongues at a time when the people were reported to have spoken but one language. The common origin of language has long interested the world's scholars and still holds stimulating attention. The origin of language is not as important to us in this study as the relation of the languages used by man in their mutual development.

Darwin was one of the first in modern times to be impressed with the universality of pantomimic response. It was his observations of the emotional responses of animals and man which later led to his more famous studies. He noted that the muscular responses in many animals and in man throughout the world are similar when expressing the more primitive emotions.

Fear, anger, and enjoyment are shown by universal similarities of response in the facial muscles. They often vary in minor details, but always agree in the general. A Frenchman, a Chinaman, a New Zealander, an Eskimo, an American, all respond to fear in a similar manner. One need not leave America to make a very exhaustive study on this matter. To visit the various districts of New York, Boston, Philadelphia, or San Francisco one can easily observe how the different nationalities respond to certain emotional conditions.

Laughter is a universal response and the same general facial activities dominate. Let us refer to an incident which occurred on Fifth Avenue near the Metropolitan Museum: a very portly gentleman, dressed in excellent attire of latest and most fashionable cut, slipped upon the icy pavement and sat bumptiously upon his plug hat. His discomfiture and embarrassment caused all who saw to smile broadly and many to laugh heartily. The look upon his face when he discovered that he had mashed his own headgear was indeed a forlorn expression. Italian workmen, coming through the park, enjoyed the situation; two French girls laughed politely; three Mexican fellows laughed loudly at first, then went to the discomfited dandy and proffered aid. When such assistance was most promptly and forcibly refused, a medley of languages and laughter greeted the now retreating figure. There was a marked sameness in facial expression, but the tones of the laughing and the words spoken differed with the individualities and their responses to the ludicrous situation.

Pantomime is universally understood; tone is understood or approximated in all the simpler situations, but words must be native or acquired by study. At a ball game in Philadelphia, we have no difficulty in understanding the pantomime of the bleachers, but we cannot comprehend all the conversation which is indulged in within hearing. In Milwaukee, a German mother may scold her young boy as he enters the delicatessen; the words may be unintelligible to some of the customers, but they understand the pantomime and most of the tones.

The world over, one may understand the language of the body. Pantomime is more universal than music. It takes a long while for the American ear to appreciate oriental music. The oriental scales are built on quarter tones while the occident builds its music with the Greek tetrachord in half tone intervals. The oriental ear is trained to a more fine and subtle degree than is the occidental. Strange intervals are heard in our Indian music. While the common ejaculations of sound to the response of the simpler emotions are universal, the music of the world is not yet so catholic. The radio and phonograph are aiding in this and the interchanges of entertainment have broken the barriers of indifference. Rhythm, being the basic factor of all expression, belongs to gesture as well as music.

Many observations aid us to determine that pantomime is the first language to be used by the race, as well as by the individual. A babe starts using words when he is about a year old. In the life of the babe, we discover gesture response almost immediately, tone responses somewhat later, and ability to use words delayed to about the year mark. Some gestures and tones are also delayed in response, such as those which develop in adolescence and patriotism.

The individual but reflects race history in his own life. Just as pantomime is conceded to be the first language in the life of a tribe or race (discussion to follow in subsequent chapter), so pantomime is the first language used by the babe. It is the first means of communication used by the babe and the last to be used by man in the parting moments of death.

Man's ability to recognize in others what they express in pantomime, does not always carry over into his own life as a personal power. When a man reaches maturity, he has often lost the ability to portray consciously by pantomime what he did so easily and unconsciously, as a child. And acting and speaking are conscious arts. A man cannot always show just what he means and what he feels. If he could, there would be no necessity for study in any speech art. We ask a man to sing, and he replies that he cannot, since he has not studied. Ask him to act, and he immediately accepts the flattering word. Yes, he can act, though it has not occurred to him that he has not studied. Because he has used his voice all his life should be ample warrant that he could sing, if the use of his body has given him the assumption that he can act.

Can one language of the speech arts detract from or annul the potency of another? This is one of the most important phases of our discussion. And it is the least understood by the average student of dramatic art. What truth is there in the old saying, "Action speaks louder than words"? Or in the other, "Seeing is believing"? Can one ignore the fact that intense emotions often inhibit and choke speech while they intensify expression with the body? "I was so mad I couldn't say a word" or "My sorrow choked me." Gesture, tone, and words should perfectly harmonize in the expression of the thought.

Which is the more important, what one sees or what one hears? Which is the more universally believed? Which carries the greater degree of meaning intended? The great majority will accept the verdict of their eyes in preference to their ears, when these two language receivers get conflicting messages. Gesture is dominant over tone. So tone is dominant over words, when a choice of meaning is necessary.

A few demonstrations usually convince the observing

student that the action of the body is given precedence over the other two departments of expression. For a familiar example: a crowd of girls were in the lobby of a dance hall, when an unwelcome relative of one of them called out from the check room, "Hello, dearie, may we join you?" The cousin turned away and with a look of utter disgust answered, "Why, sure, glad to have you." What was the verdict of the girls who had seen the gesture? The entire body said a positive unwelcome, but the tones of the voice and the words conveyed different ideas to the visitor.

You may know of a woman who believes in but one helping of any course served at dinner. Such a woman was serving and some very particular friends had been invited. Johnny, her son, seated next to his mother, asked if he might have another piece of chicken. The smiling hostess answered in her sweetest tones, "Yes, darling," and reached her foot under the table and gave him a vicious dig in the shin. To her embarrassment, and to the surprise of the company, the visiting cousin yelled out a healthy "Ouch!" The visitor's leg had crossed the son's and had received the full penalty of the aunt's indignation. The hostess had to explain that her foot had got caught as she was about to rise. Two boys understood and knew that the language of the body was more eloquent than words, and all knew that words did not convey the exact meaning of the occasion.

Numerous examples of unconscious efforts, when bodily action denies the intention of the speaker, are observed daily. A fiery orator was laying down the law in his most emphatic manner, saying, "We want these things, and we are going to have these things." All the time his head was shaking in a most negative manner, which any child would interpret as being negative—a horizontal movement of the head. His audience heard him say "yes," but they saw him say "no." Why were they unconvinced?

A fisherman sat on a river bank, very quiet, awaiting

the expected bite. An unseen couple passed by on the nearby roadside. The man said to his lady companion, "Of course I love you. Like hell." The lady replied, "And that's the way I love you." Both voices snarled out their retorts, bitter and sharp. But when they appeared at the river bend, the fisherman saw that the lady was crying and that the man looked as one doomed. Each gave the lie to the words the fisherman had heard. Each waiting the first chance to tell the other that life would be impossible without the other. And the fisherman knew that he had often spoken what he didn't mean.

Flattery is a very common tone and word contradiction. It is possible only because of this conflict.

Bodily disease has often left voice habits that do not justly represent the owner. The corner grocer came to the minister and asked him what was the matter with him, why people did not like him as they should. The minister was a real friend and told him exactly what he thought, telling him that his voice was one of a grouch, unpleasant, as if he were displeased with everything. The grocer thanked him for his opinion and stated that he did not believe the minister, as he loved people. When the pastor imitated his voice and said it was often worse than that, the merchant left with niggardly thanks. When the merchant asked his wife the same question and received the same reply that the minister had given him, his first impulse was to blame her for not telling him long ago. She had, but that was when he was sick, and he didn't care to know then and he had reproached her for telling him. As the grocer reflected upon his life, he remembered that his wife had cautioned him about his acquired, gruff manner. He now realized that the tone of his voice made politeness seem an impossibility to him. He had learned that he could mean one thing and have his friends think another, that his expressive self was a complex organism needing unity.

A look of love, a tone of love, and a word of love.

There can be no question of meaning. A look of love, a tone of doubt, and a word of uncertainty, can never convince. Great artistry depends on harmony of all agents. An awkward foot can undo much of the beauty of tone. An improper inflection can annul the meaning of the thought. Just as the great violinist works for dexterity of body and hand movements, proper position of violin and bow, an exhaustive study of musical notation and nomenclature, so the dramatic artist must work for the fluent movement of a trained body, the resonant beauty of a flexible voice, and the correct knowledge of the use of words. The most neglected of these three agents is the proper use of the various agents of the body to express one harmonious thought. Walking does not mean that a person is conscious of all the possible expression to be obtained from the feet, nor does writing with a pencil mean that a student knows all the power of expression which can be obtained from the graceful hand.

Pantomime was the first phase of dramatic art to be developed and is still the greatest agent of expression for the stronger emotional responses. It is imperative that an artist of dramatic technic must know the language of the body with all its subtle changes, and have the ability to depict consciously any emotion which is demanded in the art.

A comparison of light and sound will not be amiss at this point. We are not concerned here with the activity of the retina and its rod and conic sensibilities, nor the cochlea with its circular tonal shell, but we are very much interested in knowing some of the effects of light upon our consciousness as a whole, and the impressions of sound with similar awareness. We must keep in mind that movement of the body reaches the consciousness of the audience through the means of sight, and that voice gets to consciousness through the ear.

What are some of the chief characteristics of light and sound? To say that the retina is more sensitive than the cochlea would be stating only a partial truth. For our discussion, this is irrelevant. All observations bear out the statement that what we see is as important as that which we hear, and that the language of the body affects the consciousness of the audience equally as much as does the language of tone or words. All dramatic aspirants should keep these facts in mind. Indifference to body technic has been the greatest barrier to histrionic success. The science of language relations demands a careful attention to graceful, unconscious movement as it does to careful, melodious voice. The audience is very observant of unharmonious body technic though it cannot always explain its observations or reasons for such criticism. I recall how Paris acclaimed Mary Garden in "Resurrection." Her voice was not superior, but her acting was superb. George Arliss does not have a beautiful voice, but he is one of the most popular actors of to-day, and deservedly so. His pantomimic powers raised his "Old English" to a classic.

There are but few auditoriums where the difference in rate of speed between light and sound could make much difference. It is to be noted, however, that sound travels at the rate of 11,000 feet per second and light travels approximately at 186,400 miles per second, and the sensitiveness of the receiving agents in the ear and eye are somewhat related to this ratio. In a given space of time the eye has the ability to receive more definite impressions than the ear. The exact ratio is inconsequent here. A simple experiment will prove what is meant. Take a deck of cards and run the thumb over the pack. Try seeing and counting the number of cards as they pass from the major deck. In a second's time you may be able to count as many as twenty before the movement becomes a blur; and in doing this, you cannot form words for counting. Go to the piano and strike different keys as many times as possible, to test the ear for its differentiating powers. You will be able to detect cards over the number of tones on a basis of about three to one. You must have this done for you so as to be the audience. Otherwise the element of touch would materially enter into your determining results. This is a very crude experiment, but it suffices to arouse interest in those who further question whether the eye receives more thought impressions in a given space of time than does the ear.

In distance, we know that time elements are very important. We see the steam of the engine several seconds before we hear the whistle. By the time we have heard the whistle of the train ten miles away, we have seen the white steam which caused the whistle, we note the smoke from the engine to be very black, that the train is a long one of passenger cars, that the sky is bluer over the train than near us, and that people are waiting at the flag station three miles away—all this while the sound of the train is getting to us.

The number of visual images which you receive in a given length of time and the number of auditory images you receive in the same length of time are problems which the psychologists have worked out quite definitely, and their results corroborate our practical experience. Vision gives the most accurate information concerning the lateral extension of objects, and is the only distance sense that gives more than a rough approximation of distance in the third dimension. The extension of the eye with scientific instruments is far more advanced than is possible with any other sense. The telescope brings thousands of stars into our direct vision and knowledge and the microscope reveals worlds of microbes that exist for no other means of discernment, and makes the classifications of biology possible.

Another fact we must not overlook: the moving picture industry has appealed to millions, while the phonograph has appealed proportionately to but thousands. Millions have heard of Charlie Chaplin, the world over, while in comparison the glorious Caruso is known to but few countries. You pay for picture show privileges, while the phonograph interests spend thousands of dollars in gratuitous concerts. We can further agree that it isn't the chorus girls' singing which fills the theater. A lyric tenor will attract select audiences during a limited season, while a pulchritudinous chorus will fill a Follies house during the summer months.

How far will the talkie supplant the picture? It is one of our most natural desires to hear what we see and see what we hear. For a while there will be a tendency for the motion picture producers who have been converted to sound, to overdo the speech and dialogue part of the film industry. This will be of short duration, and already (the talkies are not yet universally used in the United States) there is a trend toward emphasizing the action of the film rather than the dialogue and voice. The novelty of recorded voice will soon wear off and action will again dominate drama of the film as it always has for the legitimate. Words convey thought of things distant better than action, but action and emotional response best reveal thoughts as affecting present environment and personal relations. Words can tell us what one saw in London, but actions best show what one feels and thinks now and here.

In concluding this brief discussion of the body and its relation to art, let me recapitulate some of the major paragraphs. Art is the embodiment of thought, and it is the thought so embodied that holds our interest in that art. Art is good art in proportion as thought dominates, and bad art in proportion as the materials of which it is made dominate. We recognize the classification of art in two chief divisions, fine and practical. The material of art is the material of nature, and, of necessity, the laws of art must therefore be the laws of nature. Each art has its respective laws of nature which govern its conduct and product. Art makes its appeal to consciousness through the five major senses; and dramatic art affects the eye and the ear through movements of the body, tone, and words (the stage being impersonal). These appeals must perfectly harmonize to produce lasting impressions and meritorious art. If there be any conflict of these three expressive agents, the pantomimic language will usually influence the audience more than tone or words. Pantomime is the most universal of all languages, and, by nature, is strongest when accompanied by appropriate tone. Gesture and tone are inherited or instinctive, and words are the invented product of the environment.

The musician depends upon his violin, piano, or trumpet; the sculptor must have his marble or clay; the painter his canvas and paints; the mason his stone and brick; but the dramatic artist reveals his thought by the power of the materials with which he was born. Godlike, with his own body and voice, he creates his art in all its strength. Man, the creator of art with the materials of nature, has his greatest art in the possession of his own body and its ability to reveal the divinity of his mind.

BODILY EXERCISES

This volume concerns itself chiefly with dramatic action, development of imagination, and control of expressive agencies. Emphasis has been almost exclusively placed upon the language of the body, rather than upon tone and words. Health, vigor, vitality, bodily control, and poise are essential requisites. The exercises following are helpful in obtaining these essentials, but must be done with an intellectual interest.

The great actor possesses imagination, health, bodily control, and poise. These are requisites for any one who would long enjoy the plaudits and admiration of the public, be he speaker, singer, dancer, or actor.

In the study of great national movements of body culture and power, we first turn to the golden days of glorious Greece. Always, the gymnasium of Greece meant more than physical exercise. Special buildings were early provided by the state and the physical and moral conduct of the youths was entrusted to special "Gymnastæ" and similar teachers. Suitable exercises and mental culture were prescribed for each person. The great buildings provided for various exercises, contests to prepare for the Athenian games and festivals, and porticos, where teachers and philosophers could lecture and instruct the members.

The young boy devoted his time to moral and physical training, to music and letters. Athens produced three great gymnasia: the Academy of Plato, the Lyceum of Aristotle, and the Cynosarges, the rendezvous of cynics. It is significant that history gives greater honor to the intellectual values of the gymnasium than to the purely physical.

Rousseau, in his immortal *Emile* called civilization to task for its centuries of neglect of the systematic development of body and mind. Soon followed by others, national teachers influenced European countries, and America eventually responded.

Physical culture of to-day means more than setting-up exercises. Dalcroze introduced a system of eurythmics, whereby each musical notation had a corresponding body movement. A quarter note meant a normal step, an eighth note a quicker step, and a half note a step and a bend. This was carried out to fullest musical notation and a student learned an instrument, body power and grace, and intellectual quickness all in one operation. This system is of greatest value for those who have the patience for its mastery. It should have greater acceptance in public schools.

Ballet has developed a series of definite movements for its various terms, and consistent results are universally obtained. While we cannot learn the dance from textbooks, we can approximate many steps and movements. Dancing gives a mental causation for enjoyable exercise. A dancer, with a definite technic, must always be cautious that such technic does not carry over to other arts, but the fundamentals of dancing cannot help giving any artist greater poise in any bodily expression.

Isadora Duncan, probably more than any other dancer of this age, combined physical and intellectual power. Her pantomime was consummate artistry. She represented the concept in its fullest portrayal and not merely in its physical embodiment. To read of her life and art is to obtain a better understanding of beauty, rhythm, and grace.

Pavlova, Rosina Galli, Nijinski, Michio Ito, the Denishawns, all portray embodiment of concept more than any physical representation. National dances differ as national minds differ. Form and tempo remain constant—national uses and selection of form and tempo vary with and as races love and hate, build and destroy, adapt to snow or heat, passion or restraint. Mei Lan Fang reflects dynasties of ages gone; Charlie Chaplin impersonates the incongruous as it has always existed in the human race. The slow grace of the velvet train varies considerably from the vigorous charm of the shortened skirt. Mrs. Helen Moody, appearing before the court of England's royalty, is a different lady than Helen Wills on the tennis court of Wimbledon. Form is a reflection of inner concept. Mental control of body is the joy of body movement.

These exercises are here presented for those who wish concentrated effort upon some definite requirement. Many have been presented within the pantomimes themselves. We need not comment further that exercise without active thinking is almost a total loss of effort and time consumed.

The practice drills are divided into two groups, relaxation and poise. For those who have a poor sense of rhythm, musical accompaniment can be employed to excellent advantage. The stage artist must have a rhythmic consciousness.

Relaxation. These exercises are primarily for those who expend useless energy and who incline to be tense.

1. Stand with heels together, chest erect and filled with good air, shoulder blades far apart and chin kept in (not protruding), raise slowly on balls of feet and stretch arms and fingers to full length, vertically, keeping palms in. Hold for count of ten or more—relax suddenly and completely. (Arms should fall limp from shoulders, head drop, and no muscle taut.) Repeat until all muscles respond simultaneously. It is understood, relax does not mean relapse.

2. Repeat above exercise, except that you clench fists tightly, as well as muscles of body and legs. Relax suddenly as a body unit.

3. Heels together, good carriage, hold arms to side horizontal, palms down. Stretch outward far as possible with arms and fingers. Hold. Relax suddenly and simultaneously.

4. Repeat exercise three, except that arms are held in front of body. Tense all muscles of the body as well as clenching the fists. Hold. Relax as unit.

5. With body erect, raise arms over head, palms facing. Rise on toes and sway arms from left to right in a half circle. Do not bend knees or body at hips. Keep arms and hands relaxed throughout, just enough muscle power to move arms. Movement should be done slowly.

6. Bending at hips, arms hanging loosely from shoulders, body parallel to floor, let arms swing with the movement of the body, from side to side. Arms relaxed.

7. Spread feet apart to a comfortable degree, hold arms to front horizontal, palms down, and sway shoulders from left to right and return. Use as big a circle as the fixed stance permits. All muscles relaxed. Feet flat on floor.

8. Clasping hands back of neck, with feet apart, swing elbows from left to right, and return. Repeat. Again keep feet flat on floor.

9. Clasping hands back of neck, raise on toes and

sway body left to right, and return. Repeat. Keep relaxed.

10. Feet flat on floor, without bending knees, touch palms of hands to floor, then raise arms to full vertical height. Repeat. Keep lungs filled with good air.

11. Hands on hips, body erect, heels together, slowly go to sitting position, until you sit upon your heels. Raise slowly. Repeat.

12. Spread legs apart and gradually assume sitting position. The slow movement demands greater effort and control. Relax all body, save leg muscles. Come to vertical, and repeat.

13. With legs apart, body erect, hands on hips, sway body so that weight is transferred directly over one foot and then the other. Repeat slowly.

14. Repeat preceding exercise with hands on back of neck.

15. With legs apart, arms held straight out from shoulders to the sides, palms down, sway shoulders vigorously, left to right and reverse. Keep feet flat on floor.

16. Arms held to front horizontal, hold arms taut and keep hands relaxed from wrist. Move hands vigorously up and down, in and out, by movement from the shoulder center. Fingers relaxed completely.

17. Repeat above exercise with arms held to side horizontal. Move relaxed hands in circles, up and down, in and out.

18. Hands on hips, weight of body on right foot, move relaxed left foot so that the sole of foot touches floor gently in successive taps, by slightly bending the knee. Take slowly and increase to quick tempo.

19. Do same exercise with right foot free. Watch for complete relaxation.

20. Standing erect, place fist of one hand against fist of other, keeping arms horizontal to the body. Push with equal vigor against the fists and hold when tension is greatest. Relax arms and hands completely. Repeat.

21. Keeping arms in front of body, permit fingers of left hand to clutch fingers of right hand, hook fashion. With forearm perpendicular to upper arm, pull vigorously until tension is maximum; hold. Completely relax after each exercise.

22. Placing hands back of head, place one fist against the other, and push to maximum power. Hold. Relax after each effort.

23. Repeat above exercise, by pushing with maximum power. Hold and relax.

24. With arms held front horizontal, clench fists tight, roll arms at shoulders, i.e., hands turn the palms up and reverse to palms down. Repeat vigorously. Relax.

25. With arms held front horizontal, clench and relax fists. Repeat, but never to exhaustion point.

26. Roll head slowly, in circular movement, from side to side. Reverse movement. All muscles relaxed as possible.

27. Body erect, fill lungs with good air; tense and relax muscles of diaphragm and abdominal regions. Endeavor to keep arms and legs relaxed.

28. Body erect, lungs filled with good air, lower and raise chest, holding breath. Keep arms relaxed.

29. Body erect, tense and relax muscles of legs. Repeat.

30. Standing on one foot, twist foot with vigor in wide circle, using ankle as axis. Repeat with the other foot.

31. Preferably with bare feet, spread toes far apart as possible, then tuck them under foot to a tenseness. Walk on balls of feet for some distance. Repeat.

32. Standing on balls of feet, heel in and out slowly. Repeat. Increase tempo of change as control is gained.

33. With heels together and legs straight, bend as far forward, sidewise and back as possible, circlelike. Repeat.

34. With weight of body resting on toes and hands, face downward, keep body straight, raise and lower chest, not quite touching body to floor. Repeat.

35. Resting on back, hands under neck, with feet together and toes pointed straight as possible, raise legs from floor to vertical and return slowly to floor. Repeat.

36. Resting on back, legs to vertical, arms spread on floor, perpendicular to body, spread and close legs. Repeat.

37. Lying on back, legs resting on floor, hands under neck, raise legs (feet together) to vertical and over head until toes touch floor beyond head. Slowly return to original position.

38. Lying on back, move legs as if pedaling a bicycle. Slowly at first, to an increased tempo. All other muscles relaxed. Let knees come to chest on down arc.

39. Lying on back, hold one leg vertical as other leg comes back and toes touch floor beyond head. Alternate with other leg.

40. Lying on back, rest weight of body on top of head and feet, gradually lessening distance between feet and head. When feet and head are but a short distance apart, roll body forward and back, permitting neck to do major work.

N.B. In all relaxation and tension exercises be careful that member consciously exercised is the only one working. Relaxation is the genius of control. Suppleness, good-shaped limbs and strength can be attained and maintained easily, provided nature was kind when you were born. Even crooked limbs can be materially aided by proper, corrective exercises.

Clothes cannot conceal ugliness or weakness.

Poise. This volume has many pantomimes which call for distinctive carriage and various walks. A beautiful carriage in walking is seldom seen. Health, radiant personality, and ease of movement are essentials, but, above all, that conscious assurance that your going is the result of purpose and plan; motivation with mental dominance. Good carriage in the animal is the result of good breeding; in man, it is surely related to a conscious relationship and assurance that you have a rightful place in the social group.

Poise is power at ease. It is the ability to move without attracting attention to movement, and the expression of symmetrical beauty in attitude.

Poise is balance in lines of beauty and grace.

May we repeat: use music when desirous of accentuating any particular rhythm. Music is helpful in any bodily practice. These exercises are closely related to the group written under relaxation.

41. With weight of body on left foot, right foot extended back of you, and both arms extended in wing position to sides, body leaning forward almost parallel with floor, pivot or turn on ball of foot, completing circle. Slow movement and constant arc. Turn in either direction.

42. Alternate foot and repeat preceding exercise. Note that leg extended makes a continuous line, not broken by sharp angles at knee or ankle.

43. Spreading legs apart, bend body backward as far as possible—until eyes can see space under body. Slow movements are best. Balance is imperative. With practice, the hands touch the floor.

44. Heels together, bend forward without bending knees, until hands easily rest on the floor. Repeat.

45. Dance on balls of feet, balancing a light balloon on finger tips.

46. Without bending knees, walk on hands and feet. Note comic effect.

47. Stand on head, with hands on floor to aid in balance. Spread legs, to further challenge balance.

48. Place two chairs close together. Put firm hand on top thereof and slowly raise weight of body from the floor by straightening arms. Raise feet from floor until legs are parallel to floor. Hold. Let legs down gently.

49. Put feet under rung of some heavy chair or bottom of divan. From lying position, lift slowly to sitting

posture, without aid of arms or hands. Return slowly.

50. Place convenient articles in sequential spaces apart, and hop over same, using but one foot at a time and coming to a complete rest after each hop. Let unused leg be carried back of you with bended knee. Repeat. Use other foot.

51. Balancing on one foot, other leg held gracefully back of you, lift a ten-pound object over your head and pivot on ball of foot. All muscles relaxed except supporting arm and hand. (Adjust weight to strength.)

52. Carry a laden basket or tray on your head as you walk. Glide as much as possible. This training gives people in certain Mediterranean countries their supple carriage.

53. With body balanced on ball of one foot, circle around by power obtained from swinging other leg. A movement seen in ballet. Keep in small area. Extend arms for proper balance.

54. With one leg extended straight in front of your body, gradually obtain a sitting position on supporting leg. Raise to standing position slowly. Alternate other leg.

55. Place one foot directly in front of the other, standing on balls of feet. Bring right leg forward as the left recedes. Alternate quickly, lighting in same areas each time. Do when arms are relaxed, and then with aid of arms.

56. Jump in air and make complete turn. Light on balls of feet and remain stationary when you alight. Alternate direction of movement. Keep body erect.

57. With a running jump, "sail" in air as far as possible and light on either foot, with equal grace and power of control. Permit unused leg to hang easily from torso, somewhat in rear of body. Alternate with each foot for the spring.

58. With body resting on either foot, come to sitting position and extend other leg in front, as you rest on heel

—alternate position of feet, each leg taking its turn in supporting the body, which is low to floor and erect. This is a step often used in Russian dances. Repeat as quickly as is consistent with balance. Put hands on hips or fold them in front of body.

59. With a low obstacle near you, jump with both feet from one side to the other, going over barrier by side movements. Fold arms or put hands on hips. Light on both feet each time. Don't hop-scotch.

60. Procure a long feather and balance on nose, walking on tiptoe in long strides. Balance arms at sides, horizontal. Speed movement as practice permits.

It is to be noted that the different exercises are developed for specific uses. We have particularly avoided saying that certain exercises are excellent for the development of the neck or the reduction of the hips and abdomen. Your doing them will be the best proof of their efficacy.

Many actors do not exercise abdominal and leg muscles sufficiently. They, accordingly, crack at joints when stooping by the safe, or walking up a long flight of stairs. A picture was delayed for two weeks because the leading lady could not go up the steps without the sensitive microphone registering her every knee movement. It took that time to loosen up the unused muscles.

The old bugbear that women should not exercise for fear of "developing muscles" has long been exploded. The most beautiful women, who keep their charm, exercise consistently, intelligently, and systematically. We are not presuming overindulgence. Beautiful women and handsome men exercise with a purpose, and eat with reason. Normal measurements mean longer favor in public eye.

Health, radiating personality, control and poise are part and parcel of the favor attained by any actor or actress in these enlightened modern times.

DISCUSSION AND REVIEW QUESTIONS

(Some of the questions asked are not treated fully within the text of the chapter, but all deal specifically with subject matter under discussion.)

1. What is meant by "awareness"?
2. When, in life, does man become most aware of self?
3. What periods in history have men studied themselves most intelligently?
4. Does self-study aid or inhibit art? Why?
5. Define art in its broadest sense.
6. Which came first in man's development, vocabulary or art?
7. Is beauty a necessary concept of art? Why? Which dominates in art, beauty or utility? Develop.
8. Explain, "art is the embodiment of thought."
9. When can art said to be "bad art"?
10. Compare nature and art. Wherein are they similar?
11. Name the various arts that appeal to the several senses.
12. What is intelligence? Define briefly.
13. Define "association of the senses." Apply to art.
14. What languages does man possess to appeal to the different senses? Which is more important and why?
15. In race history, which "language" came first, pantomime, tone expression, or words? Does that have any significance for dramatic art?
16. Develop the statement, "pantomime is universal."
17. Elaborate, "The individual but reflects in his own life the race history."
18. Discuss the statement, "Great art is conscious art."
19. How can pantomime, tone, and words contradict each other? Develop fully.
20. How does habit affect expression of artist? Can a bad habit of voice annul the potency of gesture? Give examples.
21. Which is the more important to the audience, seeing or hearing? We are thinking in terms of dramatic art when we discuss this question.
22. What are the materials of the actor and the speaker in the creation of their arts?

23. Can a "bad" man in life play the part of a "good" man on the stage and be convincing to the audience? Can a "good" man in life convince in "bad" parts? Discuss fully.
24. What are the chief differences between acting and dancing?
25. Define ballet; tap; folk dance. When were these dances introduced and for what purpose?
26. What is poise?
27. What relation does poise have to power?
28. Is fatigue mental or physical? How does it affect the artist?
29. Define health, personality, grace, charm, and character. Explain what each may do for the art of acting.
30. Discuss "Exercise should have thought motivation."

CHAPTER II

A BRIEF HISTORY OF PANTOMIME

UNTIL very recent years, the common belief was held that drama was primarily the development of Grecian civilization, and that all other dramatic activities were in some manner connected with, or affected by, this common origin. But the more careful study which has been made by world scholars in the subject of ethnography, anthropology, and sociology lead students of the drama to go beyond the Grecian and look to the more primitive groups. Especially is this true of the pantomime.

It is quite generally accepted that gesture was the first means of communication between men and that a desire to imitate is a common response to children and men of all nations and nationalities. Whether desire to imitate is instinctive need not enter into this discussion; the fact is important that all children do imitate and that the higher the type of civilization the greater is this faculty developed. The language of the body, gesture or sign language, comes first in the life of man, is followed by tone and, some time after, words are acquired. Of these three languages, the language of the body is the most universal and the least universal is a vocabulary of one vernacular. As civilization grows, there is a tendency to make language of tone and words more universal and of more general service to mankind.

The part that interests us here is that gesture is the first to develop with our babes and, until the great influence of modern civilization, was the chief means of communication in all native tribes throughout the world. Professor

Sayce in *Development of Language* says, "Man is man by virtue of language and it was gestures which first made language possible." We read in Professor Allport's *Social Psychology* that "The earliest form of expression in infancy is not speech, nor indeed vocal expression of any sort, but gesture." And in W. D. Whitney's *Language and the Study of Language*, "It is past all reasonable question that, in the earliest communication between human beings, gesture long played considerable, if not the principal part." The entire chapter in Wundt's *Elements of Folk Psychology*, under the heading of "The Beginnings of Language," is very instructive, and puts forth the gesture theory of language. Wundt concludes that gesture precedes speech in the infant, and that gesture is adopted by primitive and civilized people when they have no other language in common. The fact that deaf people communicate with each other, irrespective of nationality, is one of his strongest observations.

We must conclude with Spencer, Lubbock, Wundt and others in regard to the ability of the Indians understanding sign language. The Utes, Blackfeet, Crows and Shoshone are most adept at pantomime; in fact, they are quicker in comprehension of gesture language than are most of the other people whom I have observed. It was among the Indians that I first noticed that the greater the emotion the greater was the use of gesture and the less the use of words. I subsequently observed that this is more or less true with all peoples, though the Orientals seemed, at first, an exception to this conclusion. I have seen the Indians tell their tribal stories almost exclusively with pantomime. It is well known that the Indians of North America and the Islanders have elaborate pantomimes in a very serious vein, and that the pantomime has taken generations to acquire; that the major pantomimes are not individual, but are tribal.

But the interesting phase of this work to note carefully, is that the play of the Indian babe and the play of the white child is consistently the same. Each of these youngsters plays for the fun of it, the pleasure of body action and mimetic enjoyment. The pantomime of the Indian adult is almost exclusively grave and serious, and quite generally partakes of adult phases of life. If there is anything that makes the play of the Indian child appear more serious than the play of the white child, it would further bear out our conclusion that it is universal for children to imitate, and that imitation is as old as the human race.

The many stories of our mountain pioneers still further bear out the fact of child spontaneity for imitation and dramatization. A baby Indian was left on the doorstep of one of the pioneers with a crude note, half Indian and half English, "Baby ma die, you keep, white God he pay." The little child responded in every manner as does a white child and was very quick in imitating adult actions. She seemed to get no more joy of playing Indian than she did of being Little Red Ridinghood or Cinderella. Her Indian parenthood appeared to have little effect upon the playing during childhood. Mr. Groos, in his book *The Play of Man,* gives some good stories where the situation is reversed, the effect of natives upon the white children. He found that white children very eagerly imitated the Eskimo woman or native hunter bagging his game. A general survey of the world to-day, influenced as it has been by a very rapid rate of civilizing processes, will convince any student that pantomimic activity is natural to all races, and that all native tribes and groups have a well-defined type of sign language which dominates in the telling of tribal stories or supplicating some god. Furthermore, that we need not go back to the Greeks for the sources of drama, but that *drama was born with man himself, and repeats itself in each generation.*

To appreciate the drama as we best know it to-day, we are forever indebted to the Greeks, and all students of dramatic art should be well versed in Hellenic studies.

We find, however, that the members of various tribes were much more versatile in theme matter than were the Greeks. The Mediterranean masters indulged in many forms of revenge, fate was omnipresent, and only the aristocrat could occupy the center of action or story. With the North American Indian, the theme varied from sun-dancing, vegetation ceremonies, totemic rites, and animal representations; sometimes revenge, but more often blessing and supplication, dominated. Tribal history was recalled by enactment in pantomime, and the best means of teaching the young the elements of bravery was in the elaborate pantomime. A well-defined drama existed among the Aztecs and was found by the white man. The fact that the Greeks recorded their drama for the edification of the world (though hundreds of the best plays were performed but once and lost forever) and that the drama of the Indians and natives was performed and learned, and handed down from generation to generation with no other means of record; this fact is one of the chief reasons why we have so long started with the Greeks for the origin of drama and its related subjects.

The form given to the Augustan drama is also a motivating cause for its study. A conforming to time limitations and definite locale has had great influence on a subsequent drama when a stage or indoor theater was to be used. Much of Indian drama could not be adapted to the modern stage. Scholars of drama know that with the advent of Dionysius and Adonis, the real drama of Greece began, and that these characters came into Greek social and religious life from the Egyptians. To the Egyptians, Isis and Osiris were all important. Dionysius was but a modified form of Osiris; rites were performed to the personification of the sun, and later to the vine. Herodotus is one of the first, to my knowledge, to point out this conclusion. And such rites are still being performed by the Ute Indians of the Wasatch Mountains in the annual sun dance and bear dance pantomimes with rhythmic accompaniment from a hand-beaten drum. While we learn much of the early sources of drama from the Greeks, the Oriental and the savages, *it is best learned from the modern nursery.* If you would understand the real origin of drama and know its beginnings, study the daily life of a babe. You will discover his first language is gesture and that he has an amazing capacity to imitate: the very foundation of drama.

Brander Matthews has written in several of his volumes some interesting conclusions about gesture being the original language, and that its elaboration in tribal usage is caught up by some later poet and becomes the form of drama. In his volume, *Development of the Drama,* he states: "It is from the observation of children and from the study of savages that the comparative anthropologist has been able to throw so much light on the earlier stages of human progress." He quotes from Professor Grosse: "Pure narrative requires a command of language and of one's body which is rarely found," and that "children and primitive people likewise are indeed unable to make any narration without accompanying it with appropriate demeanor and play of gesture." Professor Grosse noted that common usage means by a drama, "not the relation of an event enlivened by mimicry, but its direct mimic and verbal representation by several persons"; and he asserts the existence of this in even the lowest stages of culture. He recognizes as one root of a more elaborate drama the duet of the Greenlanders, for example, in which "the two singers are not only relating their adventure, but are representing it by mimic gestures"; and he finds a second source in the mimic dance. "Out of one or the other a true drama gets itself evolved at last; and its slow rise in the dramatic scale is in strict proportion to the rise of the people itself in the scale of civilization." Professor Havemeyer, in his book *The Drama of Savage People,* has a very interesting chapter on savage, Greek, and Japanese dramas. For the student who is interested further in the pantomimic drama of the North American Indians, I have included several additional references in the bibliography.

The use of the word "pantomime" has varied in different periods of history. It is generally used to mean the telling of a story or incident without the use of words. Pantomime, in its truest sense, may or may not accompany words. It is body action to reveal thought. For the use of pantomime in public places and its acceptance as an art and entertainment, we first must study Greek drama. Many volumes have been written on the origin of comedy and the origin of tragedy. Most authorities are agreed that tragedy was the first to develop and that its meaning had some connection with "goat song." It is not the province of this chapter to enter into the discussion, whether the prize was a goat, or the clothing worn resembled the goat, but we are interested in the certain fact that the first Greek dramatic activities were improvisations. A story was to be enacted and a group of men were chosen to present such a story as they improvised; these spontaneous action and group adjustments could easily have assumed a certain form as some of the same players were used and tried to produce the same effects which pleased their audiences most at the previous performances. From what we glean in skimpy record, it is easy to conclude that the same story was not often produced at the same place. It is difficult to determine just when the performance came to have metrical form, but by the close of the sixth century B.C., the dithyramb had become a regular form of acknowledged literature. At the beginning, the dithyramb was extemporaneous and was confined to the worship and exaltation of Dionysius, and, according to R. C. Flickinger in his *The Greek Theater and Its Drama,* "the dignifying of the celebration was a slow process of time and tradition. The boisterous wine spirit was eventually curtailed and Æschylus presented innovations that were to have lasting effects for world drama."

The name of Thespis should be a most familiar one to all students of drama. His innovations were far-reaching and most important. He is credited with inventing the first actor; all the attendants must now look and act their parts, they must appear and behave as worshipers. With the actor he gave the chorus certain intervals of relief, and with the mask one actor could play many parts. Thespis was probably our first traveling actor, as he took his companies on wagons and gave his shows from this improvised stage wherever he could get an audience. His was the joy of acting. It was Thespis who won the first goat prize awarded at the Athenian festival. The very size of the amphitheater demanded expert pantomime by the time Greek drama reached its height. Oratory at this time had reached an important place in Grecian life and the many rules of action were early learned by the youthful student. Aristotle and Demosthenes were contemporaries, and from each we learn much of the conduct of the Grecian scholar.

It was Æschylus who first gave tragedy a place in Greek literature, as it was Aristophanes who first dignified comedy. Up to the time of Sophocles, all playwrights were actors in their own productions; it was he who probably became the first director of plays, in the sense we use it to-day. He had his actors carry out his own ideas of the play he had written; thus another step in the art of pantomime and acting was taken. But by the time of the great tragic writers, the story had become better known and more fixed than had the traditional action. The roughness of the tragedy had gradually disappeared and a new form of drama was taking hold of popular opinion. Much of the roughness that had previously existed in original tragedy was now being put to a different purpose in comedy.

Aristotle tells us, "Comedy also sprang from improvisations originating with the leaders of phallic ceremonies, which still serve as institutions in many of our cities."

We are informed that the state had official control of comedy by 485 B.C. To Susarion is given the credit of inventing the comic chorus. That there has always been a great difference in the moral standard of tragedy and comedy is determined by the very nature of their purpose. In all ages crowds have asked for laughter; the very uncertainty of the ultimate in death has caused them to go to the tragic in their more serious moments. *One thinks of tragedy in terms of self and he thinks of comedy in terms of others.* It is seldom that one laughs at self, but always one will condone or console one's self. A sense of superiority of self and a discomfort of others are the two chief causes of laughter. These are the stock factors of comedy. A study of the first comedies of which we have record will bear out these observations; present-day productions will prove them.

Little is known of the pantomime stories which were used by the Greeks, but much more is known as they applied to the Roman. The word "pantomimus" applied to the actor himself. There is ample record that Augustus showed great favor for this kind of entertainment. During the Roman period the *pantomimi* wore masks, giving no facial expression other than the grotesque one supplied by the mask. The actor depended entirely on body activity to tell his story. The choir sang the story as the actor enacted his part or parts, and the early actors or *pantomimi* came singly upon the stage and acted successively the various parts. The theme was usually some mythological love story. As the play became more complex, more than one actor was used. The most famous actors of the Augustan age were Roscius Gallus and Clodius Æsopus, who were very popular in comedy and tragedy. Of the *pantomimi,* the names of Bathyllus in comedy and Plyades and Hylas in tragedy, are the most conspicuous. The *pantomimi* were so popular that Lucan wrote librettos for the ballets (A.D. 65).

The status of the actor in social life has varied with

the fluctuating times. Tiberius forbade his senators to go to the shows and his knights to be seen with the actors. By the time of Caligula the plays and players were again popular, and the "versatile" Nero acted in a pantomime. From this time on, as long as paganism lasted in Europe, the *pantomimi* were well known. The Roman soldier introduced the *pantomimi* in England and the use of the word was not lost track of, as Dr. Johnson puts a current significance to it in his day. George Puttenham, in his *Art of English Poesie,* wrote: "Between the actes, when the players went to make ready for another, there was great silence, and the people waxt weary; then came in these maner of conterfaite vices, they were called Pantomimi." The more commonly used term in England during the Elizabethan period was "Dumb show." The first English play, "Gorbuduc," used such a show, as did the greatest English play, "Hamlet."

The Spanish were early fond of the pantomime, and used it in the form of a ballet, more on the order of the French. During the time of Cervantes, the pantomimists were very active, their clown being called "Gracioso." To this group of actors and funmakers is attributed the original "Don Juan," the first pantomime ever performed wherein Scaramouche was used and Harlequin displaced.

While the *pantomimi* were being used variously throughout Europe, it was Italy which gave them their greatest popularity and development. In her "Commédia dell'arte" came the traditional characters, Harlequin, Pantaloon, Columbine, Pantalone. Harlequin is of French origin, influenced by the Italian. Pierrot and Pierrette came later. A celebrated Italian company entertained for Henry VIII in 1596, a company of the Gelosi. The Fedeli company was in France about the middle of the seventeenth century. Tristan Martinelli was the Harlequin. The Parisian favorite was Trivelin. The evolution of the characters is one of the most interesting in stage history. The "damned souls" of legend became the demons, vices, fools, and clowns of later times; Pantalone, the Venetian merchant, survived in the uncommercial Pantaloon and the Bolognese "Dottore." The Zannis (Giovannis) were the domestic servants in this type of comedy and included the Arlecchino. From Zannis to "Scapin" was not a very far step, and shows the adaptability of pantomime to general and local conditions. These characters were become traditional in the marionettes and Punch and Judy shows. The English eventually developed their clowns and fools, the Germans their "Hanswurst," and the Dutch their "Pickelhering." In France, in the seventeenth and eighteenth centuries, the pantomime applied to mythological spectacles at the opera. The great "ballets d'action" of Noverre were pantomimic. The first half of the nineteenth century Deburau and his associates had a spectacular revival of pantomime in their little *Théâtre des Funambules.* Present-day writings as Sabatini's *Scaramouche,* Guitry's *Deburau,* and Evreinov's *The Chief Thing,* all recall these times and characters. Reinhardt's production of "Sumurûn" and Laurette Taylor's "L'Enfant Prodique" are of more than passing interest.

When we speak of pantomime to the English, it is usually connected with some form of spectacle. The dramatic history of England starts some time within the tenth century and has a continuous record from that time. From the "Quem Quaeritis" to the mystery play was a slow evolution in response to English demands. An alternating song was combined with various sorts of theatric staging from the "Quem Quaeritis." The language was at first Latin, the subject was always from the Scriptures and the performance was always in the church. The *mystery play* originated in liturgy and presented a series of events from Holy Scripture; the *miracle play* was built around the life of a saint or martyr; the *morality play* was a dramatization of an allegory for the purpose of teaching religion or some principle of life. The presentation went from the church to the churchyard, from there to the street and the market place. Latin gradually gave way to vernacular, and the priests were displaced by laymen. The procession of the Corpus Christi day was greatly elaborated and trades were represented as best fitted their occupation. Control of the drama and pageant spectacles passed from the church to municipal authorities of guilds. For several centuries most of the dramatic activities were pantomimic. The actors capitalized the comic wherever possible. The unwillingness of Noah's wife was made comic to extreme, and putting the devil in hell always gave the actor the best opportunity for farcical play. From Vice in these plays, the character evolved to the English Fool, who was first pantomimic entirely and was given words by the time John Heywood and others wrote their interludes.

The pantomime, as we know it to-day in England, started during the early part of the eighteenth century. John Rich has been called the father of pantomime. The first pantomime is said to have been produced at Drury Lane theater in 1702, by a John Weaver. The name of this piece was "The Tavern Bilkers." This same author wrote the more popular "The Loves of Mars and Venus." Colley Cibber tells of this "Mars and Venus," which was in dumb show, "formed into a connected presentation of Dances in Character, wherein the Passions were so happily expressed, and the whole story so intelligently told, by a mute Narration of Gesture only, that even thinking Spectators allowed it both a pleasing and a rational Entertainment." John Rich was the most noted Harlequin of this time, though he had a good rival in Pinketham, whom Pope called "Poor Pinky." When John Thurmond produced "Harlequin Dr. Faustus" at Drury Lane in 1723, John Rich of Lincoln Inn's Fields produced a rival pantomime called "The Necromancer, or History of Dr. Faustus." It was immediately popular, and the rivalry between these two houses helped to further establish pantomime in England, and the *Christmas Pantomime* is yet one of the chief events in a young person's life. Thackeray in his *Sketches and Travel in London* tells of the Christmas pantomimes. Fielding wrote against the pantomime in his "Tumble-down Dick, or Phaeton in the Suds," which was acted in 1744. This was dedicated to "John Lun," the stage name of Mr. Rich. Garrick wrote the following lines of Rich:

When Lun appeared with matchless art and whim,
He gave the power of speech to every limb;
Tho' masked and mute, conveyed his quick intent,
And told in frolic gesture what he meant.

Colley Cibber laid down certain rules, which prohibited giving of a pantomime with a good play. His son, Theophilus, advised the return of a part of admission for those who would leave before the pantomime. It is reported that very few took advantage of the opportunity. Garrick had to play in pantomime to satisfy the major portion of his public. Lewis Theobald was author of some of the most popular pantomimes, and Joseph Grimaldi achieved great fame in his "Mother Goose" produced at Covent Garden in 1806. Grimaldi was especially clever in devising tricks and inventing scenery for his great effects. Grimaldi used such subjects as "Aladdin," "Bluebeard," "Cinderella," and "Little Red Ridinghood." To read in the eighth number of the *Intelligencer* a description of a pantomime audience as seen by Swift:

Observe, the audience is in pain,
While Clown is hid behind the screen;
But when they see his whitened face,
With what impatience they rejoice!
And then they value not two straws
How Solomon decided the cause.
Should Faustus, with his imp behind him,
Enter the stage, they never mind him.
If Clown, to stir their fancy, place
In at the door his mirthful face,

Then sudden draws it back again,
Oh! What a pleasure mixed with pain,
You every moment think an age,
Till he appears on the stage.
He gets a thousand thumps and kicks
In every action thrusts his nose,
The reason why, no mortal knows.
While teasing all, by all he's teased;
How well are all the spectators pleased,
Who in the motion have no share,
But purely come to laugh and stare;
Provided Clown, for there's the jest,
Be soundly mauled, and plague the rest.

During the recent World War, we read in the 1918 issue of *The Stage Year Book* of London, that Murry King would produce the pantomime "Robinson Crusoe" for the provinces after its successful run in London. "Open to produce same at good theatre next Christmas." In the years of peace and reconstruction, the pantomime goes merrily on.

In America, we find but little pantomime history. George Fox in 1870 attained considerable fame in his "Humpty Dumpty" as a clown. For years, the New York Hippodrome had its pantomime. The "Ravel" family from France were very popular and traveled throughout the United States. Tony Denier obtained a reputation as a pantomimist. The Martinetti family and the Zanfretti Troupe made considerable fortune with their dumb show. Vaudeville has usurped the best of the pantomimist of to-day, except as we see them in the moving pictures. Charlie Chaplin is probably the greatest pantomimist America ever produced. His characters are superior and always show greatest care and intelligence. For most of the best pantomime of to-day, we look to the movies. When we go to a play, we are no longer assured of great acting or melodious voices. It is a hopeful sign, however, that the most popular actors of to-day are the best pantomimists; the deplorable voices and worse diction is partially offset by the power of their acting.

One need not be a great scholar of dramatic history, nor a member of a good company to be a good actor. The history of pantomime proves better than any other means we have, that *great acting is native in each individual,* dependent upon his power of observation and ability to portray such observations to an audience. Emotions which have been experienced by a race, never die in the subsequent individual, though many remain dormant until a particular situation calls them to life. Pantomime is used equally well for tragedy, as for comedy. Pantomime is man's greatest power for thought transmission and is the foundation upon which all drama is based.

Partial List of References on History of Pantomime

Attic Theatre, The, A. W. Haigh (Oxford, New York).

Aztecs, The, L. Biart (McClurg, Chicago).

Development of the Drama, The, Brander Matthews (Scribner, New York).

Development of Language, The, A. Sayce (Duckworth, London).

Elements of Folk Psychology, The, Wilhelm Wundt (Macmillan, New York).

Golden Bough, The, J. G. Fraser, (Macmillan, New York), Vol. III.

Greek Drama, The, L. D. Barnett (Murray, London).

Greek Drama, History and Criticism, W. Ridgeway (Cambridge Press, Cambridge).

History of Theatrical Art, The, Karl Mantziuz (Duckworth, London), Vol. I.

History of the Harlequinade, Maurice Sand (Secker, London).

Indians of the Painted Desert, J. W. James (Little, Brown, Boston).

"Japan, Its History, Art and Literature," *Encyclopædia Brittanica,* F. Brinkley.

Language and the Study of Language, W. D. Whitney (Century, New York).

A Brief History of Pantomime

Mediæval Stage, The, E. K. Chambers (Oxford, New York), Vol. I.

Native Tribes of South East Australia, A. W. Howitt (Macmillan, New York).

Origin of Tragedy, W. Ridgeway (Cambridge Press, Cambridge).

Plays of Old Japan, C. C. Stopes (Duckworth, London).

Poetics, Aristotle (Putnam, New York).

Principles of Sociology, Herbert Spencer (Appleton, New York), Vols. I, III.

Romance of the Savage Life, G. F. S. Elliott (Lippincott, Philadelphia).

Theatre of the Greeks, The, P. W. Buckham (Cambridge Press, Cambridge).

Theatre of the Greeks, The, J. W. Donaldson (G. Bell, London).

Discussion and Review Questions

1. Define gesture; pantomime; dramatic acting.
2. What evidence do we have that gesture developed as man's first means of communication?
3. What type of language dominated with the aborigines of America at the time of their discovery by the white man? Quote from authorities.
4. From personal experience, if possible, tell of the present-day pantomimes as practiced by some of the American Indian tribes. What is the motif of each dance-pantomime of the various tribes?
5. Develop the statement, "Drama was born with man himself and repeats itself in each generation."
6. Briefly state the main factors for general belief that drama originated with the Greeks.
7. What is meant by pantomime in Greek and English drama, and at present meaning in America?
8. Give an outline history of Thespis.
9. How did size of Greek amphitheater affect Greek acting? Compare their style of acting with the present.
10. What important part did Sophocles play in the development of the art of acting?

11. Develop the differences between comedy and tragedy, and explain, "One thinks of tragedy in terms of self and he thinks of comedy in terms of others."
12. Who is the greater actor, tragedian or comedian? Why?
13. What are some of the main reasons why society, in the different periods of our history, has failed to accredit the actors? How has this affected the art?
14. Would the practice of Commedia dell 'arte improve or retard the standards of present-day acting? Why?
15. How did early pantomime evolve from the church dramatic presentations?
16. John Rich was referred to as the father of pantomime. State reasons.
17. What part does emotion play in the presentation of pantomime?
18. Does pantomime form any part in the power of a great speaker. Explain.
19. "Pantomime is greatest when given alone." Do you believe this? Is pantomime weaker or stronger when accompanied vocally?
20. Discuss the pantomime art of your six favorite actors.

CHAPTER III

THE EMOTIONAL BASIS OF ACTING

WE hear so much about being "natural" on the stage and in the college classroom that it becomes necessary to try to understand just what is meant by this much abused term. A daily occurrence is to see a dramatic coach with one of his star pupils before him. She is trying to enact the part of, say, Portia. She is stopped in her rendition and the coach calls from the back of the auditorium, "You are not feeling your part; there is no life to it. Feel it; put some emotion into it." The scene is played again. The response is even worse because the young lady has become very conscious of self and has this ego terribly mixed up with Portia. The director asks her, "What on earth is the matter? You did her well yesterday." And the young star replies, "Well, I'm doing exactly as I did then." But she wasn't, though she was trying harder than ever before. She was "emoting" all over the stage but could not show it. In desperation, she asks, "What did I do yesterday that I did not do to-day?" "Well, in the first place, you walked in a more dignified manner; you were more learned in your demeanor and more deliberate in your actions. You weren't jerky and impulsive as you are to-day. Now get into it and feel your part." The director had told her what she had done, not how she had felt. The audience responds more to what is done than what is felt by the actor. It was natural for that girl to make impulsive movements, which did not in any way fit the character she was portraying.

There are few parts in which a person can remain entirely "natural" and be true to the stage character. Being natural, and feeling one's part, are such ambiguous terms that they should be taboo. If being natural were to be correct, then that would be the one term to use. Portia, in her gown and mien, is a vastly different person than a modern Genevieve in her gown and mien. We have to learn how to be a person of another period. We must outwardly show what is universally conceived of a well-known character to acquire recognition for histrionic greatness.

Emotion, or feeling, cannot be taught. It is a personal experience. Its form and outline can be taught and discussed. It is the outward showing of the emotions that give actors their ability to hold an audience. Just how much of an emotion is shown by the actor is not the province of this chapter, nor is the question of whether actors feel their parts a pertinent one. We all know that they *reveal* their characters, and *it is this outward showing which most affects the audience.*

A certain amount of emotion is necessary for best portrayal of some characters, but emotion is not the dominant factor for acting greatness. There are many situations where feeling is unnecessary for the actor. Walking, eating, sewing, writing, and such activities are descriptive in character and may or may not be accompanied by an emotional response. And with each of these manifestations there is the better way of doing them, and the actor has to learn this proper and better way for stage deportment. His "natural" way is often not artistic or adequate. Some actors are of necessity cast for type parts, because they do not have the ability to look like the character they would wish to assume, though they may contend they feel such characters. John Barrymore is endowed by nature to play the part of villain, saint, or hero. A Richard, Hamlet, Don Juan, or doughty captain in search of Moby Dick, each can be portrayed so that his audiences enjoy his impersonation and live in the time and place of his characters. It would be a difficult matter for Frank

Campeau, one of our greatest stage villains, to play the part of a Don Juan or Romeo, though he may have the ability to "feel" such characters and properly motivate their parts. The public would judge him miscast. Nazimova, at one performance of Joan in "War Brides," was superb, at another her interpretation was very flat. She is the "feeling" or emotional type of actress rather than the actress with a consistent technic. *Knowing* what to do is better than *feeling* what to do.

The question that confronts the sincere student of the stage is a very important one: "Why can't I do what I want to do?" A director will tell him what to do and show him when necessary. And very often the student will say, "Well, I thought I was doing just that." What we respond to unconsciously is a greatly different proposition than when we have to create such a situation consciously. What powers we have naturally are not the same to control with such ease consciously. Say the word "Wyoming." A beautiful word with mellow sounds. What did you do with your tongue and lips when you said it? Few people know. What they do so well unconsciously or naturally has to be learned or closely observed before it can be done consciously. Anything learned has to be done so many times that it becomes an unconscious process before it has value in technic of any art. By unconscious, we mean that we are not focusing the attention of our awareness upon that particular phase of the activity. It has been well said that there are three kinds of knowledge: unconscious ignorance, that blissful state; conscious ignorance or knowledge, and unconscious knowledge. It is in the latter stage that all artists must put their technic before they can have free power to concentrate upon thought interpretation. If one has to think of hands and feet, he has little ease left to develop the main object of his interpretation. If he could respond to imaginary situation as well as he does instinctively to real ones, all the world would be truly a stage, and all the inhabitants thereof would be great players.

Acting is a learned art with definite technic, and to be "natural" one must know what laws of human conduct to emphasize, augment, minimize, and ignore. What personal habits must be suppressed, what deficiencies should be hidden, and what powers played upon. Art is not life. It has so many conventions, so many phases which are taken for granted in order to assume a likeness of reality. And no art has so many conventions as does stage art. Society does not permit the individual to live a natural life in fullness, and still less does the stage allow the actor to be a law unto himself. If he be a great artist he obeys the conventional laws which simulate conditions of natural reality.

To observe man, from the period of infancy to adulthood, is one of the fascinating and profitable occupations afforded accumulating intelligence. The only time a person is really natural is for a short period of his infancy. He then comes close to doing just what he wants without the myriad of restrictions which later confront him. And if it were not for the nature of parental care, even that brief period might be denied him. The lower the form of intelligence, the less care the parents seem to exercise over the destiny of their young. A snake is hatched, and, within a short period, is endowed with the three P's of nature. It has the ability to provide for self, protect self, and procreate its kind. In its simple existence it comes close to living a real, natural life. The higher the form of the intelligence, the greater adjustments the individual makes for group and social purposes. Man has to make the greatest number of adjustments. Civilization molds man into a composite unit of heredity, environment, convention, and adjustment.

A child has few wants, and his expressive self is confined to a small radius. If he dislikes an object, he withdraws his head. The withdrawal may be on a vertical or horizontal plane for the first few times, but it is not long until the average negative response with the head is in the horizontal plane. This usage of head movement is universal; to move one's head from side to side is the most common method of saying and meaning "No." The response of the head in the vertical to mean "Yes" comes a little later, but is equally universal. The complexities of the many meanings which are positive and negative in nature, develop as the child matures. Some of the emotional responses are products of adolescence and some even of maturity.

The very simplest of responses remain constant throughout life, but the activities developed in childhood up to adolescence are often expressed only in extreme conditions and are not used sufficiently by youth to be a fixed power of expression in an advanced age. To express negation, most mankind responds at will. To express shame, most people would have to stop and think what they would do, and then they would not generally be correct. They could approximate something akin, but not have a definite picture that would go unchallenged in an audience or group.

The baby is chiefly concerned with hunger, comfort, and exuberance of health. It develops its expressive self upon these elements. From a head withdrawal as an unwanted object touches its lips, the babe soon learns to withdraw his head from the object before it touches his mouth. As soon as he sees the object, he refuses any contact with it. The step from withdrawal to refusal varies, but is usually a very short period in infancy. This action of refusal is understood by the mother or nurse who accepts its significance. As soon as this refusal is recognized by others it becomes a sign, and as such is known as a gesture. Gesture is used to convey individual thoughts to others. This sign language expands as intelligence of the child increases. Man has the most complex language of all animals. The child learns first to express his likes and dislikes through contacts with his mouth. For months the babe will take all objects to his mouth, and in first infancy knows objects chiefly by means of his mouth. Everything first means an object for eating or something unpleasant to eat. As the hand becomes more facile and learns to detect qualities in objects, the mouth is used less as a final determiner. Children put to their mouths such objects as later frighten them. The little child soon learns to express very easily his likes and dislikes. He learns that such results are obtained from such expressions. His language of gesture increases in power as he has ability to recognize the effects of such movements upon others. But for a period of nearly three years he is learning by sad experience what he can have, what is good for him, and what punishment and reward is meted out for deeds done.

Anger is early "learned" and remains constant in life, that is, a person can easily reproduce the outward body form of anger without the mental causation. Fear is early learned and it also is expressed easily by children. It is to be noted that anger is more generally expressed than is fear. Most children and men express anger many times during a lifetime, whereas but few people express fear many times in these modern conditions. Such phenomena as lightning and thunder do not frighten children nearly as much as they did twenty years ago. Parents are learning so much of natural conditions that their dread, superstition, and fear are being greatly minimized. Knowledge diminishes occasions for those emotions. Children usually become frightened with that which frightened their parents. The expression of love is early learned and fondling is the chief means of showing it. It varies in proportion as sex is the dominant factor after adolescence is attained. Hunger and sex are the two greatest factors for impelling men to acquire learning, to adjust to new conditions and other environment, to inhibit personal wants for social relations. Anger is one of the closest expressions to hunger. Love is developed from simplicity of sex, complicities of sex coming somewhat later in life.

The more we develop this phase of our subject, we are led to conclude that such *gesture responses as are used early in infancy and youth are the easiest to reproduce at will or consciously,* and such gesture responses as are used later in youth and early adolescence are the more difficult to portray consciously. This not only bears out observations but it also complies with the laws of learning. This is true of all emotional responses, that the later they are acquired in life, the less apt they are to be reproduced correctly when done consciously. It is one of the evidences we have that we are not "natural" at maturity. We do not always have the ability to portray what we think we do or what we "feel" that we do.

When the boy goes from the world of mouth to the greater world of mouth and hands, he has taken the great step to learn more of life and the physical world in which he lives. But when he goes from the world of mouth and hands, to the broader world of mouth, hands and feet, he becomes an individual of far greater abilities and acquisition. It is the use of his hands which differentiates him from most of the other animals. Most animal life is governed from the relation of object to the animals' mouths. To paw an object is not uncommon, but to handle it, measure it, determine its qualities for use other than eating or building a nest or lair, is left for man alone. Just as the head first was used to show others what the baby did or did not want, so the hands and feet later become agents of thought transmission for social purposes. The hands and feet are not used by man only for lifting and supporting, they are chiefly used to express thought. This is an observation that has escaped many public speakers and actors.

The world of the baby's home is a great educator, especially if he has a brother or two. The great period of inhibitions comes to the babe when he starts to crawl and walk. Things that were kept from him before, he is now able to get. Wants from natural inquisitiveness are now adjusted very quickly to the family and social code. Brother's top is private property; sister's doll must not have the hair removed; mother's comb must not be put in the mouth; father's safety razor is a most dangerous weapon, despite its shiny attractiveness. Stoves are hot, doors can pinch, chairs can bump, needles can prick, peanut shells can choke, cats can scratch, onions can hurt little eyes, caterpillars can sting, knives can cut, and a thousand other objects come into consciousness and must be learned if the child is to survive. He soon learns that *what he wants is a small part of his existence;* he is busy with thoughts of what he can have and what he can get. What he so freely expresses with all natural honesty, society soon confines to the walls of its own limitations. Rousseau said that man by nature was good and remained good until society corrupted him. There is much truth in such an observation. We think of civilization inhibiting man's personal wants only to that extent as will benefit him or the race. But it is true that periods of civilization have greatly retarded man and even acted against his own welfare and good. Rulers have enshrouded the better expressions of men's lives, and governments have corrupted freedom in respectable avenues. All such inhibitions have played their parts on man's life as we know it to-day. We are far from being the best "natural" man we could be in many respects. And in the same breath, we must add that it is due to the coöperative agencies of civilization that man has obtained the position of freedom and liberty he now enjoys.

This is the greatest period of enlightenment and freedom the world has record of, and the best era for the expression of happiness and achievements. But man himself is far from an ideal and has not reached near the power which lies dormant within him. Society has truly curtailed much of his greater power. The little Russian babe will act the same for some time as will a little American babe, but what of the two when they reach maturity? A little Japanese child will respond as does a Negro babe in Liberia, but what of maturity? How far does tradition affect manhood? What is meant by being natural, in any national sense? Is war a natural demonstration of the individual to-day as it was when swords and arrows were the chief weapons? It may be natural for man to want to lie in a shell hole and be gassed by an unseen enemy or torn by distant mortars. Is it natural for a man to be honest? Or does society reward him for adjusting his personal equations? Is honesty measured by personal contentment or financial returns? Why is stealing to one person only business practice to another? If a powerful company beats an individual out of his claim on a piece of mineral land, what is the natural response for each of these? Does scandal aid or retard repentance and restitution? Does publicity of rape, murder, suicide, divorce, and robbery affect the individual for good or bad? Does it aid him in expressing his natural self? Is man by nature religious? What of national sentiment on religious subjects; how does it affect the individual? If church-going were popular, how many would attend because of personal desires? Is it natural to transfer love as we would any salable commodity? Is divorce an outgrowth of society or indifference of the individual to home ties? In other words, just how far could an individual go in society if he told the absolute truth under all conditions? If he were honest and virtuous in all relations? If he did just exactly what he wanted irrespective of the conduct and laws of society? Just how far has the individual been able to accept the ideals and inhibitions of society and react in a natural manner? To the extent in which governments and society reflect the Decalogue and the Beatitudes, the individual can live a natural life, to the extent which they diverge, to that extent must man adjust and be "unnatural." Man by nature *is* good, and needs only the opportunity to live in such a manner. As he weakens in debate with conscience and practice, he lessens his ability to express with conviction the ultimate determination of his action. As he has to argue with himself what are the practices of society and what he individually wishes, just to that extent has he weakened his aptness to respond naturally.

I remember distinctly my first lie: a willful expression of a known fact. I do not remember my parents once talking to me about honesty; it was a term and condition on which I had not previously thought. I took twenty-five cents from mother's bureau and when she asked me if I had seen it, I replied "No" and left the house. I sensed most vividly that I had done a wrong of some kind. It was not that I had said "No" that bothered me, but that I had taken something that did not belong to me. Mother said it was not that I had taken the money, but that I had said "No" when she asked me. It took me some time before I saw the great issue between these two situations. I was by nature honest, though I had not carried my honesty to the extent that honesty of word was as sacred as the honesty of deed. Some other boy might have felt bad for having said "No" and still believed he he had the right to take the money. He would have responded to honesty in a different manner. Each would have a bigger significance of the deed to learn about later, as they understood social relations. Adolescence, marriage, death, travel, and business all offer new inhibitions to the individual, new adjustments which must be made before he can successfully associate with his fellow men. *Life is a continual adjustment of the natural self to society.*

Adolescence is a period of greatest adjustments to the average boy and girl. But before that time he or she has well learned the art of dissembling. When a young neighbor friend of ours had learned the chief elements of cake-etiquette he had learned much of social relations which inhibit naturalness. It started on a Saturday afternoon. The little fellow smelled the aroma of his favorite cake and went to the neighbor's back door. There was a chocolate cake in all its glory, resting in easy accessibility. The housekeeper was in a distant part of the house. All the active senses of that boy wanted that cake or a portion of it. It smelled good, it looked as good, and experience told him it would taste even better. So he responded to a natural impulse or desire and put two chubby hands well into the cake. When the busy wife came happily into the kitchen she was confronted with a most unexpected sight: her Sunday dessert was in a ruined heap and a pair of innocent eyes looked up in satisfied enjoyment. She gave the little fellow a severe box on the head, shook him and placed him outside the door with definite instructions. He obeyed the one to go home and told a tale of unjust treatment. His mother investigated and learned the harrowing details. The child was forbidden the pleasure of going over to the neighbor's where he was not wanted, but there were no fences, and memories are not so well trained in early youth.

Saturday came again, and with it another tempting smell. The son ambled slowly over to the back kitchen and leaned against the door. The neighbor was more vigilant and this time asked the boy if he wished a piece of cake. He remembered something of the last experience and his mother's admonition. He did not put out his hand and take the proffered small cake, but shook his head in a slow negation, while eyes looked "Yes." The understanding lady put the cake in his hands and locked the door. He was happy and went immediately home. There he met a new situation. Again the mother scolded him and asked him why he had taken the cake against her expressed orders. The boy told his mother that he had not taken the cake, that the lady had forced it on him, and that he even shook his head when she asked him to have it. The mother chided him more vigorously this time and told him he should not ask for anything again from the neighbor and accept nothing unless it was properly offered to him. The boy thought he had not asked the neighbor, and also thought he had done considerable by not even waiting till the neighbor was in the front part of the house before he went over.

Two weeks later when the baking time appeared the boy remained out in the yard, but whistled loudly so as to let the generous cook know that he was there. When she came to the door and asked him if he wanted a piece of cake, this time he had so far socialized that he could now add "No, ma'am" to his reluctant negation. But the tone betrayed him and she knew he wanted his expected portion, so she again presented him with a specially decorated morsel. Later, father was brought into the scene to reprimand the boy for his lack of manners.

In a short time the boy had learned to keep his hands to himself, to refrain from looking in a telltale manner and could say "No, thank you" in a most convincing manner. He had learned to lie with his body, the tone of his voice, and the very words he used. The first time the neighbor lady took him at his word and actions and had actually not insisted that he take the cake, he went to the back of the barn and talked to himself for a half an hour, in suchwise: "Why did you lie to her? Why did you say you didn't want that cake, when you know darned well that you do? What are you such a big liar for? Ah, heck, that's what you get for not tellin' the truth." His education of inhibitions had begun in conscious earnestness.

He later saw his chum, Bill, dismissed from school for admitting that he had put glue on teacher's desk, and saw Jim exonerated from breaking a window when he denied it to the inquiring principal and teacher, though most of the room had seen Jim do it. He couldn't reason social evaluation nor did he understand some of the necessary adjustments. When his mother served company he wondered why they hesitated in the choice of certain spoons, when any would have done him. And why did he have to wait to be served last when the food was closest to him from the very beginning? Why did he have to take the smallest piece when he was the one there who liked cake the best? Many such edicts he accepted, but silently wondered. And the time he and Nellie and June went in swimming in the mill creek, and June's father had found their clothes on the bank. Why were they all spanked by her father, and he, especially hard? Though he asked if he could go in swimming and was granted permission. Why did the grocer let the well-dressed lady stand by the fruit and eat just hundreds of grapes as she talked and bought nothing, when he took just one grape and got hit on the knuckles with a pickle spoon, and was buying something?

Many things he had learned by the time the great change of life came to him. He was reciting on a program the day before he was to "graduate" from the eighth grade, and was in the midst of his well-chosen oration, when a great calamity occurred. His voice slid several tones to a cracking falsetto. Nor did the attempt to cover up this personal weakness add glory to his fame, as the attempt went caroling off in a new tune. Right there in public view, he had stepped from boyhood into young manhood. The world had been his greatest sphere, now ego was to be his dominating interest for some time. He found himself more uneasy in the presence of girls and yet wanting to be with them. His hair was not as ruly as it used to be and his clothes certainly got dirty very easily nowadays. He started to ask questions that pertain to the cost of a family, and what is the best job for a man of his abilities. Games and parties take on new angles; he didn't want such a large crowd as before, just him and her and a few pals would be better. What was once fuzz turned out to be the potent evidence of blossoming manhood and adventures in mustaches led to fanciful dreams. Seventeen came upon him in all its peacock glory. He strutted where before he had ambled. Money started to have new powers he had not dreamed of before. He found himself doing hundreds of things to please his girl, things he would never have done in the olden days. In the halo of his own ego, he built his life in a new aura of what will please her. He changed ideas and habits of clothes, food, money, work, and worship.

For the girl, this period is more of a personal affair than it is for the boy. She is brought very suddenly to realize that she is no longer a girl, but a woman. Physical charms that were not hers before are now very potent. Self in sex is constantly making her conscious of herself. The imitative dressing of childhood develops into a very earnest effort to enhance personal charms and magnify every possible phase of her beauty. She no longer wrestles with the boys as she did a short time ago. The freedom of legs and arms is greatly curtailed and a greater care of position of her person is consciously watched. To be seated at ten was just to be seated, but to sit at sixteen is a conscious pose to adjust clothing with each body movement. Not even modern clothes have lessened this attention. The few who disregard conventions of this kind make the other ladies present the more conscious by their associates' indifference. There is coming a gradual status of social code in what constitutes modesty and what does not. What is nudity to one nation may be vulgarity to another. It is a pitiful indictment of civilization that as the natives are forced to dress, they become the more immoral, and that the white man introduced lax moral codes wherever he explored. It is natural for mankind to wear clothes as a body adornment and protection, and not for a covering of erotic parts.

Man by nature is an active creature and gets his greatest happiness in work. As society permits the few to lounge about and the larger group to maintain them in their leisure, the separation of moral ethics is more noticeable. Divorce was the scandal for ages; now there is more toleration. Divorce started first with the indolent and gradually reached the working classes. It was natural for young men to look forward to gainful employment; now there are various groups of young men who look forward to yearly leisure. Little work with much pay. This condition is changing man from the animal he started out to be. Environment is fighting the charge of heredity. Wild animals in natural states mate in season; the same animal domesticated mates with opportunity. Just what confinement, and man-feeding, has to do with this change is a matter for others to decide. The observation is sufficient for our purpose here.

With every new condition in which man is confronted in the modern social world, he meets a new set of inhibitions or reactions which materially change or affect his natural self. No institution is a greater tyrant than is marriage, and in its very tyranny it is the greatest institution for good which man has to honor. The sanctity of the home, which is built upon marriage relations, is the very foundation for proper government. To enumerate the many adjustments necessary for a successful home would take half a volume. When the young man first learned to smoke, it made him sick. Later, this acquired pleasure is thrown into the discard to please his affianced girl. Other marriages have been shattered because the parties involved would not give up their tobacco or liquor. The personal too far dominated the social. Hundreds of men have wished to be artists; but children, wife's ambitions, wars, and deaths have forced the quick monetary returns upon the provider and his greatest ambitions are never realized. They slumber in the power of suppressed desires or break out at most inopportune moments. The care of children has disillusioned hundreds of brides; what was romantic in honeymoon has become monotonous in marriage. The freedom of girlhood has given way to confinement of family obligations. Her family has deprived her of her great desire to star on the stage or travel around the world. She lives on a farm and she dreams of the city, or the reverse is true. Freedom of girlish movements retards to the largo of dooryard diversions. A suddenly inherited fortune disrupts the peaceful routine of family life and new methods of spending money and the meeting of flattering but envious friends change the real fellow into a popular misfit, or his wife into a bird of paradise. Death knocks at the door and convention dictates that black be worn for weeks or months and various means of advertising sorrow are indulged as traditions govern. Or white may be worn by others, as in Korea, where an entire nation mourns the loss of its erstwhile prestige. The thousand and one inhibitions to which man subscribes in civilization have added to his power of creation and usefulness, but have made him a man of learned habits and conscious adjustments. Only for a short period in infancy is he the "natural" being.

The *Forum* magazine in the March, 1927, issue, quoted several definitions of "natural." Mr. Lyon's definition is interesting. "In Shakespeare's day natural was used to describe a fool; that is, he was natural and just as God made him. The only true naturals are babies and fools for they often have a wisdom to confound the wisest. Because dogs are natural, they are better companions than some people. All things artificial are created by religion, culture, learning, and law. We pretend to love nature and all things natural, yet not one of us dares be natural. Anatole France says, 'That which distinguishes man from animals is lying and literature.' We shall never be natural so long as we *write* and *lie*."

"Nothing but the Truth" is a play built on the theme of trying to be natural for a day.

In the Los Angeles *Times* of December 16, 1928, George Arliss wrote an article, "Actor Cannot Be Real." It is so pertinent to this chapter, and coming from such authority, I think it will interest all students of the drama:

The actor cannot be real on the stage: he is artificial almost every moment. The very fact that he has to speak a great deal louder than in ordinary life compels him to depart from the purely natural way of making effects. The natural acting that "gets across" and impresses an audience is the result of training, experience, and study. I have met a good many reformers in my life, who insist upon being really natural; but their acting never gets beyond the footlights. These belong to the school that will not be bound by conventions.

Now, if an actor is going to turn his back to an audience just whenever he feels it's natural, because (as I have heard so many of the reformers say) "we do not always sit down and face one way in a room," then the audience should be allowed to stroll around after him, if they feel that they would like to hear what he is saying.

We hear of great actors and actresses being so carried away by their parts that they lose themselves entirely. . . . That happens now and then. But of course, he doesn't really lose himself. If he did, there is no reason why his emotions should not get into his legs and carry him clear off the stage and into some remote corridor of the theater. Obviously, he is all the time aware of the limitations imposed upon him by the architecture of the theater.

He is not only aware that he must remain within the frame of the stage, but also knows that, at a certain and prearranged moment, he has to cross right or left or upstage, and that if he doesn't do so, he probably mars the performance of some other characters equally necessary for the presentation of the play. There are instances when leading actors, in giving full play to their emotions, disregard these carefully rehearsed arrangements to the confusion of the other actors performing with them; but that is not so much because they have forgotten they are acting, as it is that they are remembering they are stars.

. . . The art of the actor is to learn how not to be real on the stage, without being found out by the audience.

We must conclude that acting is a conscious, learned process, that society curtails more of natural man than it augments, and only as man unconsciously obeys law can he be natural. Man's greatest power is liberated by conscious knowledge in an unconscious manner.

NOTE: References for some of the topics discussed in Chapter III are to be found in the bibliography at the end of Chapter IV.

DISCUSSION AND REVIEW QUESTIONS

1. Define the term "being natural."
2. Is "feeling" a part of "being natural"? Explain.
3. Define emotion, quoting ten or more authorities. Wherein do the various schools of psychology (e.g., Behaviorist, Psychoanalyst, and Introspectionist) differ?
4. Can emotion be taught? Can it be learned?
5. Do actors "feel" their parts? Develop.
6. Explain "art is not life."
7. Name some primary "wants" which go with us through life. How does society condition these wants?
8. Name some emotions which seldom come to the adult in our present civilization.
9. Would language of any kind ever be developed if man lived alone? Why?
10. Explain the statement, "The last acquired is the first to disappear," and apply to gesture response. Which agents of man's expression developed first? Which does he use most in adulthood?
11. Give examples from your own life showing conflict of actions in public with what you really wish to do.
12. How do our emotional lives expand in adolescence?
13. Could a person be "natural" and remain happy? Is being happy a personal or social adjustment?
14. Develop "Art is the result of a conscious, learned process. Technique is a conscious obedience to laws governing the materials of the art."
15. Defend or criticize the viewpoint of Mr. Arliss, as presented in his article in the Los Angeles *Times*.
16. What value do emotions have in dramatic art? In life?
17. Which expends the most energy, the expressing of an emotion (e.g., anger) or the inhibiting of the emotion?

CHAPTER IV

THE BODY AS AN EXPRESSIVE AGENT: SOME OBSERVATIONS ON GESTURE

THE body is the most expressive instrument in the realm of art, differing from most instruments, in that it has an animation of its own. The violin is a constant instrument, dependent upon wear and tear of wood and strings. Its shape is fixed and universally consistent. The cornet is definite in mold, and its shanks, once adjusted to the condition of the playing room for pitch purposes, remain so conditioned. Its shape is definite and fixed. So with all musical instruments. It is easy to teach musical technic for position and how to run a scale, but it is a vastly different proposition to teach music when quality and interpretation are involved. A person can learn notes but not quality, from a book and manual. This is even more true with the art of pantomime.

One can learn gesture from position, but he cannot learn emotional evaluation from a textbook. The body is not as fixed in general form as is the violin or cornet, yet all people admit readily that they cannot play music until they have learned their instrument. Neither a violin nor a cornet has to contend with heredity, environment, conceit, weak lungs, fallen arches, and other engrossing impedimenta, but is manufactured to a standard of accepted merit.

Most actors have some bodily imperfection that has to be minimized in playing a part; they learn how to magnify strengths to obtain dramatic powers. They use an ever-changing body with conscious ability but, what is significant, like the musician, they must learn how to use their instrument. The body is an instrument which is bound up with habits, good and bad, reflex actions which respond to situations despite desire or location, an instrument that telegraphs a tooth-pain to the same center which must direct the steady hand of a stage villain. The very animation of the body as an instrument makes it the most interesting of all agents for thought expression. Man, the artist, expresses his inner self only by the external evidences of his physical body. Man, the actor, must train that body, so that others may understand what the artist wishes actually to portray.

As it is impossible to teach the soul of music from a textbook, so it is impossible to reveal the genius of acting from a printed page. The best we can hope to do is to point out some pertinent observations and external forms which will enable the actor to discover his own soul or genius. It must come from within; even though its evidence is revealed only by external factors. One learns to do by doing. The best way to find the power of body expression is not so much to classify emotions, study movements, analyze plays or stage business, but actually to try out the myriad experiences which the stage calls for. All study is helpful, but is not the end. Study is only the means. Study and practice lead to technic. Technic is the habitualizing of proper form for expression. One must think properly before he can do adequately. Such thinking must become a technic in position and action, an unconscious revealing of the artist's thought.

When the actor learns that to be "natural" means to be correct, and universally understood, then he is capable of studying his art without letting that study deprive him of the joy of his work. When he learns that he may be doing many things not beneficial to his art and that a conscious technic is the only cure of these defects, then he can set about perfecting his art and profession. Only the conceited prig can be harmed by a knowledge of what he does. All scientists know that knowledge is power; artists of real merit have always been conscious of their knowledge and technic. If an actor thinks *how* he is doing his part, he senses that his portrayal is stilted and artificial. That has been the chief reason for many actors not desiring to know how they do any scene, and also their chief answer for feeling their parts. What if any scientist so reasoned? What if a surgeon so reasoned? What if any pianist so reasoned? Why should the actor be the last to understand his medium of expression?

The sincere artist knows all materials of his art. The human body is easy to observe and many kinds are daily about us. We need never lack for material. As we observe the actor on the stage, we are conscious of certain physiognomic centers. We see three major divisions for independent study; the head, the trunk, or torso, and the limbs. Most people look to the head and its component parts as the greatest agency of expression. This is, no doubt, due to the fact that the receptive avenues of our major senses are situated chiefly in the head, and that voice also emanates from this center. The torso is that agent which we observe has the major activity in expression of affective relationships. Many think of the torso as the center of heart activities, and conceive it to be closely allied in the expression of all strong likes and dis likes. This is partially true, because of the discernible blood pressure and heartbeat variations for the different emotions. At least, we all observe that the lover holds his lady close to his bosom in tenderest affection, as does the mother when caressing her babe; or that the body is turned from any disliked person, though the eye may look upon that person. Such actions of like and dislike cause the torso to be recognized as the agent of affection. So the legs and arms have very particular parts to play in the gamut of expression. The long stride of the man in violent anger is much different from the walk of a thief. The arm movement for fear differs greatly from meditation. The legs and arms are observed as being more of the physical in expression than is the head or torso. From some such general observations we deduct the more specific and reach some pertinent conclusions.

No discussion of the body as an expressive agent could be properly presented unless we understand that the mind is situated in all the body, and not in just the brain. The mind is more properly understood when we think of it in terms of the nervous system. The central part of the nervous system is focused in the brain, but no small part is found in the spinal column areas and the thousand nerves which inhabit the body. The centralizing of the mind is important, as we shall observe later, but we must not forget that the mind as a whole is situated in all the body. A telephone system does not exist in central alone.

The mind can reveal nothing of itself except through the body. This great dependence, each upon the other, must not be lost sight of in the study of dramatic technic, or life itself. The late Leland Powers used to say, "As the hand gives shape to the glove, so the mind gives shape to the body." Modern psychology has not yet determined just how far we can go with the statement that "The body affects the mind as much as the mind affects the body," but we are getting more evidence daily to make that statement seriously worth our attention. Empirical knowledge reveals that years of grief permanently mark our countenances; that a Scrooge has a hard time eradicating expressions of distrust and greed; that trades affect our appearances, and that one cannot be sad if his whole face is smiling.

We are truly led to believe that every little movement has a meaning of its own. The knitting of the brows, the clenching of the fists, the raising of the corner of the lips, various positions on the feet, all reveal major or minor thoughts of the individual. Life is a struggle of encouraging proper wants and inhibiting bad wants, or of encouraging the bad and belittling the better desires. These struggles mark themselves definitely upon the conduct of man and are revealed minutely in every expressed thought. Conduct is the only criteria for man judging man. Bumps of the head, lines of the brow and of the palm, are, at best, broadly suggestive of certain general observations. Man is only what he does. The raising of an eyebrow is as much a part of man as the raising of his arm. How he stands on his feet is as important as how he uses his eyes. Thought is expressed by all the body and its various parts must harmonize properly to express thought. Each position and movement of the body as a whole, or its agents in part, expresses some integral thought of the human mind. By knowing these body positions as they are universally understood, we gain the ability adequately to express thought as desired. All thought, as it affects the individual, is expressed by a definite position or movement of the body. And this is an excellent comment: when a person knows the language of the body for the United States, he has learned a language that is understood throughout the world.

The Head. Because of sight, hearing, taste, and smell being centered in the head, this agent receives the greatest attention from casual observers. The activity of these sense centers are immediately shown by the response of the head and its agents in the most conspicuous manner. A scene is distressing to you; your brow and lids are among the first agents to reveal such reaction. An unpleasant odor is present; your mouth puckers or the upper lip lifts, and the nostrils tighten as if to shut out further inhalation. A glorious song comes floating across the water; your ear is inclined to the source of pleasure as if to get every vibration. You bite a piece of candy, forgetting it is April the first; your tongue will usually protrude and your entire face be made awry. Your boy or girl friend comes up to you; your eyes dance and smiles move the mouth. It is this concentrating of the sense centers in the head which gives it such importance in daily life. That such adjustments are being made with other parts of the body is usually unobserved, though they are equally important to the student and the actor.

Most emotional responses affect more than one part of the body. To cite an example commonly observed: we see a person in controlled anger; his head is usually tilted from the object of his ire, his brows are knit, the lids are raised, the nostrils are tense, the mouth is tightened, the chest often raised, the muscles of the arm are stiffened, the hands are clenched, and the body is poised over the center of the advanced foot. Such a picture may have variations, but is consistently true. The mind is situated in all the body, though it is centralized in the head.

For study purposes, the head conveniently divides itself; the head proper, taken as a unit, and the face as we see it with the brows, eyelids, eyes, nose, cheeks, and mouth.

The head is the only agent of the body which does not change its shape in expression. It is purely an agent of attitude. For an excellent study of head positions, one can profitably go to the masters of sculpture. Sculptors, of all the artists, have been the keenest observers of body position in its entirety. Phidias, Donatello, Robbia, Berrocchio, Michelangelo, Cellini, Giovanni da Bologna, Lombardo, Bernini, Jean Houdon, Rodin, and some of our Americans, such as Gutzon Borglum, Dallin, French, MacMonnies and others, offer ample opportunity to study head positions in definite and fixed attitudes. Each piece of great sculpture reveals years of study in the portrayal of that particular attitude of the figure portrayed. Students of dramatic art can well afford to be interested in sculpture in all its phases. It leads to greater power of observation in life itself.

Inasmuch as the head is unable to change its shape, as can the face, the brow, the mouth, the hand, etc., we are primarily concerned with its positions. It moves freely about, with the neck as the center of its activity. A complete circle is described if we observe the head movements in their entirety. It moves to the right or left as far as the shoulder and it goes well forward and backward with all the accompanying degrees in between. As man becomes older, he seldom uses the entire gamut of head expression. This is more or less true of all of man's agents of expression, except his mouth. The shoulder line becomes a convenient line dividing the head activities. (By shoulder line is meant the line drawn from left to right shoulder.) All positions are either in front and below the shoulder line, or in back and above the shoulder line. (The one exception being the head held in its most vertical position.) A very humble person comes to you and his head is held in front or below his shoulder line. The varying degrees in which a person holds his head above or back of the shoulder line mark degrees of self-assertion, and the degrees in which a man holds his head below or in front of the shoulder line expresses proportionately his attitude of self-suppression. In extreme happiness we throw our heads back of the shoulder line and in extreme grief we drop our heads in front of the shoulder line. We thereby observe that the vertical line of head movement or position reveals what a person thinks in terms of himself, just as his head moving from or towards an object proves that the horizontal movements of the head show what man thinks in terms of the object. If the object of attention is on the left of a person, and we see that person move his head to the right, or from the object, we readily observe that the person is expressing some kind of disapproval or disagreement with the object. If the head of the person is seen to move toward the object, we register that there is some form of approval or agreement. The fact that we go toward the things we like and from the things we dislike, is as old as man, and we but respond to natural phenomena. The head is one of our best agents to reveal thoughts of agreement and disagreement, just as it is the best agent to reveal what we think of ourselves.

After the eye has determined the object of attention, it is very easy to register agreement or disagreement, as the head goes toward or from that object. To register anything else would be to confuse the audience. As one stands erect and drops his head vertically in degrees, observation soon teaches us that he has shown self-suppression in some such progress; concentrated thinking, scrutiny, forms of humility, and ultimately reaches shame or guilt. If he holds his head at normal and gradually raises in the vertical, he has shown self-control and attention, animation, pride or conceit, exhilaration and, ultimately, exaltation. Forms of distrust are shown when the head is held below the shoulder line and from the object. Degrees of adoration or reverence are shown when the head is held below the shoulder line and toward the object of attention. As the head is held above the shoulder line and from the object, variations of scorn and disdain are revealed, and when the head is held toward the object and above the shoulder line, we register degrees of protection, affection and kindness. Just as great musicians vary in playing a Chopin nocturne, so actors vary in revealing thoughts, but the audience always knows what is being played. Man cannot improvise to the extent that nature's tune is not recognized. We must speak in the universal, the language biologically imposed, if fellow men are to understand. The head adjusts for every variation of thought and harmonizes with all other agents in expression. It cannot remain a fixed block and expect to animate character or reveal a proper interpretation.

There are but two inflections or movements of the head that are universally used. When the head moves in the vertical plane, up and down, all the world interprets affirmation or "yes"; when the head moves horizontally, left and right, all the world understands that the meaning is negative or "no." The head is primarily an agent of expression depending upon attitude or position. Being in such a conspicuous place, it must be thoroughly trained for best results in dramatic expression. The major ideas which come to us from the puppets and marionettes come almost entirely from attitude or position. We cannot overstress the importance of a thorough knowledge of the positions of the head.

The Face. When we include the brow and lids, the eyes, the cheeks, the nose, and the mouth, in the one word, face, we speak of the greatest agent of human expression. Great in the sense of its multiplicities of adjustments and intricate muscular changes and important as an agent in the expression of the emotions. We can run the category of emotions and will find few, if any, which are not in some manner revealed by the face. To name at random such different emotional responses as anger, fear, hunger, pity, anxiety, contempt, doubt, joy, despair, and vengeance, we readily recognize the part the face registers in each. There are emotional responses whose bodily patterns are confined primarily to the face, but no major arm, hand, or foot responses which do not also reflect on the face. One would conclude that the focusing center of emotional activity is usually in the face, irrespective of the length of the pattern as it extends to other agents of the body. The seeming exceptions to the above conclusion are some of the interesting developments in the controversies of modern psychology.

There are about twenty-four pairs of muscles in the face, eighteen of which are used in showing the unpleasant responses and only six are used in registering the pleasant. This study alone is worthy of a full chapter, as it effects a fuller knowledge of dramatic art. But a comment only will be made.

Inasmuch as all emotions can be studied best in their relationship to responses, pleasant and unpleasant, we are vitally concerned with any study which clarifies their expression and existence. The very difference between the tragic and comic in life is paralleled with the study of facial expressions. By the laws of biology and results of evolution in man's development, we recognize the force of the grimness of early struggles in man's life. He has evolved a nature which responds to the unpleasant approximately three times as readily as he responds to the pleasant, or, there are many more ways to react to the unpleasant than to the pleasant in life. A catalogue of emotions further verifies this statement. In all animal life the opportunities of meeting the unpleasant are far greater than those which afford the pleasant responses. The enemies of life far outnumber the privileges of enjoying tranquillity. The hunt for food, being hunted for food, the change of elements, the finding and accepting of a mate, fire, pestilence, and famine are but a few of the conditions which keep animal life in a state of unrest. The males fight for hours for but a short period of mating, or the pleasure of a small area of forage.

Centuries of wars and unrest have left their external marks on the face of every human. The very struggle for existence is a serious business and but few men know how to get pleasure out of it. Civilization depends more upon man's mental adjustment to his surroundings and associations than it does upon his fitness to adjust to physical relations. To give freely is a great joy to one; to give at all, a begrudged separation for another. The human face reveals much more of the latter in man's development than the former. A Moses came in the distant past to raise man's concept somewhat higher than the better beast; a Messiah lived to aid man more fully to appreciate his dependence upon his fellow man; what the future generation holds for civilization will be revealed in the face of the current citizen. Most of the baser emotions can be expressed on the face of the higher forms of animals and but few of the better emotional responses ever form in their muscle response. Man has developed to the extent of expressing more of the pleasant responses, but has lost none of the expressions of lower or baser emotions. What will be the appearance of the human species when his major life is expressed in altruism, loving service, and tolerant patience? In a million years the answer will be written immutably on the face of man.

Most actors wish to play the tragic part in preference to all else because they have discovered a greater versatility and scope in expressing the unpleasant emotions than in the pleasant. Our greatest plays have been tragedies. Our greatest players have been tragedians.

The study of conduct as revealed by the human face is one of our most fascinating subjects. It must be left here, however, with a hope that all students of the drama will contribute some new ideas to life which will further enrich mankind.

As we analyze the face for expression, for our purpose, the cheeks become associated with the eyes and the mouth, and the chin can be associated with the lower lip. The nose shows animation only in the closing or expanding of the nostrils. Under extreme vital emotions, the nostrils expand and with extreme depressive emotions, they contract. The nostrils are of importance to but few emotional responses. Great care should be exercised that they do not intrude unnecessarily, as closing of the nostrils greatly affects resonance of voice in head cavities. The nose is especially important in showing disgust.

The Eyes, the Brows and Lids. These agents of expression just as often act independently as they do together. The eye, in a general usage, is understood to be the combination of three agents. In dramatic terms the eyeball, the brows, and lids are decidedly three independent agents.

The eye or eyeball in the great majority of cases is the first agent of expression. It is the determiner of attention; it reveals where the object is to which attention is focused. It shows the direction which others take in locating a person or object under consideration. The eye has been accepted, above all other agents, as being the universal director of attention. Great actors have that coveted power of easily using their eyes; they become a part of the scene when not speaking by using an attentive eye; they dominate and concentrate the scene when talking or acting by using their eyes in such an unquestionable manner, that all actors and audience know to whom remarks or actions are directed. A commanding speaker sweeps the room with his eye and talks directly to those within his compass. An eye which wanders from person to person aimlessly, or from object to person indifferently, can never maintain power with or over its associates. It is disastrous for an actor to take his eyes from the players and look at his audience. There is only one audience for the actor, and that audience is always on his stage. He plays *for* the audience in the auditorium, but he plays *to* the actors on the stage. His eyes must live within the realm of the play, and not in the freedom of the auditorium. The public speaker who lets his eyes wander out of the window to note a passing car or airplane carries some of his audience with him who may never return.

There is an observation about the eye which could help many of our actors and amateur Thespians. It is easily observed that a baby has a very open, round eye and that the adult seldom has a full round eye. There must be some pertinent reasons for this marked change. When we observe the babe in the crib for the first few weeks we see the head lies quite still and the eyes wander in all directions of the compass. This ability to move the eyes easily from left to right, up or down, without moving the head, carries on well into childhood. But by the time the child is able to move his head by the strength of his own neck, he starts gradually to use his eyes less in their entire radii and depends more upon the flexibility of his neck. When this person is adolescent, he uses his eyes almost dominantly up and down, as he follows the wink or the closing of the eyes. When any side attention is necessary, the neck becomes the greater pivot and the eyeball adjusts itself only on an up and down basis. As this process is carried on into maturity the side muscles of the eyes become less and less used, and the pull on the inside and outside of the eyes is minimized until these side muscles are weakened and the eye logically lengthens and the roundness of the eye is diminished. It accordingly becomes longer on the sides and more narrow between the brow and the cheek. This lengthening of the lobe of the eye plays many tricks with vision and is one of the major causes of eye trouble and need of glasses, the bugaboo of the actor's profession. If the thoughtful person would exercise all the muscles of the eye, the four side ones as well as the two which move the eyes up and down, he would have round eyes and thus greatly minimize the use of glasses.

By the time a person is adult, he seems to have a desire to smell everything he sees. He points his nose almost directly at the object of attention, whether that attention is of major or minor importance. So universal is this practice, that we could rightfully conclude that man must have been in the smelling age for some centuries, such an influence has been cast upon his conduct. Some people have been accused of putting their noses in other people's business; many more do this than they realize. Dramatic art demands that the actor have the ability of looking to the right or left, without dragging the nose along with the eyes. (The chin is the best face focus.)

That the iris of the eye contracts or enlarges in expression, there can be no doubt. But that it should be a matter of control, does not interest the actor. The chief concern is that the eye be well rested, sensibly used and exercised, and that it have the ability to move without the aid of the nose or neck. The dark eye carries farther with its expression than the light eye, chiefly because of visibility to the audience, not because the light-colored eye is any the less in expressive power. The larger eye has a decided advantage over the small one. The former can be lessened when necessary, but the latter cannot be made larger at will. The eye has been called the most beautiful thing in nature. Its color is less important than its power of expression.

The eye is the first agent to be used in expression. The *sequence of gesture* is the eye, the face, the chest, the foot, and the arm. This is invariably true, except when they are used simultaneously. To move otherwise is to appear awkward and ungraceful.

The Brows and Lids. There seems to be a very marked difference in the kind of gestures resulting from the use of the frowning and knitting muscles. The long muscle which runs over the top of the head to the base of the upper brow, very often condenses the forehead from three to six folds. The muscle which opposes the wrinkling one is situated at the base of the brow and pulls the forehead toward a center between the two eyebrows. This causes a knitting of the brow, or vertical wrinkles. These two activities constitute the chief methods of revealing thought with the brows. The brow may be taken up (horizontal lines), down (vertical lines), or complex (upper part of brow horizontal and the lower part perpendicular). The complex brow shows worry, grief, or sorrow. The brow has its greatest variety of expressions in coöperation with the lids. For the brow as an independent unit, there are four positions. Up, normal, down, and complex. With all the remaining agents of the face remaining normal, these four attitudes reveal forms of indifference, attention or animation, displeasure, and worry.

The lids not only move over the eyeball to keep it moist, thus causing the wink, at more or less frequent intervals, and also to shut out light from the retina for a refixation process, but they are also used for definite expression purposes. It is usual for the eyelids to respond together, though each may act independently of the other and it is advisable to acquire such control for comedy acting. The lids vary in degree of opening in which they are normally held when looking at an object in ordinary attention. Some people seldom open their eyes to the full. Usually the upper lid adjusts over the eyeball so that it just clears the pupil and does not extend past the iris. When the upper lid opens beyond the iris, the eye is given an awed look and if carried permanently is indicative of being awed with everything which is seen. Such a person is stupid or an imbecile. When the lid is held at a rational normality, the eye denotes attention, self-control, or a form of animation. The drooping of the lid, in its various degrees, when no other agent of the face is active, shows some form of weariness or fatigue. The closing of the eye indicates a desire to exclude avenues of thought reception, so as to concentrate within. When the eyelid is closed for a physical reason the world interprets as some form of sleep or the resting of tired eyes. If the brows and lids combine in thought expression, several easily recognized responses occur. With the brow down and the lid up, we see the commonest form of anger. With either of these agents lazy, the registration upon the audience is very uncertain. With the brow up and lid down, disdain, loathing, scorn, and insolence are shown, as the mouth and head positions vary. With the brow down and the lid down, man assumes his most used attitude for concentrated reflection. The brow and lids should be two of the most used agents of gesture.

The Mouth. The muscles about the mouth are the most flexible of all the face muscles. We daily see the lips contracted or stretched out, the corners move independently of the lips, both up and down, the upper lip may snarl on either side, while the lower lip often protrudes with little activity from other parts. The angle of the lips and the thickness thereof greatly affect the entire appearance of the face. The general disposition of a person is indelibly stamped on the flexible mouth.

The mouth is doubly conspicuous because of the many parts it plays in life. It is the great creator of speech, the agent of sound and words, and its every movement is therefore important. The mouth expresses many dozens of emotions, irrespective of the vocabulary it must master. The mouth is the first agent of expression in most individuals with its intimate love-making and affection. Kissing is the quintessence of touch, the nectar the poets acclaim and lovers aspire to. Some mouths move in speech as smooth as water over mossy falls—others gyrate as wobbly fish-wheels in the turbulent spring. Shakespeare had to admonish his players not to mouth their words. Teeth are integral parts of mouth beauty and must be preserved and respected as any agent of expression. Whiteness and cleanliness are essential and retainable. Many a beautiful face is ruined when the person opens his or her mouth. When a person is endowed with a huge cavity for a mouth, he should be grateful for the fact that great speakers and most great actors have had large mouths.

The corners of the mouth and the lips combine to perform the major expression of the mouth. With the corners of the lips down, the negative in attitude is registered. Corners down and lips closed, we recognize forms of disgust, discontent, displeasure; corners down and lips ajar, we see types of grief and sorrow; corners down and lips open, we register terror, horror, and fear (other facial agents, such as brows and lids, accompany these). With the corners even, and lips closed, we get a form of attention, firmness, or determination; corners even and lips ajar, we see eager attention, expectancy, and animated listening; corners even and lips open, we recognize awe, wonder, amazement, and forms of surprise. If this attitude of corners even and lips open is permanent, it is evidence of stupidity and even idiocy. Very often such a person drools and words are spoken in a lazy, incoherent manner. The tongue is sluggish and hangs out. Clutey

John in "John Ferguson," Bud in "Sun Up," and William in "The Devil's Disciple" are characters of this type used with excellent dramatic effect. Very often the Jester in "Paolo and Francesca" is interpreted as one below the level of the moron. When the corners are up and the lips closed, we see a smile of amusement; with the corners up and lips ajar, we recognize a hearty smile and enjoyment; and laughter is shown with the corners up and lips open. Loud laughter is not cultured, nor is a painful flit of lip muscle ever construed for laughter. We needs must get a temperance in all things. Laughter is a hearty exercise and a good relaxer of all abdominal and face muscles. The raising of just a portion of the upper lip is used to show utter contempt. Children will protrude both lips, especially the lower one, in pouting. Not that I would confine pouting to children as far as life is observed, but it is primarily a puerile gesture.

The lower jaw is often projected as a method of showing meanness and rowdy spirit; it is sometimes taken in to aid in showing childish disgust. Other than these two responses, the jaw serves little in expressional purposes. It should be used but little in speech, being kept well open and relaxed.

I have known people who could move their ears at command. It added but little to their expressional powers, but it did furnish a sense of comedy in its unusualness.

The face is one of the most interesting objects of study in the realm of man's consciousness. All the mind is reflected in the face and its powers of expression have seldom been approximated. As one conquers the technic of face expression, he finds a ready synchronization with other parts of the body. As the average man and woman settle down to the mediocrity of complaisant marriage, routine of content, and ever-diminishing circle of friends, the lexicon of countless emotional experiences of youth dwindles into a monody of listless motions and effortless expression. God's greatest creation lies flattened to a mold of inexpression—the human face.

The Torso. The trunk or torso of man is the least visible of all his agents in the use of expression. Most people keep the face uncovered at all times. As civilization develops and suffrage is made equal, this is becoming universally true. Bare feet and arms have been generally accepted, but the torso has been usually covered in civilized races. Just what constitutes civilization, only scholars in the distant future will be able to say, but it is a notable fact that clothing came to be used by the aborigines when white men abused the social relations among the darker skinned natives. As "civilization" spread, clothing became more prevalent. When previously worn for protection purposes only, the prude and the *roué* later had clothing worn by the natives for moral purposes chiefly. With the appearance of restrictive and superdecorative clothing, suppleness of the body gave way to obesity and awkwardness. The more advanced and complex the civilization, the less folk dances have been used. Folk dances have always been great aids to body grace and health encouragement; they have now almost disappeared from the globe despite our efforts to catch and preserve their flitting shadows in university gymnasiums.

Clothing has had considerable effect upon our conduct and body deportment. And its greatest effect has been on the torso. There is a considerable difference between nudity and lewdity. Lewdness is often most conspicuous in people overdressed. The moral code was never so low on the English stage as it was during the eighteenth century, and the clothing worn by its women has never since been so abundant, nor have men ever again worn such fantastic laces, ribbons, and abundance of befuddled clothing as in this period.

Possibly corsets have affected the torso as much as any apparel conceived by man. Supple bodies were replaced by absurd stiffness. A natural waist of twenty-eight inches was displaced for a modish eighteen. The wasp form became the rage and Venus de Milo was a forgotten model. The present generation has not effaced the effects of several generations of tight lacing. The entire method of proper breathing was undone and the small waist prohibited good health and great singing. Diaphragmatic breathing is done in minimum when the belt is unduly tightened or the clothing excessively confining. The small of the back is curved in and the torso is considerably distorted.

Instead of the walk centering from the upper chest, in a series of forward fallings, that is, having the chest lead in forward body activity, the walking is centered in the hips and an ambling process of motivation results. The long, full muscles of the front torso have been pinched and made inactive and walking is purely a hip and leg exercise, rather than a full body development. Grace is impossible when the center of gravity has been displaced from its natural position. When man distorts any member of his body, he has affected all his body. The most damage that can be done is any which affects the freedom of body movement. The neck, the arms and legs, all come from a common center—the torso. None of these agents can perfectly function if their center be inhibited in freedom of activity.

The proper carriage of the torso is to be erect, chest held high, but not rigid, and the shoulder blades far apart. This latter is very important, as so many think they have a good position if the shoulders are thrown back and the upper chest tightened. Chest capacity for breathing is as dependent upon proper carriage of the back of the torso as it is of the front. If the chest is never dropped, there can be but one method of breathing, and that the proper way, diaphragmatic. Proper carriage is not only necessary for grace, it is imperative for proper breathing.

The day of the flat chest has just about gone. When clothing is worn, it best adorns a body of developed proportions. All the art world knows that the most beautiful line and contour is the curve of a woman's breast and shoulder. (The greatest line of beauty suggesting power is seen in a man's thigh.) With or without adornment, the breast of man or woman must have an erect body to give it the best position and beauty.

Possibly the person who suffers most from a bad posture is the tall young woman. There is something almost universal in her mental attitude. She stoops to appear less conspicuous, and attains the very opposite of her desire. She becomes more noticeable and in an unfavorable manner. Her very slouchiness calls attention to itself. But what is more attractive than a tall woman who carries herself with a queenly mien? The size of such a person is less evident and the proportions of the body are more evenly balanced. Power and attractiveness are shown in every movement. No stooping makes a person really shorter; it does hurt breathing and wearing of good clothes, and becomes a factor of itself for observation.

Because of the importance of the head on the neck and the arms from the shoulders, the upper chest receives a major importance in many of our gestures. It should be accordingly honored.

As we observe the torso for gesture purposes, we see three distinct zones: the upper chest, the heart region, and the abdomen. I can possibly explain this division with a homely example by showing the relation of the torso as affected by smell. Not that we smell in these regions, but that our gesture centers are affected by subtle differences. When we put ammonia to our nostrils, we inhale very sparsely, as if the fumes could go only a way past the larynx, and our hand could stop them; when we breathe the perfume of violets, we often put both hands over our heart and inhale freely; when we stand near the table and the kitchen door is suddenly swung open, the aroma of soup is wafted to us, we see hands put over hungry stomachs as we inhale to the very depths of our lungs. Such examples could be multiplied to a great amount. The upper zone is often called the "honor" zone. That is a very good designation. Most gestures of the arms should be done in this area, that is, even with the shoulders. So many people do all their gesturing of the arms in the "material" zone, or low in the plane of gesture. They live in the "inferior" planes. A man in life with a high sense of honor invariably gestures with his arms even with his shoulders. Exceptions are of interest, only as they prove what has just been said. Petty people and sensualists gesture around the hips, men of high ideals in honor gesture in the shoulder zone. *No laws can be stated that will regulate conduct, observations can only be expressed which may aid the judicious.*

The torso, being affective by nature, best shows likes and dislikes. When we turn the body from a person it is our best means of revealing some form of dislike, even though we still look at the person. This must not be forgotten on the stage. So many actors expect to express all their thoughts with their heads and hands. The torso is the dominant affective or volitional agent of expression.

The Limbs. The legs and the arms offer the most interesting study of human expression, except the face. The legs, as expressive agents, do most of their work with the various positions on the feet. The carriage of the legs is not so important in revealing thought as the carriage or bearing of the arms. When a person stands so that his knees bow outward, he is a victim of physical deformity. When he stands with his elbows held well out, he is manifesting a very evident degree of self-importance. The leg and the foot cannot change their form as easily as the arm and the hand. Both are less flexible and, consequently, the leg and foot show fewer thought expressions. A multiplicity of expression is revealed by the ever-changing hand and very flexible arm.

The limbs are the great "doing" or "acting" agents of man. Cut off a man's limbs; he is helpless indeed; he has but one major expressive agent left, and that is the mouth. Huxley and others have said that man is man because of his hands and his use of his hands. Man is a greater man in that machinery is but the extension of his hands. A study of the arm and leg as units leads to the observation that the limbs are the "doing" or "vital" agents of the body. Characters of power, or strength, of physical vitality, will use their arms and legs to a greater degree than a character who gets most of life in terms intellectual. The gestures of a dynamic fullback are considerably fuller and larger in scope than the sophomore dig. A Robin Hood will be much more vital in action than a Richelieu. Katherine will have more vigorous lines of action than will Bianca. Holbrook Blinn liked the vigorous character just as George Arliss prefers the mental.

We conclude, by studying life in a broad plane, that the head is the mental agent of the body in expression, the torso is affective in nature, and the limbs are vital. Such general observations can but lead to specific results in the studious actor.

The Feet. Most of man's thought expressed by the feet is by the position of the body over the feet. It simplifies itself with relation to center of gravity; man's response in evolving to the upright, in opposition to the animal's general position of the horizontal. Why do animals walk on all fours and in the horizontal, and man walks on but two feet and tends toward the vertical? This question is one of the most interesting in the realm of expression. The fact that kangaroos use their hind feet and tail, or that birds use only two feet, does not lessen the importance of the above question, as observation proves. The base of the kangaroo is considerably larger than man's in proportion to his body, and all fowls fly in the horizontal. Animals tend to have a horizontal body position and man tends to the vertical.

In order to focus the discussion, without multiplying too many examples for proof, I shall start with a statement suggested by the much misunderstood François Delsarte,[1] "Mind activity, or intelligence, is expressed proportionately to narrowness of base."

Intelligence and Base. To state that "mind activity or intelligence is expressed proportionately to narrowness of base" is very ambiguous, unless we predicate some qualifications and examples.

By base, we mean, as in physics, the distance between the points of contact on the supporting surface. For the animal, it is the rectangle made by drawing lines between the four feet. For a human, the distance between the two heels and the front of each foot. These bases are variable. For a cube, the base is a constant square. For a grand piano, the base is a triangle. For a ball, the base is a point. Whether the body is balanced, depends upon the relation of specific gravity to its base. If the center of gravity passes within its base, the body is balanced. If the center of gravity passes without the base, the body will seek a balance, unless counteracted by some modifying circumstance or condition. If a human loses control of

[1] Monsieur Delsarte died before he had opportunity to formulate his notes into a logical philosophy, but many of his principles, on the verge of a proper unfoldment, were so misunderstood and misquoted, that elocution became a byword in all America and has not yet risen from the stamp of disapproval put upon it. Some of the better teachers in America clarified and amplified much which was started, but never finished by Delsarte. Psychologists and dramatic art students must do the rest. Delsarte could not be used to-day in his fantastic entirety, any more than Grecian laws of rhetoric could prevail. But we can give honor where honor is due. Michelangelo and Shakespeare were not understood by all the artists of their day, but their works have not been wholly denounced by the present generation. And much of modern sociology was anticipated by humble teachers of dramatic art. Pages could be written of Corax, Delsarte, Salvini, Calvert, and Steel Mackaye, but that belongs to another discussion. Because of the transitory nature of acting, its great teachers have been unhonored by history. Their memory but lives in the imperishable mind.

his senses, his body succumbs and will fall as any innate physical matter, so as to seek the first available position for balance. Active intelligence has been the factor for keeping the body upright, has been the agency for keeping the body poised upright over the feet.

It is interesting to observe a babe's struggle for this upright position. At birth, he lies sprawling in the crib, the length of his body. He sits up in the course of a few months, and then we see him crawling. His next advance is to lean on bits of furniture until he can stand. From this, he lets go of his support and toddles, walking with a wide base. In the course of a few more months, he has become able to support himself on one foot and stand erect. He has developed from the babe of a broad base to a potential man of a small base. His intelligence has correspondingly increased, at least as far as his adaptability to his environment is concerned. He has developed so that his body can be supported on his legs, and he remains upright to be the better able to move in any direction with the least amount of effort, and at the same time keep his arms free to carry out the mandates of a reasoning mind. This struggle to reach the vertical position necessitates a narrow base and makes man different from any other animal.

When man reaches maturity he may walk erect to the speakeasy, procure his hip bottle and his friends later notice his unsteady walk, his base becoming broader as intellect is clouded, and later in the evening his eyes are blurred and the walk has become a lurch. When friends again see this alcohol addict, he has lost complete control of his senses and lies prone on the street. As the use of his intelligence lessened, his base broadened to the full horizontal.

The coarser characters in life stand with a broadened base; a gentleman stands erect. As has been stated previously, trades reflect themselves upon character; character is shown to an interesting extent by position on the feet. A low type of intelligence can build a flat hut; a generation of intellectual giants are responsible for sky-scrapers. It is natural for intelligence to build up, accumulate, collect—hence the *significance of vertical lines in gesture.* It is natural for materials to be subjected to the law of gravity, which tears down and spreads out. Hence the *significance of horizontal gestures.* This ever-present struggle within man, to build up or be weighed down, is evident in his foot positions, and in his major planes of gesture. Vertical lines affirm and build up; horizontal lines deny, tear down, and overthrow.

Man stands erect on a small base because he has learned it is the best way to stand, to do the most efficient work and accomplish the greatest intellectual efforts. Compare a champion of liberty and a philosopher of the country street corner, or an alert broker and a river stevedore. Notice how they stand when at their work. From such a starting place, we place characters in various categories, or, better still, we watch the same person in many standing positions.

We easily observe that man first stands on his two feet, and on the middle of his two feet. That is, the foot has three positions through which the center of gravity can pass, and man maintains his balance; the ball, the middle (when foot is entirely on the floor, from heel to toe), and the heel. A person may stand on the toes, but that is a terpsichorean exercise and is properly left to the ballet dancer. It has little province in expression, except as an exaggerated position of grace. From these three positions which a babe early learns, nine foot positions are eventually used. Three on both feet, three on the advanced foot, and three on the withdrawn foot.

As man stands upright on two feet, if he be attracted to an object, he discovers that the weight of this body is on the balls of his feet, or forward. When an object of unpleasant aspect comes to his consciousness and he withdraws, he observes that his weight is on both heels. He is standing on the middle of the foot when neither vitally active nor vitally withdrawn. The first step in a baby's life is a very important event. The child graduates from a simple base of two feet to a complex base. He is now able to stand on either foot, with all three positions on each, each position having a very definite meaning.

On the withdrawn or back foot, degrees of vitality are expressed progressively. The least vitality is shown on the heel and the most is revealed by standing on the ball of the foot. This relationship applies to the advanced or forward foot, and also to both feet. By withdrawn or advanced, we mean our relation to the object of attention. If I could observe myself in a state of fear, to a point of prostration, I would note that the weight of the body would be on the heel of the withdrawn foot. A more easily observed experience is to watch hikers reach the top of a great snow mountain. In 1923, I was the first of one hundred and fifteen to reach the top of the great glacier mountain, Timpanogos, of the Uintahs. The ascent was mostly on snow and ice and shale rock. As I sat near the flagpole on the twelve-thousand-foot level, I waited for the long string of hikers to reach the top. Most of them arrived in a state of near exhaustion, and one hundred and four dropped to the snow or rocks with the weight of the body on the heel of the withdrawn foot. Six did not sit at all, more inspired with the magnificent view than anything so personal. The remaining five dropped to the snow on their knees and hands. This ratio is consistent with the responses we observe in the average human conduct. There are always a few who do not conform, because of certain mental differences and adjustments to environment.

The responses as indicated in the chart below are universal and all understood. Exceptions are personal and not to be used for stage purposes, unless adaptable to some eccentric or comedy character:

Back Foot

HEEL	MIDDLE	BALL
prostration-fatigue weariness	concentrated thinking mental repose	defiance active resentment

Both Feet

HEEL	MIDDLE	BALL
respect servitude	ease (vulgar ease)	uncertainty indecision

Front Foot

HEEL	MIDDLE	BALL
suspense anxiety	animation exuberance	vital or explosive response

What was said of the position on the heel of the withdrawn or back foot could be elaborated in analysis of all other positions. To comment upon but a few: What is the difference between a command, when the person stands on the middle of his withdrawn foot, or on the middle of his advanced foot? If an actor were to say "Go" and stood on the advanced foot, it would imply physical force; wherein the same command and standing on the withdrawn foot, would be less of the physical and imply mental power. Such a difference as one would observe in Macbeth and Hamlet. Defiance is seldom seen. A lifetime may pass before we actually see it. Watching for these attitudes for years, I have seen defiance but four times and shame only three. Yet drama calls for both of these attitudes many times in the course of a career. Many actors have to portray emotions they have never personally witnessed, experienced or felt in all their lives. Respect is one of the most universal of standing positions. Soldiers and servants the world over so stand, when listening to a superior officer or employer. Gentlemen stand in this manner when being presented to a lady, though courtesies are fast dying out.

The Latins are the most courteous and graceful of the gentlemen, and best know how to honor a lady. Their feet are always graceful and deportment is a conscious part of their training. Will Irwin, as special correspondent with the Herbert Hoover party to South America, wrote an article on the importance of Latin manners. He advised American firms to send only such men as could assimilate the courtesies of deportment. "To do otherwise not only is bad business, but poor patriotism." With the equality of sexes being more generally established, there has grown a greater disregard of man's respect for women. This should not be a criterion for man's respect of man. Manners is the training a people gives its citizens for deportment among its own kind. It is a serious breach of etiquette and understanding not to honor such manners when visiting these people. Foreigners look askance at American feet.

No refined person stands with his feet far apart. Should three women stand so on a street corner, with their hands on their hips, the remarks of passers-by would convince us of the status of such women in society.

There seems to be a certain let down in the responsibility for our feet when we get seated in a comfortable chair. Poiret, the French haberdasher, condemns the modern short skirt on women, as it leaves so little to imagination. He must have visited some American or English parties, where the distance between the feet is inhibited only by the expanse of the skirt. It is as imperative to have good deportment of the feet when seated as it is when standing. This is just as true of the beach as it is of the stage. Irrespective of the length of the skirt, the knees should balance the posture of the leg and the body. Gentlemen on the stage should also be cognizant of this. As a law of grace, the knees should not be far apart, and should be consistent with the line of grace from the hip to the foot. Even though we represent a character at rest on the stage, we must not forget that the character is at rest in public.

In general, the more advanced our weight is placed, the more vital or active is the scene or character and the more withdrawn we stand, the less vital or active is the scene or character. When the weight of the body is on both feet, it represents a less definite attitude of mental or physical response. The nine actual positions of weight distribution should be consciously learned and unconsciously used.

The standing on the sides of the feet is seldom used, and then only for a very uncouth awkwardness, such as might be used for a Topsy or a Sis Hopkins. In standing before an audience, the extended line from the heel of the advanced foot should strike the arch of the withdrawn foot. Inasmuch as most people are right-handed, the left foot will dominate in public speaking

On the stage, we regulate base and arm movements to the character addressed. There is less of right- and left-handedness on the stage than there is in life. We must learn poise and action for either side of body activity. "Crossing" of the leg or arm is to be avoided, except as we wish to appear awkward. By crossing, we mean to be standing on the right foot and fling the left leg over to go right. To use the upstage limb is not only better for "looks," but also economy of movement.

Many observers of health and dramatic art have hoped that the ridiculous high heel would be but a passing fad. Its popularity in urban circles for the past fifteen years, and the styles yet in vogue, cause it to be considered seriously. It can no longer be ignored. Many pretty girls on the stage wear the most extreme patterns, and college girls in daily class work can be seen rubbing throbbing arches. Lest it be misunderstood, we readily admit that the high heel on the shoe very often gives it an excellent line and beautifies the appearance of an otherwise ordinary foot. The only defense for the high heel is that it may add beauty to the appearance of the maid. Short girls are the most flagrant users of the extreme high heels. Their reason is as untenable as the drooping of the tall girl to make her shorter.

The high heel is one of the greatest destroyers of grace. It may add good lines to a clumsy foot but it does not add to the grace or carriage of the body. For every part of an inch over an inch and a quarter to an inch and a half for the heel, just that distance must be paid for by the knees or the small of the back. To clarify such a statement, we may ask the interested to stand on the floor in stocking feet. Walk several yards and note carriage of the body and legs very carefully. Then put on a heel just an inch in height and again note carriage. The center of gravity remains approximately in the same areas. Raise that heel to two inches, then three inches, and one of two things happens; the body remains straight and the knees bent for balancing purposes and the person walks as one about to squat, or, the legs are straight (and the body has to bend over, which is seldom done) and the body is bent where nature has already provided a balance point, the curve in the back just over the hips. This is the danger point we especially note. But few women walk with legs bending much at the knee; they make the body adjust to gravity by bending the back farther forward. This bending of the spine forward cramps the spinal cord and becomes one of the chief vertebræ sections enriching the chiropractor. The straighter the back the less pressure of nerve centers in the vertebræ. The higher the heel, the sooner a person strikes the sidewalk or stage with a wooden thud. Instead of walking being a series of falling movements, the leg is thrown sidewise until the heel has reached a sufficient distance in front to make it possible to take up the additional three-inch height. If a girl thinks the hip is the center of walking balance, then she does well to wear high heels—she positively accomplishes her result. If she knows that body guidance is controlled from a higher source, then heels will be worn commensurate to her personal charm, grace, and health. Health is not the least element in radiating personality.

Extreme high heels inhibit graceful walking, throw the spinal cord out of proper alignment and make walking a conspicuous clatter rather than a pleasant transportation. The bones and muscles of the foot once misplaced over a period of time, never again regain their vigorous power and buoyancy.

The Arm. The arm is divided into three physiognomic groups: the upper arm, the forearm, and the hand. The upper arm is the great power agent, the forearm is the dominant agent for showing the affective relations, and the hand is the great thought revealer of the arm.

The arm has three general ways of carriage, which we universally recognize. By carriage, we mean the manner in which a member is habitually held. Elbows out, revealing importance or assertion of ego; elbows normal, self-control; and elbows in, revealing timidity, or self-suppression. Elbows out tell people to get out of the way; elbows drawn close to the body, say "excuse me for living." The carriage of the arm is therefore important as revealing attitudes of self, just as were the vertical positions of the head.

The general laws dominating the grace of the arm are very important and must become a thorough application of unconscious technic. The Grecian philosophers and sculptors were very careful with these laws, which may be briefly stated. In *all gestures of unfoldment or evolution,* the wrist leads the hand and the elbow shows the extent or direction. This is in obedience to a law which is seen in operation in all phenomena of life. A tree shoots out a limb, then the branches unfold, and ultimately the expanding leaf. We watch a foundation being laid, bricks follow, and eventually a roof. This sequential development may be broken by arm movements and awkwardness results. If the hand spreads out and later the arm is straightened, we have grown the leaves before the branch was developed. Such effects are used in weird witch dances, but not in graceful technic. *In gestures of enfoldment or involution* (turning in), the fingers lead the wrist, and the arm makes a related curve. The joints of the arm should never be conspicuous as joints and diversion points for changing direction. If the hand is being taken to the chest, the fingers should lead just as the tip of the morning-glory petal first turns when the blossom folds for the night. We never see the calyx fold and later observe the petal turning. Nature folds back to a center in the reverse order in which she unfolded. Man must obey these fundamental laws if he would be graceful and conserve energy.

Another observation about the arm is very important. The head opposes the hand, the chest opposes the forearm, and the torso opposes the upper arm. This great *law of opposition* is of tremendous interest. It reverts fundamentally to the law of balance, which is matter in obedience to gravity. If we pile books on one side of a reading stand, it eventually tips over. If we place the books on opposite sides, the stand holds a burden to its maximum capacity. A great tree is a balanced beauty. Almost to a pound, the limbs and foliage measures equally to either side. (This is always true unless environmental adjustments are necessary.) When we walk, the right arm opposes the left arm and parallels the left leg—when the right arm goes out the left arm goes back. Balance of the body forward and backward is equally essential. When we tip our hats, our hands go toward the head, else we should never get the hat. That is opposition of the head and hand. When the athlete gets ready to put the shot, his left leg extends to front as he leans back with the weight in his right arm, then as he throws the weight his right arm extended forward and his left leg extends backward. Helen Wills Moody is champion woman tennis player of the world, chiefly because of her marvelous body opposition. She is always in perfect balance. We readily recognize the athletic body on the stage—it is regrettable that a beautiful voice does not always accompany the beautiful body.

The division of the space on the canvas is one of the chief concerns of the painter. He very carefully obeys the law of opposition—his perspective with his opposing areas, is the real artistry. In music, harmony is nothing more than opposition, just as melody is its unfoldment. In four-part work, the alto is continually opposing the soprano, and the bass the tenor. Study any score of merit and note how an up of the soprano is met by a down of the alto. Certain instruments in the orchestra are always opposing each other in the same manner. If one would be graceful and harmonious, he must learn obedience to fundamental laws of nature.

The Hand is one of man's most powerful agents of expression. While it is the great doer of man's desires, it is primarily the mental agent of the arm. With the hand we indicate, classify, mold, describe, and other such purely mental activities. To write a letter is really to form syllables. The hand is divided into three significant areas: the edge, the back, and the palm. The edge of the hand is definitive, the back is affective, and the palm is executive, or vital. If we see a girl resting her cheek on the back of her hand, we give it little heed, except as it indicates some attitude with sentiment, but when we see the palm of her hand over her cheek, we immediately think of toothache; especially is this true if both hands are used. When the arm is extended in front and bent at the elbow, so that the forearm is parallel to the body, it makes a great difference whether the palm is toward the object or from it. If we go toward a person and we are confronted by an extended arm and straightened palm, turned in, we readily know we are not welcome. The hand is the great indicator of the arm. It is to the arm, what the eyeball is to the face. The French are very facile with their hands, and they recognize keen psychic uses even for the fingers. The thumb is the vital member, the two outer fingers are the mental, and the two inner fingers are the affective agents. The world recognizes the first finger as the pointing or index finger; the little finger is next in importance for pointing out. Only the coarser types of people point with their thumbs. Scratch your lower lip with the index finger, as if thinking, and then do the same with the little finger, and your discernment will tell you why the French call the index finger an agent of "masculine sagacity" and the little finger "feminine subtlety." Except for vital gestures, which extend activity and decentralize movements, the two inner fingers are best kept together for grace and beauty. The two outside fingers should also have similar vitality given to them. A study of statuary will further reveal the importance of position for grace and power of hand gesture. It is well to keep in mind that vertical gestures affirm and horizontal gestures abnegate or deny.

An ugly hand can be made to appear graceful if the person learns the laws of opposition, unfoldment and enfoldment, and practices movements until the most beautiful lines have become unconsciously employed.

The hand has been written about in many books. Eleanora Duse had such beautiful hands that D'Annunzio wrote a very powerful play to call especial attention to those hands and Duse played the part in "Giaconda" with consummate success. Bernhardt was also superb with her hands. In "La Dame aux Camillias," she did even more with her hands after the amputation of her leg. A movement of a little finger said as much in the later years of her career as the whole body of an average actress. When Haaj, the Beggar (Otis Skinner), playfully drowned the cruel Wazir in "Kismet," it was the feet of Skinner which conveyed the comedy, and the hand of the Wazir, as it slowly disappeared in the harem pool, which revealed his tragic ending.

The movies have endeavored, from time to time, to show great struggle by showing only the hand rather than film the usual agony of a suffering face. The grim hand clutches desperately in the slimy mud and a soldier disappears in the horror of a trench of death. The suggestion of the hand creates in imagination a stronger impression than actuality itself. Lon Chaney liked to silhouette, in a grotesque shape, a bony hand playing over his intended victim. The Gish sisters use their hands more than any other agents of expression to show nervousness. No actor on the American stage to-day shows greater power or better acting with the hands than George Arliss. His is a consummate technic of masterful artistry. From "The Devil" to "Old English" he has talked with his hands.

For those who must know the meaning of "prone" and "supine" I have included a list of references. It is difficult to write fully of the hand because much of its strength lies in movement. It has many attitudes or positions which definitely convey thought, and an indication of some of those attitudes may prove of interest.

The hand conveys thought in varying degrees as it concenters itself in a clenched fist, to decentralizing itself by spreading fingers far apart. The more clenched, or to a center, the hand is used, the more it conveys mental struggle, and the more spread out, or from a center, a hand is used, the more the active or vital is shown. From the accentric (to a center) attitude of the hand (being most accentric when clenched) to the most eccentric (or spread apart and hand back on wrist) the hand shows in successive positions of unfoldment, the following attitudes: mental struggle (all fingers and thumb tight together—with this special injunction, never clench a fist with thumb inclosed; that is left for the weak-minded); detection (thumb against tips of fingers is the most common, though drumming on table or rubbing of forehead by finger tips, are both familiar); agony (curved fingers and thumb, spread apart, hand facing body); weariness or fatigue (with fingers reposed, except thumb dropped in); repose and ease (with all fingers easily curved and not too eccentric); tenderness and affection (the hand in easy curves with fingers and thumb and palm down toward object); exasperation (fingers spread out and tips curved in, and palm facing from body, differing chiefly from agony wherein the palm faces in and fingers are more eccentric); mild surprise (with palm out and fingers almost straight); and extreme surprise, such as fear, terror, etc. (when fingers are straight, far apart, and palm very still, facing object).

The hand is very helpful in the descriptive gestures, but not less used in the manifestative. For the attitudinal gestures, as briefly described in above paragraph, we note a dominance of the manifestative. The gestures themselves are self-explanatory. With descriptive gesture, words usually precede or accompany. Such gestures as the following will better indicate: the hand defines (edge active, in vertical line and hand straight, thumb not hugging the index finger), it supports (palm up and straight), it affirms (palm down, hand straight, with such a thought as "Don't touch it—leave it there"), it rejects (hand at right angle with wrist, palm up and spread out toward object of rejection), it assails (palm toward object, with fingers eccentric), or caresses (palm toward object and fingers curved but not too much, and note that the thumb is out and even with the fingers). These are merely indicative and show the many uses the hand possesses in expression of varied thoughts. Truly man is great because of his hand.

Emotions in Expression. It is not the province of this brief to present a symposium of the some hundred and one definitions of emotion. They are yet one of the most interesting problems and studies for the psychologist. What we care is, that they exist in the live human body and are a part and parcel of dramatic art. They are peculiar in that they seem to live in pairs or opposites: defiance and submission, joy and sadness, conceit and humility, severity and tenderness, to name but a few of a great number. They are the product of thought in nerve and muscle response, and have well-defined patterns. By assuming the form of an emotion, a trained actor can quickly assimilate the emotion. The amount of "feeling" put into any emotional response can be controlled. This is imperative to dramatic art and all speech arts. The person who cannot control and call up emotions as occasion demands will never be a great artist. Some players become so mechanical in long runs that their parts are but automatic responses and lack the virility of first weeks. A great actor makes his exterior self do most of his work and supplies just enough emotional fervor to affect his voice and enliven his character. To reiterate, a great actor is one who can arouse his audience to emotional responses. Emotions are not transferable, though they do have group effects. A person clapping in an audience often starts dozens of others who had no intention of such applause. What makes one cry, very often makes another laugh. A dramatic situation reacts differently within the audience. Many men cried when they saw and heard Al Jolson in his first singing picture, "The Jazz Singer." Others were embarrassed at such "weakness" and laughed at their neighbors. It is a wise showman who knows just how far he can "pull" the emotional strings. The saturation point to-day is much more easily reached than it was in the sentimental novel period and in the days of weeping heroines. Sarah Siddons could work an audience to such an emotional pitch that riots were not infrequent in London.

Emotions, like other controllable commodities, have their days and their fads. Race questions become very ticklish in some quarters of the globe, to be forgotten in a few generations. Slavery is no longer the burning issue of the South, though there are yet a few who carry over some of the traditions of its presence, and they often show this in an audience response. Sex and gang plays have their day, and like mist in the sky vanish from playgoing interest overnight. To break a woman's heart was once gossip for an entire nation; now it receives less attention than a drop in the price of aluminum combs. The ultra-sensational which fills our daily papers, and consequently our lives, has almost washed the American face dry of the finer emotions. There are very few Lincolns to stop and turn a bug over on its feet. The sublimity of mother is more difficult to find in casting type than is the habitué of the night club. That is but a reflection of a phase of national life. The interest in aviation, prohibition, biography, and sports are all being shown in the current drama. Even companionate marriage must have its day. The playwright tries to catch the peak of a national interest and profit in a commercial or popular show. Shakespeare lives as no other dramatist, because he depended less upon emotional fads and more upon eternal principles.

One of the richest experiences in an actor's or student's life is to portray some hundred emotions to a group of friends. His vanity will receive a terrible shock. The degree of efficiency of recognition depends upon two factors, the experience of the audience and the ability of the actor properly to portray. In a group of trained students and observing actors, the ratio of accurate recognition is considerably higher than it is when the audience is picked at random. Most of the tests recorded to date have failed to recognize this important fact. The actor must also remember that the audience before him is usually "picked at random." [2] This difference of ability to recognize portrayed emotion between a trained group and an untrained group, is just as true as it is that artists see much more in paintings than do ordinary laymen. Actors paint their canvas upon human minds. When those minds have been

[2] The New York Theatre Guild and Pasadena Community Players have picked audiences and correspondingly produce better plays.

trained consciously to observe human action, the actor will, of necessity, paint better pictures. The painter can be reasonably sure of his oils and canvas; the actor never knows just what fabric sits before him, and quite often his picture is blurred and even runs, because of the poor quality of its texture.

The hope of American and world drama lies as much with the audience as it does with the actor, though the actor should lead the way. The American audience has a greater opportunity for a varied emotional life than any public in the world's history. This should redound to a greater drama and a greater actor. The Latins have seldom learned proper control of their emotions; the Anglo-Saxons have almost submerged them. The future American must strike a happy medium to be anything of the superman, or the great actor, for which we aspire.

Of all the materials of dramatic art, the emotions will ever remain the actor's greatest problem and greatest power.

GESTURE AND EMOTIONAL RESPONSE

Books of Outstanding Interest and Merit

Acting: A Book for the Beginner, Crafton and Royer (Crofts, New York).

Art of Acting: discussion by Coquelin, Irving and Boucicault (Columbia University Press, New York).

Art of Pantomime. The, Charles Aubert. Sears translation (Holt, New York).

Artistic Anatomy, J. Duval, revised by Peterson (Cassell, London).

Art of Speech Deportment, The, Anna Morgan (McClurg, Chicago).

System of Delsarte, Genevieve Stebbins (Werner, London).

Elements of Speech, O'Neill and Weaver (Longmans, Green, New York), Chap. V.

Expression of Emotions in Man and Animals, Charles Darwin (Appleton, New York).

Fundamentals of Speech, C. H. Woolbert (Harpers, New York).
Masks and Faces: Psychology of Acting, William Archer (Longmans, London).
Philosophy of Expression The, M. T. Brown (Houghton Mifflin, Boston).
Physiognomy and Expression, Paolo Mantegazza, English Edition (London).
Psychology, General Readings in, Robinson and Robinson (University of Chicago Press, Chicago).
Psychology from the Standpoint of a Behaviorist, J. B. Watson (Lippincott, Philadelphia).
Social Psychology, Floyd Allport (Houghton Mifflin, Boston), Part II.
Talks on Expression, Leland T. Powers (Groom, Boston).
Technique in Dramatic Art, Hilliam Bosworth (Macmillan, New York).
Technique of Pantomime, Florence Lutz (Sather Gate Book Shop, Berkeley, Cal.),
Theatre Practice, Stark Young (Scribner, New York).
Thirty Six Dramatic Situations, G. Polti, L. Ray translation (Reeve, New York).

Acting

Ambrose, G. B., "Can Actor Create Real Acting?" *Mask,* Vol. 9, 1923, pp. 12-14.
Bloom, Vera, "Tyranny of Tears," *Theatre,* Vol. 27 (April, 1918), pp. 214-215.
Brewster, E. V., "How They Make Us Laugh," *Motion Picture Magazine,* Vol. 30 (August, 1915), pp. 40-41.
Calhoun, Dorothy, "Crying Real Tears on the Screen," *Motion Picture Magazine,* Vol. 29 (July, 1925), pp. 32-33.
Cohan, G. M., and Nathan, G. J., "Mechanics of Emotion," *McClure's,* Vol. 42 (November, 1913), pp. 69-77.
Cook, B. C., "Manufacturing Stage Laughter," *Theatre,* Vol. 23 (June, 1916), pp. 359-360.
Cowl, Jane, "Is Stage Emotion Real?" *Theatre,* Vol. 23 (May, 1916), pp. 145-146.
Eubanks, L. E., "Emotions: How Worked Up," *Motion Picture Classic,* Vol. 5 (October, 1917), pp. 31-34.

Grein, J. T., "Acting and Feeling," *Illustrated London News,* Vol. 163 (November 3, 1923), p. 810. Replies: *Ibid,* November 23, 1923, p. 954*ff*.

Landis, Carney, "Expression of Emotion," in *Foundations of Experimental Psychology,* C. Murchison, Editor (1929).

Patterson, Ada, "When the Smile Meets the Tears," *Theatre,* Vol. 38 (June, 1923), p. 27.

Pratt, J. A., "Should the Actor Feel His Part?" *Quarterly Journal of Speech Education,* Vol. 11 (February, 1925), pp. 64-67. Reply by I. Perego, *Ibid.,* June, 1925, pp. 288-292.

Schloppisch, S. J., "Expressing Emotions on the Screen," *Motion Picture Magazine,* Vol. 12 (August, 1916), pp. 46-48.

Smith, F. J., "What Moves Actors to Tears," *Photoplay Magazine,* Vol. 23 (May, 1923), p. 325.

"Emotionalism, Exit: Enter Charm," *Sunset,* Vol. 22 (May, 1909), pp. 493-501.

Stage Fright

Fiske, M. M., "Effect of First Night upon Actors," *Critic,* Vol. 39 (1901), p. 317.

Gillette, W. H., "The Illusion of the First Time in Acting," *Nation,* Vol. 101 (December, 1915), pp. 606-607.

Gruenberg, E., "Stage Fright," *Musical Quarterly,* Vol. 5 (April, 1919), pp. 221-230.

Moses, M., "The Best of Them Get Stage Fright," *Everybody's,* Vol. 54 (May, 1926), pp. 95-98.

Wilson, B. F., "Stage Fright," *Theatre,* Vol. 44 (September, 1926), p. 18.

"Stage Fright Not Suffered by Novices," *Pearson's Magazine,* Vol. .2 (August, 1909), pp. 226-229.

General Articles

Austin, M., "Gesture in Primitive Drama," *Theatre Arts Monthly,* Vol 11 (August, 1927), pp. 594-605.

Bosworth, H., *Technique in Dramatic Art* (Macmillan, New York), pp. 16, 29-30, 49-52, 87-97, 152-164, 201-220, 235-240.

Gray, G. W., "Problems in Teaching of Gesture," *Quarterly Journal of Speech Education,* Vol. 10 (June, 1924), pp. 238-252.

Malecot, L. L., "Note on Gesture and Language," *Quarterly Journal of Speech Education,* Vol. 13 (November, 1927), pp. 439-442.

Mandikeshvana (Rev.), "The Mirror of Gesture," *The Dial,* Vol. 62 (June 14, 1917), p. 532. Review, *Nation,* Vol. 104 (June, 1917), p. 716.

Pardoe, T. E., "Language of the Body," *Quarterly Journal of Speech Education,* Vol. 9 (June, 1923), pp. 252-258.

Winkler, J., "What Stars Are Made Of," *Liberty Magazine,* March 5, 1927, pp. 15-18.

The Head

Aubert, C., *The Art of Pantomime,* pp. 51-57, 97-150.

Brown, M. T., *Philosophy of Expression,* pp. 129-144.

Lutz, F., *Technique of Pantomime,* pp. 53-56.

Stebbens, G., *System of Delsarte,* pp. 217-230.

The Face

Allport, F., *Social Psychology,* pp. 200-232.

Aubert, C., *Art of Pantomime,* pp. 58-77.

Bosworth, H., *Technique in Dramatic Art,* pp. 61-69 (the eye).

Brown, M. T., *Philosophy of Expression,* pp. 202-258.

Duval, J., *Artistic Anatomy,* pp. 291-339.

Greig, J. Y. T., *Psychology of Laughter and Comedy* (Dodd Mead, New York).

Guilford, J. P., "An Experiment in Learning to Read Facial Expression," *Journal of Abnormal and Social Psychology,* Vol. 24 (1929), pp. 191-202.

Langfeld, H. S., "Judgment of Emotions from Facial Expression," *Journal of Abnormal Psychology,* Vol. 13 (1918-19), pp. 172-184. *Psychological Review,* Vol. 25 (1918), pp. 488-494.

Lutz, F., *Technique of Pantomime,* pp. 40-53, 74-80, 81-87, 96-102, 102-110 (head and face).

Stebbins, G., *System of Delsarte,* pp. 231-242.

The Body as an Expressive Agent

"Facial Expression and What It Means to the Player," *Theatre,* Vol. 8 (March, 1908), pp. 70-71.

The Torso

Andrews, W., *Acting and Play Production* (Longmans, Green, New York, 1926), pp. 1-27.
Aubert, C., *The Art of Pantomime,* pp. 33-37.
Brown, M. T., *Philosophy of Expression,* pp. 116-128.
Lutz, F., *Technique of Pantomime,* pp. 56-59, 60-66 (torso and limbs).
Stebbins, G., *System of Delsarte,* pp. 207-216.

The Arms

Aubert, C., *The Art of Pantomime,* pp. 37-50.
Brown, M. T., *Philosophy of Expression,* pp. 145-183 (hand and arm).
Lutz, F., *Technique of Pantomime,* pp. 59, 131-138 (arm and hands).
Stebbins, G., *System of Delsarte,* pp. 191-206.

The Hands

Aubert, C., *The Art of Pantomime,* pp. 78-94.
Duval, J., *Artistic Anatomy,* pp. 232-251.
Kleen, T., "Hand Poses of the Priests of Bali," *Asia,* Vol. 24 (February, 1924), pp. 129-131.
Lutz, F., *Technique and Pantomime,* pp. 66-71.
Stebbins, G., *System of Delsarte,* pp. 173-190.

The Legs and Feet

Aubert, C., *Art of Pantomime,* pp. 13-33.
Clayton, B., "Language of the Average Person's Feet," *Green Book Magazine,* 1913, pp. 915-918.
Duval, J., *Artistic Anatomy,* pp. 268-280.
Stebbins, G., *System of Delsarte,* pp. 135-172.

Discussion and Review Questions

1. How is the body an instrument of art? Compare with other art instruments.
2. Why must the actor understand his instrument?

3. Name some specific activities which the various agents of the body possess in expressing thought.
4. Explain "The mind is situated in all the body."
5. Does the body affect the mind as much as the mind affects the body? Develop.
6. Develop "Conduct is the only criterion for man judging man" and "Man is only what he does."
7. What emotions are best revealed by the head?
8. How may the face condition head gesture?
9. Why does sculpture, especially, offer such excellent study for the gesture of the head?
10. What important function does the eye possess for most gesture response?
11. Explain "The focusing center of emotional activity is usually in the face."
12. Wherein does the face reflect race history?
13. Develop "The chin is the focus of facial gesture."
14. What emotions are revealed by the brows and lids? By the mouth?
15. Does clothing affect gesture? How? What is the chief purpose of clothing, protection or decoration?
16. Explain "Mind activity is expressed proportionately to narrowness of base."
17. What is the significance of a vertical and a horizontal gesture?
18. Give your reasons why most people are careless in expressing thought with their feet.
19. How do high heels affect body carriage?
20. Define law of opposition in relation to the arm.
21. Is the hand used more for physical action, or for expression of thought? Demonstrate.
22. How is the hand so closely aligned with speech?
23. What is the difference between manifestative and descriptive gesture?
24. What is the importance of emotions to dramatic art?

CHAPTER V

TECHNIC OF PANTOMIME WRITING

PANTOMIME writing is a different art from writing for the drama or novel. We can take more liberties with description in pantomime technic as we wish to give more privileges to the actor in his own interpretation. The dramatist says little of the exact manner of action, letting the conversation carry over such action as is necessary. The novelist describes the minutest action, almost to a state of word excess.

To illustrate with a simple scene: an old man goes to the general delivery office and is told there is no letter.

The scene takes place in a western post office the day before Christmas. It is five o'clock in the afternoon and the snow can be seen hanging on the window sills. The one lamp is burning, as the last ray of sunlight pales over the corner grocery store. An old clerk, dressed in a pale blue shirt, is peering through the stamp window. He looks out to see the exact time of the wall clock. He is anxious for quitting time. He turns his back to the audience as an Old Man comes sauntering in.

OLD MAN: [Going up to window.] Have you got any mail for John Sparks?

CLERK: [Recognizing man as one who has been in for the last few days.] No. Nothin' for you.

OLD MAN: Why, you haven't looked yet. I expected a letter here for the last five days, and if it doesn't come, it'll be. . . . Won't you look again?

CLERK: Say, who's runnin' this office? Don't you think I know what's here?

OLD MAN: I know, but it seems so queer to me as she said it would be here before Christmas, and I loaned it to her to help pay a mortgage. You see, mister, I can't work any more and that was all I had. She was my only daughter and she wanted the money just for a month. . . .

CLERK: Yes, I know. You told me before. Cox, eh; no, nothing here. [He pulls down the window as the clock doles off five.]

OLD MAN: That's the first time she ever—did he say Cox? Say, mister, my name is Sparks, not Cox. [He pounds at the window.] Did you say Cox?

CLERK: Say, old fellow, do you want to be arrested for disturbing Uncle Sam? [Opens window but a little at first and then full up to make his final speech the more imperative.] Well, get out of here. . . .

OLD MAN: Sparks, not Cox. [Yelling louder.] Sparks—Sparks—*Sparks*.

CLERK: [Looking surprised.] Sparks! You said nothing but Cox. There's been a registered letter here, for [Gets letter from a drawer.] for John O. Sparks, for the last four days. [By now, it is evident that the CLERK is quite deaf.] That your name?

OLD MAN: Yes, mister. [Shows his G.A.R. badge with his name.] I couldn't believe [As he reaches for the letter.] I couldn't believe she would forget. You don't know my Millie, or else you would excuse my insistence. Sign here? [His hand is trembling and his face has brightened to a boyish glow.] Thanks, mister. You have made me so happy . . . there you are. [Returns the pen and takes the envelope.] Merry, merry Christmas for you.

CLERK: [Still impatient, though relenting.] Same to you, Mr. Sparks. Next time speak more plainly. [CLERK returns the badge and pulls the window down for the last time. The OLD MAN pins his badge on clumsily and slowly opens his precious envelope. He counts five one-hundred-dollar bills, looks gratefully heavenward as he places bills back in the envelope. Turns toward window as if to again thank the CLERK when he thinks better of it and smilingly turns to go. He is met by a tall cowboy, with a blue handkerchief tied over his lower face.]

COWBOY: [Coming further into room and covering OLD MAN with six-shooter.] Stick 'em up, old-timer, and damn quick about it. Hand it over. I saw you countin' it through the window. I need a little cash myself. [He grabs the envelope from SPARKS, who is smiling as if one of the boys were playing a joke on him.] Don't yell or make a peep, or I'll blow your damn brains out. . . . Thanks. . . . Merry Christmas! [The COWBOY dashes out of doors and hoof beats are heard on the crisp snow.]

OLD MAN: [Reaching out his hands.] That's all I have to live on. . . . I can't. . . . [Sinks to the floor as the terrible reality bears down on him.] Oh, God. Millie! Millie! Why couldn't we have waited just another day. . . .

Whether the scene be written in the drama, novel, or pantomime form, it is well to remember that dramatic elements are necessary for motivation purposes. There are, arbitrarily stated, five elements of drama: action, contention, suspense, characterization, and dialogue. And the chief of these is action. Without action, the drama lags; without contention, the scene lacks interest; without suspense, there is poor material to lead to a climax or restriction to time; without good characterization, the principals fail to hold our sympathy or attentive interest; good dialogue is food for the masses as well as the intelligentsia, but is least missed by the crowd. Action appeals to all alike. Either the scene must have actual action or the dialogue must contain a majority of speech images of visual value. Pantomime, by its very nature, is dominantly made of action, and may well contain contention, suspense, and characterization. The novel differs radically from drama and pantomime in that it may spend much of the time in description. Pantomime must reveal only the present; drama may elaborate the element of time by use of dialogue; the novel can portray any time or any place as long as it has a thread of continuity. Those novels are the most appreciated which dominate in dramatic situations.

A few paragraphs depicting the little scene mentioned above are now used to portray the novel style. All the scene will not be written; just enough to demonstrate the method of usual novel writing.

It is Christmas Eve in Beavertown. The snow is blue-white in the distant hills and the one street of the little village shows recent evidence of a two-foot fall. A flurry of wind blows the fine-grained crystals against the log frame of the post office window, and a tilting drift has almost covered the back part of the general grocery store on the corner opposite. As the sun sinks between two Douglas firs, a faint red paints the higher hilltops as a lingering evidence of his friendly visit. A coyote howls out his initial challenge for a night's pillage of unguarded chicken coops. An unsaddled horse, gangly with winter hair and belly icicles, whinnies to his companions in the big red barn near the frozen pond.

From the valley below, a lone figure is trudging his way through the unbroken road. A dog barks from a roadside farmhouse, is greeted by the somber figure, and each becomes unmindful of the presence of the other. As the bulky figure reaches the general store, the light of the front window falls full upon his face. Steel gray eyes are surrounded by white hair, shaggy eyebrows and a grizzled mustache. The massive shoulders of a once powerful man are now stooped. A face of power mellowed by the defeat of old age. He has come to this western retreat in the hope of effacing from society's memory the great catastrophe of his whirlwind life. But of that. . . .

When General John O. Sparks stopped at the little post office doorway, he hesitated about going in. He had called at the window for the last five days, and wondered if this were to be the final bitterness of his life. Why hadn't he received that which was his? that which he had salvaged at such a cost so late in life? But perhaps his daughter was like her mother, after all—her mother whom he had spent his life upon in the hope. . . . But he would have no such thoughts about Millie, his faithful Millie. She had sent the money, of that there could be no doubt. He kicked the snow from his shoes, opened the snow-covered door, and hesitated. Why should he make his troubles the worries of others? He closed the door slowly and stood in deep meditation, as the scowling face of the clerk looked at him through the open delivery window.

Henry Markle was clerk for the post office, a post office which acted as distributing base for many miles beyond—miles of sparsely inhabited woodlands. Markle had been appointed years ago, and Congress had forgotten that he was there. Didn't know that he had grown deaf in his frost-bitten ear. Nor would Henry ever tell. To be postmaster, even of Beaverville, was no insignificant position. Especially as it carried with it the responsibility of informer-in-chief of all village gossip and foreign events. He knew every person for miles around, and almost all of their business. An occasional woodsman, trapper, or farm hand would pass his way, and more at Christmas than at any other time. Yes, he knew them all or something about them, but this new man, with no previous mail, and no known pedigree, bothered him. Kept asking for a letter which hadn't come, and, 'most likely, never would come. Wiping off his heavy, gold-rimmed spectacles, he peered through the delivery window and noted that the clock was about to toll off the official hour for quitting Uncle Sam and reporting to a more insistent boss who was waiting for the front-room logs and consequent fire. Always on Christmas Eve he made the fire in the front room and she would be waiting. But a few minutes to five and to-morrow would be a holiday for him, as well as others of the valley. Nobody coming for mail at this hour of the day and he could use the few minutes to good advantage. His package had come from Sears, Roebuck and he allowed he could open it on "company" time. Yes, he would close the window and open his package right now. As he turned his back to pick up the promising present, the old man of insistent manners stumbled against the door, opened and quietly closed the door. . . .

"There's nothin' for you here, stranger. There ain't no use yuh askin'." And the postmaster put his hand upon the window, impatient to bring it down for the day.

"Why, you haven't even looked yet, mister. Surely you have some mail for John Sparks, John O. Sparks. She never failed to send it to me, wherever I was. If it doesn't come

. . . well, I'll just have to. . . . Won't you please look again?" And the old man put his head closer to the window as if to read the names of the protruding letters in the lettered boxes back of the counter.

"Say, Methuselah, who's runnin' this here place? Want to get in trouble with Uncle Sam? Well, yuh can, mighty fast —I tell yuh, there ain't anything here for any Cox." And the window came down with a slam, almost striking the chilled fingers of the unbelieving visitant.

The scene of the drama, from this point on, would take several hundred more words to depict in the novel style. In the novel, we can digress with happenings of the past and hopes of the future, as well as elaborate what is being thought, in addition to the words actually spoken. Drama must motivate the living present and cannot long delay for time digressions in dialogue. Many good plays have been ruined because they have been neglected in this very important principle.

The pantomime is harshly insistent in its demand of present action to depict present thoughts.

A pantomime of the above scene would enact somehow in the following manner:

Scene is laid in a small western post office. A self-satisfied clerk stands behind the one window. Looks out through window and sees the time on the clock on wall. Time to close. Is about to close when a stalwart old man, whose glory has faded, enters the room, kicks off snow from shoes and goes slowly to window. Clerk looks at Old Man and shakes his head, without looking at his letter files. There is no letter. Old Man looks helplessly at Clerk and starts to walk away, though unconvinced. Clerk pulls down his window. Old Man stops by doorway in bitter meditation. Suddenly thinks of possible aid. Takes off his Grand Army badge from under inner coat and walks determinedly to window. Pounds window with his fist. Clerk raises window hurriedly, having pair of ladies' stockings in his hand. Indignant at sight of Old Man. About to slam window when Old Man holds window and shoves badge in Clerk's face. Clerk moves back, but looks at badge. Surprised and looks at badge closer. Points to the C file, but gets a letter from drawer. Holds it up to Old Man, who becomes exuberantly delighted. Grabs at letter impatiently, but the Clerk has him sign, satisfied that Old Man should get letter. Gives letter and Old Man wishes him best of luck. Clerk looks at pair of stockings in hand and jerks them down suddenly. Closes window. Old Man stands looking at envelope, turns it over, and clasps it to his heart. Opens it clumsily with his fingers. Pulls out letter and reads slowly. Tears in eyes. Takes money from envelope and counts five one-hundred-dollar bills. Puts money back in envelope and is about to leave when a tall cowboy, with face half covered, comes quickly in. Covers Old Man with revolver, snatches money from him, bows in mock thanks and dashes from post office. Old Man too surprised to speak, but tremblingly falls to floor. His voice fails him, and he grabs heart in convulsive gesture. Holds hands up to heaven, then falls forward, weeping bitterly.

Pantomime is merely a structural shell which suggests to the actor the main current of thought. Anger means all the power of the full meaning of the thought, from the foot to the eyebrow. Conversation is inconsequential only as it suggests portrayable thought. What people think matters little, only as it is and has outward form of expression. Old Man must be shown in carriage, walk, look, head movement, facial fixity, and tempo in gesture. Not any old man, but a very definite old man, actually conceived with definite proportions and consistent actions. No art can ever have power if figures remain indefinite in the portrayer's mind.

Pantomime is condensed dramatic action.

Review and Questions

1. Briefly compare the necessary elements of drama, short story, and pantomime.
2. When is a situation "dramatic"?
3. Is a dramatic situation necessary for a good pantomime? Give reasons.

4. Write a five-minute short story. Put same in pantomime form.
5. Write a five-minute drama, complete in itself. Convert same to a pantomime.
6. Do words aid the story as given in our text? If so, why?
7. When is pantomime without words the strongest form for art expression? Illustrate.
8. Why has the old pantomime theme of Pierrot and Pierrette fallen into disuse? What was the usual plot of these stories?
9. Give five original pantomime themes and chief points of interest.
10. What attention should the paying audience receive in the writing and acting of a pantomime?

CHAPTER VI

PANTOMIMES FOR THE HEAD

THE notes at the conclusion of each pantomime are an integral part of the study and will be found very helpful for the observing of the underlying principles involved in dramatic expression.

Pertinent Pointers for Head and Face

The eyes are the best agents to indicate the object of attention. The face should follow the eye, which indicates attention level and focus. The chin is the chief focusing agent of the face; that is, head gesture should pivot from the chin rather than the neck. Most people "smell" every one they address. "Keep your chin over your wishbone" is an excellent adage for head government. By using your chin as pivot of head gesture, the whole plane of 180 degrees can be used for audience purposes. Dropping of the chin does not obligate one to project the chin. Unless your own head carriage and face responses conform to the universally accepted, you will always be considered different or incorrect. Acting is not a personal gratification so much as it is entertainment for others. An oddity of mouth or eye gesture may be capitalized for character parts, but it must be done consciously.

1. Grandmother Talks with Her Eyes

Old Lady sits near window reading. She looks out and sees two children playing. She admires them immensely. As smaller one falls the Lady becomes very anxious and concerned. A little boy from across the street runs over and strikes the fallen child, for which the Lady is angry. A passing stranger gives the child a piece of candy and sets her on her feet, and the Old Lady joys as the child scampers off. Her grandson enters and gives her a bouquet of roses, reminding her of her birthday, which she had forgotten. She is perplexed at her own loss of memory and delighted with the gift. Grandson gives her a letter he got from the mailbox. She opens and takes out a hundred dollar bill. Second page of letter tells her of death of her aged brother. She gently cries, then sits in deep meditation, which resolves into a daydream. She is indifferent to her grandson's invitation to go for a ride. At her request, he hands her the family album. As she turns its pages she registers wonder, disgust, disdain, pleasure, reverence, distrust, and finally comes to her favorite picture. She folds her hands over it and leans back in pleasant memory.

(The eyes are chiefly used to denote focus of attention; with the brows and lids we register emotional variations. Above exercise is helpful in this. The pantomime of this type has insufficient action for good theater, unless we make the eyes talk so unmistakably that the audience can accurately approximate the thoughts of the grandmother.)

2. *The Sore Neck*

Person has stiff neck. Comes in and looks around the room. Sits down in chair by table to write letter. Chum runs in and slaps him on back (displeasure). Sees who chum is (extreme pleasure). Several people heard coming off right; he listens attentively as they pass on. He writes letter, asking chum to excuse him while he does so. Asks chum to sit. Writing of letter is sad duty. As he moves his head quickly to left to reach for blotter, pain. (Does most of pointing with his eyes and wears the smile of one who has suffered long.) Refers to picture on the wall as he writes. Finishes letter. Asks friend to button up his shoe. Also asks chum to adjust the sunlight from his eyes. Starts to rise and sinks back in chair. Asks to be excused and watches friend out, refusing further aid.

(Watch levels for eye use, the various focus for eye heights. Definite objects must be imagined if pantomime is to ring true. We cannot picture *anything,* it must be *something.* The first three pantomimes of this group are written for slow tempo and all agents of expression coördinate.)

3. Pictures—Living and Dead

An old actor comes into room, looks around, salutes pictures on the wall. Drops arms limply and shakes head dejectedly. Takes off coat. Pulls out pocketknife and cuts seam of his coat sleeve. Draws out a fifty dollar bill. This will pay his debts. Goes to desk and writes a predetermined letter. Bids farewell to six of his actor friends, as if they were present in their photographs on the wall. He pictures each one differently, as bitterly, tearfully, reverently, disdainfully, respectfully, and quizzically. Gives one grand salaam, then procures revolver from his hip pocket and without looking at it, raises it slowly to his head. He nerves his finger for the pull, as the door opens slowly. He watches a young woman enter. His daughter! All atremble, he lets gun slip from his hand to the table. Takes two steps back and raises arms slowly. Walks toward girl, who is crying silently. As he is about to embrace his daughter, he moves faster and says, "Marie."

(All action must be slow, deliberate. The pictures should be above the eyes of the actor. In recognition of the girl, let the eyes go first. She is not as tall as her father. Let there be a sequential resolution of the body. The word, "Marie," should contain the lament of a yearning soul.)

4. The Little One

Little girl comes into room on tiptoes. Looks around the room to find her doll. Under table, chairs, on table, buffet, on the mantel, and under some clothes on a sofa.

Sees doll hanging from picture frame. Looks around for the mischievous brother. Gets chair and just reaches doll, pulls on it and picture with doll tumbles to floor. Doll is broken. She stoops down to pick up pieces and cries.

(Let the eyes lead in all gesture. To represent a dainty person is almost beyond most actors and actresses. Grace and body rhythm are necessary. The audience must see the eyes, if picture is to be understood. The crime is not so much in turning back on audience as it is in not presenting best picture for interpretation of part.)

5. *A Courtship Witnessed*

Boy looks through keyhole. Sees big sister and lover. She is edging closer to him on sofa. Boy tells companion by pantomime. Sister kisses lover. The boy is disgusted. Lover pulls out box of candy. Boy's anticipation—pleasure—yearning. Sister places box on piano. Comes back to sofa. Lover pulls out big diamond ring. Boy greatly surprised. Girl falls in lover's arms. Boy at first delighted with fun, then deep disgust as girl sits on lover's lap. Pulls out pocketknife and beckons his friend to come on while he fixes a pole for fishing.

(All action of occupants of room to be shown by the eavesdropper, who transfers thoughts to companion. Eye and facial expression paramount. This demands face to audience at such times when picture of room is conveyed to companion.)

6. *The Blind Man*

Blind man comes in with stump cane. Seldom winks his eyes. Finds table. Sits down. Finds fork, knife, bread and butter. Maid comes in with food. He smiles thanks. He gropes for food and she helps his hand to find it, which he greatly dislikes. Jerks hand away. Then finds food in front of him. Starts cutting meat. Picks up salt shaker. Misplaces spoon, finds it quite a way to right. Takes corn, several spoonsful, puts pepper on it.

Maid enters. Trips and spills coffee. Burns his hand. He doesn't scold, but is in pain. Allows her to put some salve on it and wrap it up. Rises from table. Gets cane and goes out of door.

(Control the winking of eyelids and make blindness seem real. This pantomime may be effectively done with one or two characters. A blind person usually expresses less with face than people with normal sight; what little is used must, therefore, be impressive.)

7. *A Park Flirtation*

A young girl, flapper type, walking in park. Sees handsome fellow putting his bank roll in his pocket. She drops glove, and receives it from him, graciously. As he holds her hand, she flirtatiously withdraws. She accepts invitation to sit on bench. She takes some proffered popcorn. He ties her shoelace. They eat ice-cream cones which he buys from a passing vender. Drops some on skirt. He brushes it off with handkerchief. Profuse thanks. She arises to go. He wishes to call a taxi. She refuses. He insists. She refuses, more weakly. Finally, she accepts. He hails taxi. She is about to get in when he discovers his wallet is gone. He hails policeman. She, at first, is indignant. Then starts looking, searching with him. Policeman arrives. Man accuses girl. She shows surprise, then scorn. Policeman searches her; she is indignant. He finds man's purse in her parasol. She smiles and admits it. Problem.

(In this, watch especially the face changes of thought on part of girl, whether she be taller, or shorter than the man. Watch character level, and note carefully the manner of stealing the purse. Properties are not necessary for this type of pantomime.)

8. *The Crown Prince Receives*

The Prince is now of age and has been asked to indicate his choice of feminine beauty and matrimonial partnership. He has agreed to make his choice after he has seen all prospects pass before him, as he watches from an unseen position of vantage. His father stands by him and tells him the connections and name of each candidate. The two drink a toast to matrimony and the Prince awaits the passing of the ladies. As they pass, he reveals to his father just what he thinks of each. In order of their passing, the son shows he thinks the first too haughty, the second too demure, the next too inquisitive, another too small, and another too fat. One appears to him foolish, another humpbacked, another too squint-eyed. As others pass, one he distrusts, another he disdains, another he pities. The last one appears and the King stops the Prince and wants to know his game. Son indicates that he wishes to see last girl before he makes his final choice. The last girl finally enters, and passes. The Prince becomes joyous to an exhilarating degree. Asks father to have her brought before him again. King tells him to summon servant and send for girl. Prince pulls bell cord and servant enters. Prince writes a name on his card and dispatches servant. Puts arm around father in filial affection and awaits girl. She is shown in. Instant recognition between Prince and Lady. King surprised. Explanations follow. Problem.

(Ingenuity of creating impressions by pantomime is the secret of great acting. "Explanation follows" is to be shown in pantomime by the Prince. Various endings suggested create interest in themselves.)

9. *Thespis in Mold*

The old actor, of tragedian forte, comes augustly into room and throws a letter upon the center table. Puts two fingers of right hand into his vest front and declaims against contents of letter. Goes before full-length mirror and carefully examines his face for wrinkles. Stands with look of disgust, then of determination, and again of disdain. He picks up letter and spurns it and changes to anger, as if paper were a living thought. Looks upon letter with awe and then surprise and turns with indifference. Turns fiercely, looks aghast at letter, then registers horror, as if demons were leaving the words. He stands in deep meditation and slowly walks the floor as if in grief or sorrow. He finally kneels and supplicates his unseen employer for another chance, rises and mournfully looks at his watch. The hour of rehearsal has passed. He puts five coins on table, pulls trouser-pocket inside out, and surveys his fortunes. Deliberately walks toward his old sword hanging on the wall. Plays at foils, at first carefully, then fiercely, fighting his merciless employer in phantom movements. A loud knock at door startles him. He lays sword on table, combs disheveled hair as he walks toward door. Receives telegram from messenger. Slowly tears envelope and reads telegram. Ecstasy! A new job! Gives messenger three of his coins. Puts plug hat on cockily. Spurns old letter and walks majestically out of door, talking to telegram.

(The grandiloquent is no longer encouraged. It had its few merits and was always stylistic. There are actors still living who made good money with the long black cloak and long mustache. They often overdid but everybody knew what they were trying to do. They were always acting, very self-conscious. They knew where the audience was.)

10. *His Ardor Lightens*

A fastidious entymologist comes into garden with net and glass. Goes to rose bush and smells rose and pricks finger. Looks through glass and becomes interested. Plucks leaf and brings close to face under the lens. Turns leaf around and satisfies self. Pulls out notebook from side pocket and makes notes. Butterfly flits in front of him and he carefully watches, becomes excited, and starts with net. After two futile attempts catches butterfly and brings it reverently toward him. Pulls out bottle and places specimen carefully in. Puts top on bottle. Puts glass to eye and examines his catch. Exuberant joy. Puts lens on his lap as he looks at his winged beauty. Gives jump and grabs lens, when sunlight fires his trousers. He places bottle down and slaps smoldering cloth on his leg. An acquaintance passes, whom the professor hails and shows his prize, pointing out its salient points of merit. Picks up net and looks about him for any leaveovers and goes off limping, but joyfully gesticulating. Points to hole in trousers and laughs as he disappears.

(The eccentric character is so often made inhuman that it becomes a joy to see a good characterization within the bounds of veracity. A mental character works and gestures in a small radius, expansive within this scope. Such characters are excellent to work for minute detail. When a serious man laughs, it is more conspicuous than when a smiling person laughs. Absent-mindedness is not uncommon to certain scientists; don't abuse in art.)

Review and Questions

1. Explain "normal carriage" of the head.
2. Give examples of five character-types who do not carry their heads in normal carriage. What is significance of each variation? Use studies from this group.
3. How does the use of the chin as a focus for all face activity aid the actor before the microphone?
4. What is the chief function of the eyeball in dramatic art?
5. What do the brows and lids best reveal in relation to the eyeball?
6. Which agent of the face best shows joy and merriment?
7. Explain "character level" in pantomime.
8. How do joy and sorrow affect carriage of the head?
9. Why do blind people usually express less with their face and head than do normal vision persons?
10. Analyze the changes registered by the Prince in *The Crown Prince Receives* (*8*). Could these differences be shown with an inactive eye or mouth?

11. What caused disappearance of old style villain? *Thespis in Mold* (9). Why do we have "styles" in acting? Are styles ever necessary?
12. What best reveals character and general demeanor in statuary, position of the head, or attitude of eye? Develop.

CHAPTER VII

PANTOMIMES FOR THE TORSO

Pertinent Pointers for the Torso

THE chest is the center of all trunk activity. The chest leads in the walk and is the center for all affective gestures. The dropped chest can never show virility of character and minimizes gesture action. Shoulder blades must be kept far apart, not only for voice purposes, but for pantomimic strength. One is close to the mortician when the belt is larger than his chest expansion.

Much bodily bending must be practiced if actor or actress would keep agility and power of movement.

The body must always obey the laws of gravity and the torso is man's chief concern in this. Grace and ease is obedience to law with least effort.

11. At the Costumer's

A young girl goes to the costume house in search of a proper carnival dress. The obliging clerk permits her to try on several outfits. Girl parades before the long mirrors with different clothes, adapting carriage to costume:

(*a*) A Chinese lady before the Emperor
(*b*) A sales model for fashionable Fifth Avenue mart
(*c*) An Irish washerwoman of Harlem
(*d*) A Spanish señorita of Seville
(*e*) A Dutch girl of Leyden
(*f*) An Apache queen of Montmartre
(*g*) An Indian maid of Hopi village
(*h*) A Hawaiian beauty from Waikiki
(*i*) An Eskimo belle of Chilkoot
(*j*) A country lass of Nebraska plains

She goes back to the Apache garb as best befitting her style.

(Watch for flexibility of torso and audience relation. Despite our realism, it is no crime to act *for* an audience. Such an exercise may be done with or without costumes.)

12. Courtship in Spats

A young man enters room timidly. Offers hat and cane to girl. Sits on sofa. Uneasy. Collar too high. Gets out box of candy—it sticks hard in pocket—eventually offers it to girl. He accepts small piece. Keeps feeling in various pockets, cautiously. Finally locates ring. Looks around room. Takes girl's hand. Drops it and takes it again. Smiles foolishly. Mops brow. Gets on knee. Starts in proposing, and then gets back again to sofa. Finally proposes. Can't find ring. Mops brow. Sits down, and grins foolishly. She gets it from inside vest pocket for him. Gratified look. Puts it on wrong finger for her. Starts to kiss her, but doesn't dare. She kisses him. Takes his breath. Foolish grin. He is about to embrace her as little sister enters. Problem.

(Watch character level, audience front, and proper sitting position. He must, for best business, be on left of girl; the best business is usually the planned business.)

13. A Southern Gallant

A proud Colonel and wife are giving a welcome party for their West Point son, home on furlough. The son, Robert, stands in the receiving line and meets the guests, old and new friends. LaNelle, the girl of his boyhood fancy, enters the room, escorted by a notorious card cheat of New York. Both Robert and LaNelle are surprised and delighted at the change in each other. He has military dignity and manliness to a superlative degree; she is a radiant southern beauty. They cannot take their eyes from each other and their hands linger longer than politeness directs. Callow, the card expert, touches Robert on the shoulder and leads LaNelle from the line. A dance is started and Robert excuses himself to his parents and goes immediately to LaNelle. She is delighted but Callow intervenes and taking LaNelle's hand shows Robert an engagement ring. Callow walks away with LaNelle, and Robert watches them form a group in the minuet. The father comes to Robert and cautions him against foolish dreams. Robert starts to tell the Colonel of Callow, but refrains. A Negro servant enters and brings the Colonel a letter, he reads and rereads it, then turns it over to Robert. Colonel is shocked but Robert is perplexed. The Colonel turns to Negro servant and gives an order. Negro goes out and soon returns with detective, who dispatches servant for Callow. Callow follows Negro into room as LaNelle remains in archway. Detective shows badge to Callow and signals him to follow. Callow, taken so easily, steps up to Robert and strikes him flat-handed. The Colonel is about to strike Callow with cane, but Robert stops him. Robert bows to Callow as detective leads him off. LaNelle runs up to the men. The Colonel is going to show her the letter, Robert tries to stop him, but the Colonel insists. LaNelle reads letter and almost faints. Robert catches her and leads her to side chair. LaNelle takes off engagement ring and gives it to the Colonel. He immediately writes a note and dispatches Negro servant after Callow. LaNelle and Robert walk slowly from room; Colonel takes his wife in to the dance, as a couple come in to inquire after them.

(Ease of bearing and gallant deportment are almost lost to present stage. The minuet, square dances, and old southern chivalry could do much to rehabilitate what is a part of the heritage of every gentleman.)

14. The Bell Ringer

An old bell ringer of the monastery has just climbed the winding stairway. He is evidently in pain but tries to deny his trouble. He looks at his large watch, winds with a key on his fob chain and then waits for a few seconds before ringing. Puts his watch in pocket, after last look, and methodically counts five. Then begins to pull rope of great bell. He reaches high on rope and pulls with all his weight. He has pulled but five times when his face is distorted in agony and he grabs at breast over heart. With great pain he pulls, one-handed on the smooth rope. After three pulls he lets go the rope and gently falls to the floor. His hands relax and fall limply to his sides. The great bell tolls the death of the faithful ringer and a smile fixes on his benevolent face.

(Falling is an evolution of sequential movements—nothing segmental or jerky. Avoid falling with feet to audience. There is a predetermined place to cover.)

15. The Rubber

An old Scotch grandpa has been inveigled into taking a hand of bridge to fill up a table. He gathers up his thirteen cards and looks at them quizzically over his glass rims. He is very sleepy, but gamely obliges. The spades look like hearts and he holds cards first close, then far from eyes. He "byes" and waits for results. Partner bids and grandpa lays his cards on table. He follows the game for first five tricks, when he begins to falter. His head bobs ominously and wakes him, temporarily. He looks around and smiles. By ten, his head is low, and at twelve tricks, he has fallen asleep. His partner wakes him up with a bang. Knocks glasses off as he straightens. Tries second hand but cannot finish, this time lets his head fall back. He sleeps with healthy noise. Awakened, apologizes and sheepishly excuses himself to guests.

(Gentle relaxation takes considerable practice and feigning sleep is good exercise. Easily overdone and artificial.)

16. An Intelligent Automaton

Two young girls have just returned from a matinee of "Tales of Hoffman" and are standing before a full-length mirror. They put on an orthophonic record, as if prearranged, and get ready for the dance. Joan tells her "manager," Stella, to wind her up and she will dance. Posed for winding, Joan is gradually keyed up to a high machinery vitality, and with all joints properly functioning, she walks as she saw the mechanical doll. Movement is made only from joints: ankle, knee, hip, neck, shoulder, elbow, and waist. All parts move as sections, a solid foot, with no bend at ball or arch; a fixed hand with no resolution of finger movement; eyes fixed in stare. Joan walks around the room (partially guided by Stella); finally she begins to run down. All movements slow up and she falls in a very awkward position, head and feet on floor, arms in air and angularly bent at middle. Joan is wondering how she can get up mechanically, when a sorority chum enters the room. She is astonished and the two girls surprised, but they go on gamely playing the part. The record has reached its finale and turns off. Joan gradually jumps her head and feet close together, waves her arms and stiffly gets to standing position, helped by Stella. She is wound up again and regains her full mechanic strength, and with placid face Joan jerkily walks toward the now wondering chum. As she reaches the newly arrived friend, she suddenly slaps face of girl, who is startled. Joan dissolves the automaton and laughs heartily. All join in, though the friend hesitates at first.

(Excellent exercise to inform us just what grace really is. There are no joints in grace, as they disappear in evolutionary movements of entire body.)

17. Slow Motion

An expert coach is explaining to his basket ball squad that coördination of body is essential to good team play. He is demonstrating by slow-motion movements. He takes the basket ball and holds it properly in his hands. Then he stoops slowly as his knees bend outward and the ball is lowered almost to floor. As his back gradually straightens, his arms come closer to his body and take the spring from back as they go full length up and forward. The feet leave the floor simultaneously and the fingers remain lengthened and spread as ball goes toward basket. He shows how the ball thrown from a height above the shoulders is but the final part of the full-body toss before. Each member of body is a synchronized part with all other members, the fingers getting the full transfer of power.

A golf club is procured and the coach shows how the stance, the raising of the club, and its full swing of a complete circle, is but a blending of energies into graceful unfoldments.

A tennis racket is held in hand, and coach shows how the stroke is made, first with the weight from the back foot, then by meeting ball with a full swing and by carrying that swing into a completed circle. No segmental movements for a champion; weight is ultimately transferred to front foot. The ball receives the full power of accumulated effort, not the delayed power of disintegrated parts. The hand projects what was originally started by the foot and completion of grace circle makes possible a new start for stroke power. Grace demands perfect bodily balance and it is a series of actions, right arm versus left arm, right leg in opposite direction to left leg. A sequential line for balance to follow—no sudden shunting of the center of gravity.

As a final demonstration, the coach gets the jumping rope and takes several skips. He then discards the rope and shows how arms go down with the rope as the feet leave the floor, and that the feet are preparing to jump at a point when hands are highest in the air. Head is best held back slightly as arms are going up and slightly forward as arms are coming down. Power and grace is coördination. Fancy steps with the rope and change of direction under perfect balance and adjustment give additional power. Class will now demonstrate their skill.

(The human body is like a checkerboard—every time a lower member is used an upper member moves to meet it. It differs from checkers, in that no men are lost on either side. All are kings and can move in perfect strength to assist each other. The body lives in a compass of power and grace, as far as the fingers and toes reach. To use less is to minimize strength.

A good statue or bodily attitude, always shows what was, what is, and what is to come. The present must reveal the past and predict the future. Awkwardness always eliminates one of these essentials.)

18. Cupid on the Wing

A room in Paradise. Judgment has not yet been pronounced and it is visiting day in Nebulous Chamber. Mercury, in all his glory, passes through on winged feet, paying little heed to Josephine, Cleopatra, and Calpurnia. They are talking of the past and wondering what they would do if they had it to do over again; and had they lived in the same times, which one would have won the greatest man. Cleopatra is combing her hair with an asp comb, and Josephine has a vanity box, emblazoned with an eagle. Calpurnia has a magazine called *March Winds*. Dido enters with Beatrice, each still looking wistfully sad. They make an excellent pair as they stand near the starry window. Peg Woffington bustles in and all the drapes seemed to be moved by a restless zephyr. Peg has a date book and is absorbed more in that than the presence of her sisters, who eye her askance, all except Cleopatra. She seems to understand Peg and she goes over to her and shares her confidences. Juliet comes in with Carrie Nation. Carrie understands feuds, looks rather hopelessly upon Juliet. Carrie has a hatchet and a broken beer bottle. It looks so belligerent compared to the innocent little phial which Juliet wears about her neck. Marie Antoinette and Guinevere come in with Hester Prynne. Marie's big hat is splendid, though there is a pronounced red line around her neck. Hester carries a little doll, on which the ladies see a scarlet A. Guinevere is radiant. She is the only one who enjoyed a lover, was forgiven by her husband, and died in peace. As the ladies are grouping according to their natural habits in life and mental ambitions, Queen Elizabeth comes excitedly and apologizes for being so late. But she has certain privileges, being English and also the only one who died a virgin. For such a distinction, it is her honor to establish the custom of drinking tea. She is the only one whose engagement finger is free. Four maidens from the palace of Haroun Al Raschid bear in trays with Lipton tea and present each with a cup. The trays were made in America, by Tiffany, as his stamp is beautifully embossed in plain view. As the women are seated or standing, as befits their temperament, an elevator girl from a skyscraper, enters and calls out in dolorous tones, "Gentleman caller from the Earth, to discuss future plans of his marriage—Charles Lindbergh." All drop their beverage and stand in a gossip phalanx, ready to tender confidential advice, as terrific whir of motor is heard. Motor stops, voices are heard off stage as clouds blur the picture from mortal eyes.

(To dress and deport in costume is one of the greatest needs of our present stage. Each period has its idiosyncrasies and graces. Careful study and research is necessary before an actor or actress can live properly in a period play. Even the movements of hands and feet differ, though general carriage divergencies are more pronounced.)

19. A Mexican Wall

A lonely highway and an old abandoned adobe house. Six Mexican bandits stop their horses and dismount. They appear before wall of house and have an American rancher bound and gagged. His hat is off. The heavy-set leader, Pancho, chucks the American's chin derisively. He gives a sharp command and the four Mexicans step back and get their guns from the youngest, who has them ready. American stands against wall and looks anxiously right and left. A Mexican girl throws herself in front of the American. She covers his body with her own and faces the bandits. Pancho takes his short whip more firmly in his hand and walks slowly to her. She pleads for young rancher, receiving a contemptuous smile. For his freedom she would go with Pancho. American resents such aid and begs bandits shoot. Pancho stops them and pulls out his pistol. He whispers few words to American, takes Mexican girl by hand and drags her away from rancher. He orders bandits to mount and wait for him. They disappear. He takes deliberate aim at young American and fires. Rancher falls in heap. The girl jerks herself away from Pancho, who laughs heartily, tips his hat grandiloquently and strides off. Horse hoofs clatter and die away. Rancher gets up quickly to consternation of the girl and looks at hole in adobe wall. She clings to him, as he smiles. He bows heroically to receding leader, explains what Pancho did, as they go off.

(A painted wooden log can be substituted for adobe wall and the hole for bullet, previously made, should be covered by American's head, as he stands by wall. To fall naturally is one of greatest accomplishments of stage. It takes much practice and skill. Avoid stiff arms or any stiffness, if you would minimize personal danger.)

20. *The Chair Must Fit*

An eccentric couple enter a novelty furniture store. The man is nearsighted and erect in carriage. The woman is rheumatic. Clerk is very patient in displaying his wares. Each sits on a very heavy plush upholstered chair, sinking deep into the cushions. That seems comfortable but hard to get up from. A morris chair is tried next and is too far back. A colonial rocking-chair offers hope but is a little stiff. An oak rocker of ample space and broad arm rests sets at about right angle for the gentleman, but is a little hard for the lady. They try a tapestry *chaise longue.*

The lady is delighted, at last a real resting chair. Gentleman doesn't like the foot rest and lady wouldn't have chair without it. Old man goes back to the oak rocker and decides on that. The price is high for *chaise longue* but by persuasion and compromise they take both chairs. Lady had to get part of her money from her stocking, as gentleman didn't have enough for both. They go off, expecting early delivery.

(In sitting in chair and rising, do not bend body too far front and move upward in sections. Avoid putting hands on knees and pushing up. The lady in this pantomime may resort to this but be conscious that it is not graceful. Let chest lead and move body from foot under you, not at side of chair. Most people rise from a chair by leaning forward in a stooping position until free of chair, and then straighten up. It is better to let strength of leg support the weight and have chest lead body to standing position by keeping torso fairly erect.

Walking, telephoning, rising, and sitting, meeting friends and grouping gracefully but seemingly unconscious of efforts, can all be made a part of interesting practice for stage or study. *Motivate all action by proper thinking.*)

Discussion and Review Questions

1. Give reasons why chest is center of trunk or torso gestures.
2. Which character in pantomime *At the Costumer's (11)* is generally the most erect? Which the most stooped?
3. How much does race history affect individual carriage? Give examples.
4. Show how the following emotions affect the carriage of the same individual: bashfulness, annoyance, vanity, anger, agony, guilt, indifference, and surprise.
5. In pantomime, *Slow Motion (17)*, which sport calls for greatest torsal activity? What are body habits of the respective sports?
6. How does carriage affect wearing of costume? Explain by comparison of ladies in *Cupid on the Wing (18)*.
7. Why is a conscious fall usually difficult? Outline tech-

nic of falling as called for in *A Mexican Wall* (*19*).

8. Why do people in life usually stoop over, before rising from a chair. Why do we avoid that, for most characters, on the stage? Is getting up a pushing up from the floor and seat, or a rising as if chest lifted the lower body?
9. What is significant of the torso in study of statues by Michelangelo, and Rodin? What are their lines of power and grace? Do they approximate an ideal for the human? Why? Can statues show movement?
10. Explain "Grace and ease is obedience to law."

CHAPTER VIII

PANTOMIMES FOR THE LIMBS

Pertinent Pointers for the Limbs

THERE are nine positions of the feet, from the inactive attitude of weight on the heel of the back foot, to the attitude of activity with weight on the ball of the advanced foot.

The broader the base, the coarser the character. Man is a one-legged animal, in most of his activities. Each character has a particular type of stance.

The hand reveals the real grace of an actor. The thumb is the vital agent of the hand, the great balancing factor for power and grace. The index and outer fingers usually parallel in their movements for grace. The two inner fingers are best kept together. The best sculptors and actors know this.

The head and hand oppose each other in most gestures.

"Double jointed" fingers need special attention.

We can be "pigeon-handed" as well as "pigeon-toed."

Thought flows from finger tips, if not segmented at elbows or wrists.

Crooked arms can be made to appear straight by careful management of elbows.

21. A Medley of Walks

A young man has been informed that his job at the local stock company depends upon his ability to walk properly for many characters. He has, as his audience, two younger sisters and a baby brother. He walks in front of them, as upon a stage. He calls his part:

(*a*) A Negro dude with corns goes to flower shop
(*b*) A Chinese vegetable peddler, heavily laden, passes by
(*c*) A chic co-ed with tight shoes meets her beau
(*d*) A prisoner with ball and chain trudges on, watching boys at ball game
(*e*) An old mother leaves court room, after hearing her only son convicted of murder
(*f*) A Spanish señorita flirting with a wealthy American
(*g*) A little girl leaves her doll in a restless sleep
(*h*) A husband walks up to his wife's paramour
(*i*) A pal, momentarily uncertain, meets his boyhood chum for first time in years
(*j*) A hunter, cornered and with knife in hand, advances to meet a staggering bear
(*k*) A bandit, shot, staggers to shelter of a big yellow pine
(*l*) Football boy, with big toe broken, lurches to sidelines
(*m*) On rainy day, prima donna walks on her high heels across the sloppy street
(*n*) Gallant carries a heavy maid across the same street
(*o*) A father leaves his office, dismissed after thirty years of service

(The old actors tell us that the walk, as an art, is just about gone. Their judgment is vindicated when we visit our variety stage. The graceful walk starts in the chest and the heel should be the last phase of movement. People who carry burdens on their heads walk more easily than those who have nothing on their heads.)

22. *The Model*

A French sculptor has advertised for a model with beautiful hands. His atelier received but few applicants, as he had each aspirant pose for him. Finally a beautiful Italian girl poses for him as he dictates. Unaffected grace is paramount.

(*a*) You are wearing the famous Pelazzi diamond; show it to our guests
(*b*) A butterfly rests on the back of your hand. Walk around with it

(*c*) You are holding in leash two beautiful cheetahs. Power is necessary.

(*d*) Kindly serve tea to three guests. Each wishes sugar and cream

(*e*) Fan yourself, first with a large feather fan; next with a dainty ivory fan

(*f*) You are in the opera box. Arrange the bouquet at your belt, fix the one capricious lock of hair, and use the glasses as the curtain rises. Pass the glasses to your host. The King is looking on

(*g*) As a flower girl, sell violets and roses to patrons as they pass your booth in the fair

(*h*) At a reception, your hand is kissed by one you loathe and immediately afterward by one you like

(*i*) Register terror as bomb blasts further end of room

(*j*) Sign this contract for a thousand francs a week

(The hand can change its form more completely than any other body agent. Its three faces, the palm, edge, and back, must be used as intelligently as the brows and lids, or lips. Great sculpture and painting tells us to observe life, and note that the graceful hand separates the index and little finger somewhat away from the two center fingers. Only in extreme vital gestures are the fingers equidistant apart.)

23. Falstaff in a Flat

A tramp climbs through a window into a dark room. He uses flash and gets lay of room. Puts hand on center table and sees thickness of dust. Convinced house is unoccupied, goes to wall back and switches on light. Agreeably pleased. Goes to mantelpiece, stretches on toes to reach vase. Takes vase down and turns upside down; jewelry falls into his hand. Hurries over to table to better ascertain value. Bonanza. Looks about him, listening throughout the scene. Goes back to mantelpiece, stretches to put vase back and lets it drop to hearth. Breaks vase. Tramp kicks bits toward fireplace and is startled by sharp noise at door. Goes slowly over to wall and turns out lights. Waits by door, then slowly unlocks it and hurriedly throws it open. A cat comes purring in.

Tramp stoops down and picks it up, as he looks out, then closes door and locks it. Turns on lights and puts cat on table. Looks at hand prints on table and then at his hands. Wipes dust off with sleeve of his coat. Plays with cat for a moment and then goes over to buffet. Opens decanter drawer and finds good supply of vintage. Samples the several kinds and gradually gets drunk. Problem.

(The tempo of gesture is consistent with the rate of life. The tramp in above will vary his gesture tempo as he goes from uncertainty to assurance and to drunkenness. From the carefulness of the thief to the indifference of the toper is quite a transition. Note, also, the great change in eye activity.)

24. The Boatman

A vigorous old man with a peg leg is standing on the river side with a long rope in his hand. He ties a knot over a pole on wharf, and is about to leave when he sees a man and a girl overturned in a boat some sixty feet out in river. He signals for help. Pulls in small boat to which his rope is attached, undoes the rope and hurls it mightily up stream in river. He watches girl and man disappear for second time and then grab frantically at their boat. Fisherman again signals and calls for help as life belt reaches the drowning people. Old man starts pulling with all his might. He has pulled some thirty feet of the rope when the girl lets go and the man follows. The fisherman frantically calls for help, then throws off his coat and plunges into water.

(This exercise is to develop transition from prosaic calmness to extreme excitement. The stiff leg needs more observation than is usually given it. With such a leg, a man uses his weight very differently from the normal way. Either the comic or tragic can be brought out in this.)

25. The Mirror

A young girl (or boy) comes in from bath and stands partly dressed before mirror of the room. She poses as various characters. She first represents September Morn. Then she changes to Nellie at the Bridge, or Terror, then she defies the villain and as Nellie supplicates for her life, she rejects his offer and declares herself innocent before the multitude. She becomes a judge and lays down the law. She then enacts a tyrant. A quick change to an avenging brother with a murderous dagger. She is now the captive with chains on her wrists as she takes several steps to and fro before the mirror. Presto, the hero of rescue and pleading for life of the heroine—she sees her father's face mirrored in door back of her. Embarrassment. The father laughs heartily and she goes off resentfully.

(Such practice is helpful for weight transition and bodily change. Note that the hand changes as often as does the face or feet. Arm, also, shows general attitudes. Be conscious of all of these in practice until a technic has been established.)

26. The Prisoner

A man is in prison, standing in deep thought. He is aroused from his reveries by a slight knock at the door. A veiled figure enters, whom the prisoner thinks to be his betrayer and his whole attitude is one of defiance. A closer and more scrutinizing look proves the visitor to be the King, for whom the prisoner has utmost respect. After a moment's visit, the King looks around the room and goes out. Prisoner goes to door and then crosses toward table where he is undecided whether to write at the desk or read letters on stand behind him. Chains are heard to clang ominously outside the door. The court executioner, black-hooded, enters and hands prisoner a letter. Prisoner reads it avidly. Pleads with executioner, who is powerless. Prisoner dedicates self to God and falls back, prostrate.

(All of this pantomime is best registered only by the prisoner. Every possible position of the foot is called for, as used in normal life. This, of course, excludes standing on sides of foot, etc.)

27. *An Awkward Courtship*

A youth sitting on sofa between two girls. At the right is his mischievous sister. At the left is new-found love. He is trying to get rid of his sister. Offers her half-dollar which she refuses. This he does while conversing with his girl. Girl looks at his frat pin. He kicks his sister in shins while his girl is admiring the pin. Sister kicks back at him fiercely, while he smiles at girl. He shoves sister off edge of sofa. Both he and girl rise as she falls. He apologizes profusely as sister goes out indignantly. He stands awkwardly and bashful. Girl comes up close to him, as he shyly takes off frat pin and pins it on her. He steps toward sofa as she turns to walk away. Goes quickly toward her, slides his hands down her arms, takes her hands and pulls her to the sofa. Girl sits at his side. He is waxing eloquent. Problem.

(A complexity of hand movement takes extra moments of conscious training until desired effects are obtained. Duality of gesture is more effective for comedy than tragedy. Avoid overdoing, even under temptation of audience encouragement.)

28. *At the Game*

A young girl at ball game on top seat of bleachers. Sees kick-off. Watches ball go through goal posts and thinks that a goal has been registered. This is explained to her and she becomes delighted. Sits down. Watches scrimmage as home team gains forty yards. Drops her hat through bleacher seats. Stands up looking for same. Nearly falls backwards. Sits down in state of jocular faint. Gesticulates to little boy to throw her hat up to her. She almost catches it the first time. On second throw she kicks lady in back, but grabs hat. Apologizes to lady. Turns around and sits on hat. Quick movement.

Hat is crushed but the pin was effective. Asks interested fan about game. He ignores her. She resents it. Buys hot dog, as she leans forward over the man in front of her, he pinches her leg. Indignation. Game is still going on.

(This purports to be purely an exercise for limb movement. Reckless indifference to balance affords good comedy, if done innocently. A good pantomime must be written so that action can reveal all sequential thinking. Thought, of itself, can never be effective pantomime. Acted pantomime is effective if, when repeated, it resembles original plan.)

29. Trials of a Mother

A mother and child come into room. The little child skips from table to cupboard and back to table. She is asking for some cake. Mother walks toward cupboard. Takes out cake and puts it on table. Starts to cut cake, but lets little girl finish cutting. Little girl cuts finger. Mother hurriedly goes toward kitchen cabinet and gets medicated gauze. Fixes little girl's finger as girl impatiently stands operation. Mother kisses injured finger, and puts cake in other hand. The mother puts cake away and brushes off crumbs from table. Sends little girl out and then she takes letter from pocket and rereads crushing news. She staggers back toward cabinet. She cannot believe its contents. Knock is heard at front door. She hurriedly wipes away tears. Straightens hair and goes out with proud dignity.

(A pantomime for eye-levels and emotion transition. The hands are especially active in this exercise. Household cares are not especially conducive to grace, yet an actress need not be awkward in such a scene. Practice management of letter until business is perfect, leaving consciousness for contents of letter.)

30. Inebriety in a Boarding House

An old drunk tries to thread needle. Several attempts, different ways. Loses needle. Goes to bottle. Gives a toast to picture on mantelpiece. Offers drink to picture. Registers refusal. Surprise on his part. He drinks for her. Sits on needle. Extracts. Offers chair a drink. Holds needle and pours wine on it. Puts down bottle and finally succeeds in threading needle by running thread along the chair top. Can't find button. Sticks needle in picture. Gets bottle. Starts singing lustily. Is interrupted by landlady. Offers her a drink. She throws water in his face. First smiles, then is very peeved. Wipes face with arm. Looks for bottle. It has disappeared. Goes staggering out door, after her, protesting.

(In this, watch location of table, size of bottle, also stamping and crossing of feet. So many actors put too much "sole" into their footwork. Learn to walk quietly, though you may represent unsteadiness. A drunkard's hand acts more of a unit, as does an imbecile's. His balance is very adjustable.)

31. John, the Peddler

Peddler stands selling pencils on street. He pretends to be blind. He moves several steps to right and left as if blind, calling "Pencils, pencils." A young urchin runs up to him and puts an apple in his pocket. As customer comes toward him, man gestures boy away with his foot. Drops twenty-five cent piece. John is about to pick it up, then changes his mind and holds out cup. Little boy picks up the money and runs away with it. The old peddler tries not to show his anger in his pretended blindness. The customer gives him fifty-cent piece which he pretends not to know. As customer leaves, John hurriedly pockets the fifty-cent piece and looks around for urchin whom he sees in front of bookstore across the road. He shakes fist at him as policeman turns corner. He changes gesture into one of scaring flies and as policeman comes close to him he still presumably scares the flies. He watches policeman out of corner of eye and starts to walk away hurriedly as he sees policeman turn around. Changes his walk to one searching his way. Shakes his fist at boy across street.

(The searching walk of the experienced blind is much different than the unsteady walk of the inebriate. The hands are used differently, in that the finger tips are especially active, and each finger has a vitality of its own. The fingers are the eyes for the blind.)

32. A Tryst Fulfilled

A young girl enters the room hurriedly, excitedly. Takes off her hat and gloves. Puts them on the table, center. Goes back to door, listens. Walks to wardrobe across room. Pulls out upper drawer, hurriedly writes a note. Footsteps at door, R. Turns letter over. Stealthily goes to door. Opens quickly. Man staggers in. Surprise. She pulls him up and lifts him to chair. Finds money clenched in his hand. She tries to rouse him. She takes the money, counts it, takes letter from table, tears it up, kneels by her lover and starts crying. Severe knock at door. Problem.

(This pantomime is to see that the work is done for audience and that location of table is consistent. Watch kneeling and rising. Carrying of imaginary burdens calls for muscle tension. Kneeling in present-day skirts demands attention of direction. Though an actress may be used to a one-piece suit on the beach, such freedom does not carry over to all the audience, and clothing demands certain deportment. A bare leg on the beach is different from the same leg under a skirt. Such is our prudery, but it must be respected.)

33. The Broken Engagement

A girl comes quickly into a parlor and stops before the radio. She turns dial and hears a jazz one-step, to which she responds joyously. Suddenly spies letter on front of table and stops dancing. Picks letter up and sees it is addressed to her. Quickly opens. Reads it in deep thought. Rereads and almost swoons. Collects herself and stands momentarily in attitude of defiance and then looks at ring on her finger. Takes it off and flings it on couch. Stands in mock respect before imaginary admirer and then paces floor in despair. She starts toward her own room as ominous bell rings in familiar manner. She starts to turn toward doorway but decides to go to her room. She is further undecided by ringing of the phone. She goes to phone and stands at ease while listening. News is joyful and she hangs up happily. She walks around room rapidly, and cheerfully, as door bell rings again, in same manner. She looks at letter in her hand and stands in suspense, wondering how voice of her lover over phone and his familiar ring could be so close together. She tiptoes to couch, gets ring, puts it on, and goes cautiously to front doorway, and stands listening. Surprised as her brother enters, and she reads his smiling guilt. She grabs him by shoulders. "Did you write that letter?" "You did!" Boy runs out and she does not follow. She is too happy.

(In this pantomime, all positions of feet are used. Watch, also, the opening of letter and use of phone, especially if this be done without props.)

34. *Blind Girl in the Garden*

A young girl, blind, walks carefully into the garden. She stoops and feels for flowers about her. She picks a bouquet of violets and smells their fragrance. Pins them on her waist. Feels for pansy bush and picks up a doll. Fondles it and rocks it to sleep. Puts doll on low hedge. Reaches again for pansy and puts hand on toad. Shrinks, wipes hand, but not frightened. Finds little stick and pushes toad away. Cautiously reaches for pansy, locates it and plucks it. Puts it in her hair. Rises and goes toward garden gate. Is met by her father; she is startled but smiles as she recognizes the figure in the gateway. Puts her hands to his coat lapels, smiles assuringly and rests her head on his shoulder. Gets violets and pins a few on him. They walk off together.

(Many movements of the hand are suggested in this number. Note how people show their responses to the pleasant and unpleasant. Again we note that the fingers are the eyes of the blind.)

35. *Versatile Musician*

A young Italian artist comes before his audience, bows, and gives nod to his pianist. He gets position for his violin, checks accuracy of strings and plays "Träumerei." Acknowledges applause, puts violin down and gets 'cello from table. Seats himself and plays "The Spring Song." He further proves his accomplishments; he takes the piano, as accompanist leaves and plays for his vaudeville audience "Rustle of Spring." As a grand climax, he takes up a large accordion and plays "Poet and Peasant" most dramatically. Bows low and sweepingly as if for body exercise, and leaves the stage. Accepts the encore by bowing and kissing his flexible fingers. Leaves stage again, in hurried manner. Returns with a bound, pushes his hair from face, bows to all the house and the orchestra, and triumphantly departs.

(Nothing is more pitiful than an actor or actress trying to play an instrument in absentia. One must actually know the management of such an instrument if the real music offstage is to synchronize. Many an anecdote can be told of such deficiencies and consequent chagrin.)

36. *Another Haaj*

A beggar, cross-legged, sits on the flat stone near the mosque. The afternoon sun strikes his face and wakens him. He stretches and yawns several times. He arranges his belongings, chiefly rags and leather goods. He puts out his hand to a passer-by, receives nothing and spits at departing figure. He sees two merchants approaching and lets his left arm hang as if paralyzed and assumes doleful attitude. Holds out right hand. "In the name of Allah." Two merchants enter mosque, one of them drops the beggar a copper coin. Both hands are immediately active, as he places coin in well-filled leather pouch. He looks to see that none observe. A woman passes and drops a piece of paper in his hand, a picture of a hyena. Beggar is infuriated and rises quickly imprecating passing reformer. Gesticulates madly. Sees merchants coming—drops as one dead and assumes attitude of deep slumber. Merchants pass on and beggar kneels, sitting back on heels. Takes out dry crust and nibbles.

(Many rehearsals have been conducted on the assumption that a person will sit all right on the night of the show. Nothing is to be taken for granted in a good show. Seeing is believing. To sit on one's own feet takes considerable practice. Haaj is really a very vigorous beggar.)

37. Julio, the Jester

A humpbacked jester is seated at the foot of a throne. He is studiously reading a large book. A Duke and a Duchess enter and are surprised that Jester should be reading the Royal Book. Jester closes book slowly and bows to Duke and Duchess. Duke pulls bell cord hastily, goes to Jester and strikes him viciously across face. Jester winces and bows. Preceded by an armed attendant, King Fernando enters and goes to his throne chair. Duke bows to King and immediately informs King that Jester had been reading royal records. King is indignant and orders Court assembled, attendant hurries out and large gong is sounded. Lords and Ladies enter from either side of Court hall and the King stands till Chancellor arrives, coming in hurriedly. Kisses ring of King. King seats himself and commands Jester to come before him. Jester kneels low at foot of throne. King informs Chancellor that Jester had been seen reading the Royal Record. All the Court is astonished. The Duke asks for instant execution for such breach of Court confidence. Chancellor approves of immediate attention and King looks at Jester in his humble attitude. Jester rises and with distorted hand begs for clemency. King hesitates, as Jester is a merry fellow and a real wit. Chancellor counsels death and King reluctantly consents. Two attendants carefully seize Jester and start away. King stops them and King orders Jester to once more make him laugh. Jester takes opportunity readily and clears circle around throne. Takes a pillow and pretends it is a baby. Spanks the pillow and as he hits it, the corners poke out. One of the corners pokes out and hits the Jester in the eye. This supposedly provokes the parent of the pillow and with mad antics Jester throws pillow about circle, striking at it vigorously. The pillow is thrown toward the Duke and the Jester gives a lunge, striking the Duke full force upon the face. The Duke, so caught unawares, trips and seats unceremoniously. The King and most of the Court laugh heartily, until Duke gains composure and draws sword to strike at Jester. King, still laughing, raises hand, but orders Jester away. The Princess intercedes with King, but Duke demands the proper penalty. Chancellor turns to front of book and reminds King of the law: death for the reading of Royal Records without regal permission. King, still hesitating, drops his head in compliance, when Jester takes paper from his belled cap and jumps to throne seat, hands paper to King. King looks at Jester wonderingly, but sees look of deep concern on Jester's face. King reads paper and pales. Slowly rises and hands paper to Chancellor; he in turn, is astonished. Both King and Chancellor look accusingly at Duke. Chancellor holds paper in front of Duke's face, who trembles and drops on his knees. Treason! Attendants hurry Duke off as Duchess drops at foot of throne. The Jester kisses the King's hands as King draws the freed Jester close to his side. Court dismisses in consternation and Duchess weeps bitterly, as King looks off in great distance of oncoming events.

(Group ensemble is the bugaboo and joy of all producers. A joy, if the actors know how to express their thoughts consistently. Regality and humility offer excellent contrasts. Agility in awkwardness is demanded of Jester.)

38. An Affair of Honor

A small dance hall is partially filled with people. Most of them are dressed in dark blue sweaters. The ladies wear short skirts and the men tight-fitting trousers. A few sit on side benches. There is an air of apprehension. Most of the eyes are fixed on Sylvanus, handsome fellow with cynical smile. He is trying out his foil, proud of its temper. Two novices parry and thrust half-heartedly for a few strokes, and then join a small group toward corner. A beautiful girl enters in main doorway and all eyes turn to her. She is frightened and goes quickly to a large chair on side of hall. Her nervousness is apparent and she recognized but few who greeted her as she passed. Sylvanus, assured and already the center of attention, bows in mock heroic style and turns his back upon her. It is evident Sylvanus is not popular with most of the crowd, though he has some ardent supporters. A clock strikes five and all eyes go toward the office door. As last stroke ends a small gray-haired man enters from office door and bows to crowd. Fencers all go to their accustomed places, all except Sylvanus. He walks slowly toward the Maestro and taps him flippantly on shoulder. Sylvanus bows, mock heroic again, and points to Rosina, the beautiful girl, now partially veiled. The Maestro bows solemnly to Sylvanus and then to the lady, as he undoes his sash and puts it on the lady's lap. As he walks past Sylvanus, a resounding smack startles Sylvanus as well as the students and guests. The girl rises and runs between the men already poised with drawn swords, tips removed. As Maestro protests her interference, Sylvanus clips him on the shoulder. The crowd shows menacing displeasure. Two men force Rosina to her chair. The Maestro and Sylvanus dance nimbly about, thrusting, guarding, and parrying with lightning rapidity. Sylvanus again makes point when he clips the Maestro's left arm. The fighting is now in deadly earnest. As Sylvanus passes Rosina, he deftly grabs the scarf and throws it at her feet with cynical smile. The Maestro fences with cold insistent precision, not to be outwitted by rash movements. The crowd is in tense excitement. A heavy-set fellow has volunteered as referee, and maneuvers as necessary, ready with uplifted cane. The Maestro points Sylvanus, going deeply into his chest. The smile leaves face of younger man and a greater fury comes from his determined blade. As the Maestro tires, Sylvanus presses him closer and closer to the girl. When near her swords are locked and Sylvanus almost forces the Maestro upon her. The referee has cane raised for any emergency when the Maestro hurls Sylvanus from him and they fight furiously. With a clear thrust, Sylvanus is stabbed over heart and grabs piercing wound. Drops his foil in pain and falls back on floor. Maestro staggers to referee, bows to Rosina. She comes quickly to him and brings his scarf, kisses it, as she places it in his hand. He bows, apologizes to Rosina and tries to walk away, but falls in a heap in the arms of the students, who tenderly carry him to his studio.

(Of all the arts, fencing is the best to develop foot and arm agility. It is a form of superanimate dance. Many accidents could have been avoided, had the actors been adept with foils. Many romantic actors have failed in this. Crowd ensemble demands every eye on the one focusing point of interest. Shakespeare offers many opportunities for sword work and crowd participation.)

DISCUSSION AND REVIEW QUESTIONS

1. Explain what is meant by "active" foot in dramatic art.
2. How does a daily occupation or "job" affect stance?
3. Develop the "broader the base, the coarser the character." Does the size of foot determine base?
4. How do illustrators make feet appear graceful? How can we approximate their art? Do we?
5. Name five characters in drama demanding a broad base for proper delineation.
6. Pick out four nationalities and describe their walking

and arm habits. E.g., Scotch, Italian, German, and Hindu. Do likewise for the Negro.

7. Which is the most difficult "walk" for you to enact in *A Medley of Walks* (*21*)? Why?
8. Why are some psychologists interested in hand movements when accompanying speech?
9. Could awkward hands mar effect of a good speech? How?
10. Explain "Most arm gesture is done on character level." Demonstrate.
11. Develop "A drunkard's hand acts more of a unit" than when he is sober. Why do his fingers move more independently in sobriety?
12. Write an original pantomime which calls for twelve or more hand positions.

CHAPTER IX

PANTOMIMES WITH WORDS

Pertinent Pointers for Word-Pantomimes

GESTURE precedes speech, unless it is descriptive. The greatest element of drama is *action* and it therefore places emphasis of burden on gesture for great acting. Intellectual and talking drama have their places, but they are limited to a smaller group. A good voice enhances proper action.

The pantomimes in this series may be done with or without properties. Nonuse of properties greatly enhances imagination. Clarity of diction is as important as accurate gesture. The well-bred person reveals both.

Best pantomime is manifestative, hence the best scenes in plays have one or more strong emotions, to which all else is subservient. One must never forget that action, emotion, tone, words, all are useful to that degree in which they reveal thought.

A very significant observation: the face is equipped with emotional response on a ratio of three to one for the unpleasant emotions. Of the twenty-four sets of muscles, approximately eighteen are used for the unpleasant emotions. The more intense the emotion, the more restriction is experienced in all vocal utterance. Anger may even choke speech, as may sorrow. The actor, therefore, must physically portray the emotion and consciously relax the vocal muscles. This is another important reason why great actors must be conscious actors.

39. Crazy-Patch Cross-Plots

The following exercises have proved excellent vehicles to develop imagination and emotional response:

Character	*Words Spoken*	*Character*	*Emotion*
An old miner	Thou	Colored mammy	Kindness
A giggling girl	Please	Irish maid	Hope
Stupid boy	I think not	Jolly ice-man	Anger
Deaf fireman	Get out!	Corpulent cop	Sorrow
Negro fisherman	Jump!	Ticket scalper	Doubt
Retired banker	Move quickly	Animal trainer	Jealousy
Chicago chauffeur	I love you	Hotel maid	Contempt
East-side tie-vender	I can't	Stocking salesman	Agony
Reformed gambler	Spurn me not	Rotary secretary	Wonder
Swedish sea captain	You'll pay	Eccentric painter	Surprise
Iowa farmer	Piffle	Sentimental florist	Adoration
Texas cowpuncher	Won't you?	Stage manager	Pride
Indulgent brother	Oh, heck!	Modern flapper	Bashfulness
Rocky Mountain miner	Love me	Nearsighted ticket-man	Fear
Hawaiian swimmer	Stop	German fräulein	Guilt

Some of the situations may prove incongruous, but not any more than life itself. Practice those from which you derive benefit. Fifteen characters in each group, speaking to any of the remaining twenty-nine, from a selection of fifteen sentences and fifteen emotions, give the actor or student some twenty-five hundred sentences to practice with voice and pantomime. Examples:

An old miner says, "I think not," to a jolly ice-man.
A modern flapper says, "Piffle," to a Chicago chauffeur.
A corpulent cop says, "You'll pay," to a Chicago chauffeur.
A Negro fisherman says, "Jump," to a colored mammy.

(Enact the character speaking, so that entire carriage responds to the accepted type.)

40. *Life Is Like That*

"Ouch! I've got my finger caught in the door! Ouch! Open the door, I tell you—you're crushing my finger! Ya big fool, didn't ya hear me yell? Don't touch me. You did it on purpose! Mind your business! Leave me alone."

(Resolution of an emotion, with the physical dominating. Agony is a very complex emotion, and when it expends itself into anger, becomes dangerous. An emotion is so much physical energy which must be expended in physical channels. Swearing is the usual emotion-vent, when person is angry or embarrassed.)

41. An Aged Inventor

"For forty years I've worked on this invention and now, when it's completed and they're coming to-day, I can't demonstrate—I've gone blind—blind, I tell you—did you hear me—I've gone blind! Why should I live for a day like this? My invention—my life—all, all gone! Why did I drink that damnable stuff? Curse the vile demon who brought me poisoned alcohol! My invention demonstration to-day! Blind! Oh, God, strike me now or let me see just once more and I'll never— What's that? Voices? The Committee! And I can't see! Oh, God, let me see! I must see! Don't let them in until I can see! Don't—don't—"

(An emotion growing in power, until vocal expression is impossible. Another agony type, which increases in this example, just as it decreased in one above. Gesture portrayal must not hamper voice accuracy.)

42. A Traveling Salesman

"Last night as I came along the street I saw one of the funniest—ha-ha-ha-ha—sights I ever ha-ha-ha—ever saw; a fat woman going around the corner and she ha-ha-ha-ha-ha-ha-ha—slipped on the ice and you ought to have seen —ha-ha-ha-ha-ha—as her parcels dumped ha-ha-ha-ha—and she sat on her ha-ha-ha-ha-ha— She was so mad that ha-ha-ha-ha-ha-ha she didn't notice ha-ha-ha-ha-ha—that she lost her—ha-ha-ha-ha— It's the funniest ha-ha-ha-ha-ha—thing I ever saw—ha-ha-ha-ha-ha—"

(A mixture of vocalization and emotional impulse. Laughing needs much practice to be kept real; it must come from the diaphragm. It is laughing which man does, that gives him an expression entirely foreign to animals. Laughing is a great relaxing exercise, and, therefore, worthy of encouragement. See last exercise in this group for different kinds of laugh.)

43. *The Burglars*

"Listen. Don't make a bit of noise. Be careful, they're asleep. Where's that paper? Not that one, the diagram—that's it! Now, be very careful. Turn on your cigar lighter. Let me see; that's right. Here it is—three feet from the floor, two feet from the northeast corner, to the left, press brick. That's good. Be careful. Watch your step. Over here now. All right. Northeast corner, three feet. This about it? Be careful. Anybody coming? I've got it. Here it is? (Explosion.) Oh, I'm killed. Trap-door explosion. I'm burned. I can't see. Who did it?"

(Two men enter from side door, revolvers leveled.) Chief Detective Maloney—"I knew you'd bite. That's just a little photograph powder. A little smudge, that's all. You're all right, and to think I've got you both! Not dead but alive, and the goods on you! Casey, put the bracelets on—attaboy! Hand me his rod. And you walked into it like babies. Ye gods, won't the chief smile at this. Get a move on you? Out you go, you whimpering boob. You'll see soon enough."

(A sudden transition of emotion must not be anticipated by actor. Rhythm of movement and words must be consistent. Aspirate tones of precision accompany very clear-cut and definite gestures. Watch carefully how you manage suspense—joy—terror—surprise transitions.)

44. *Sambo's Ghost*

"Boy, you has all done got me wrong. Ah never was no fightah. Ah never was anything else but a good runnah, and if you think ah's gonna stay heah and converse intimately with any ghosts, your brains am a long ways from your intelligence. Me and ghosts ain't never met. Oh! Lordy, what was that? Oh—me and dese ghosts is goin' ta be the least friends of what ah's got. Oh, Lordy, some more of that! Which way does ah done run? Oh!

Lordy-me, preserve your innocent child! Ah ain't done nothin', ah neveh was goin' ta do nothin', and the only blessing ah ask right now is ta put more life inta these shaking dogs. Feets, does your duty and wipe out any existent distance between me and dat ghost. Oh! Lordy, which way is dose noises?"

(A simulation of direction to express actual uncertainty, demands more practice than most actors give. An excellent comedy situation if acted well—but usually quite flat. Suspense is another element of drama often worked almost to a frazzle, or is it frizzle, in the modern mystery play. We exaggerate the vocabulary of the Negro as much as the dramatist does his suspense; both incongruities afford good comedy if properly managed.)

45. *The Mortgage*

Two girls come hastily into room which is the abode of their governess.

JENNIE: Do you think we will be able to get away with it?

NORA: Well, I don't know. She certainly was very peeved to-day.

JENNIE: We've got to get it, that's all. It won't hurt her to give five dollars. I don't ask her every day.

NORA: I don't know. She certainly needs it. But I'll stick up for you if you ask her. Here she comes now.

(Enter OLD LADY. She is nearsighted and slightly rheumatic.)

OLD LADY: Who's that? Who is there? What are you doing in this room?

JENNIE: We thought we'd find you here, so we've come to have a few minutes' talk with you.

OLD LADY: Yes, I guess so. When you come to talk to me there's something up. What is it?

NORA: Well, you know, Auntie, that is, that—

OLD LADY: You shut up. You wouldn't tell me anyway. [To JENNIE.] Come on now, out with it.

JENNIE: Why, we've got to have five dollars and we want it by noon.

OLD LADY: Five dollars? You might just as well spare your breath. [Turns haughtily toward chair.]

JENNIE: Is that so? All right, Nora, lock the door, because we are going to get five dollars. [JENNIE walks toward OLD LADY.]

OLD LADY: Don't you come near me, you little hussy, or I'll have you reported and dismissed. Don't you touch me!

JENNIE: The door locked, Nora? All right, you grab her arms. I'll do the rest. [OLD LADY tries to struggle and pain makes her cry out. JENNIE switches her around back to audience, and takes out from under her waist a purse filled with greenbacks. She opens it.]

JENNIE: Why, you old miser—here's fifty—ninety! Why! here's over three hundred dollars. You stingy old miser! Hold her, Nora, while I count. You old skin-flint—over seven hundred dollars! And to think what you have been doing to us. Stop her bawling, Nora. Put your hands over her mouth.

NORA: Oh, don't do that, Jennie. Let's take five and get out now.

JENNIE: Yes, I will, I'll take a hundred dollars. Besides, she never told me how I got in this place anyway.

NORA: She's treated you a little better than the rest. You've got to admit that.

JENNIE: Cut out the chatter. I've got this hundred dollars put in the bank. [She taps her chest and gives OLD LADY a shove to the floor. Girls run to the door and rush out. The OLD LADY drags herself to chair and piteously calls for help. YOUNG MAN comes in, stops near door and looks at her.]

OLD LADY: Jennie—Nora— [Points to door.] She took all my money.

YOUNG MAN: [Looks at floor and sees greenbacks partially stuffed in purse.] Auntie! That's your mortgage money. How much did she take?

Old Lady: Oh, Fred, I don't know and the agent comes to-day. My retribution. Why didn't I tell her that I am her mother. That all this estate is hers, but now—we've lost it all. Just for a few paltry dollars that have taken me nearly five years to get together. I don't care for myself, I want to die. Every bone in my body pains, but Jennie—oh, why didn't I tell her. [She falls weeping in chair. The boy counts money.]

Young Man: How much should it be, Auntie? Here's six hundred and fifty dollars. [Knock heard outside.]

Old Lady: Seven hundred and fifty dollars.

Young Man: [Going toward door.] Auntie, it's the agent. What are we going to do? Perhaps I can catch Jennie. [He goes off calling, voice dying in the distance. Agent knocks.]

(Try each part and note contrasting action and tones and observe sudden transitions. Extremes are usually more easily made than partial blendings. Only the best actors know how to reach and sustain a climax. This is good exercise to consciously work for stage balance.)

46. The Auction Sale

The scene is laid in lodge room, at a lady's bazaar.

"Ladies and Gentlemen—I have been asked to step up here and help sell a few articles for the bazaar. I have here a bunch of roses, beautiful red roses [He pricks finger.] with one less thorn than a previous moment. How much am I bid? Come on, Sid. Get this for your Rosie. How much? Fifty cents. A gentleman of means offers fifty cents! Sold. Sold for charity, each blushing rose for less than five cents. Charlie, get the money. Here we have a book of etiquette, autographed by the mayor of the town. A golden-edged book of proper deportment. In this chapter, 'How to court.' In this one, 'Which hand to use first and where to place it in the dance!' And here's a page on 'Meeting mother-in-law for the first time.' And the handwriting of the mayor! How much am I bid? Two dollars. Good for Jones, he thinks it worth two dollars to know how to act in the presence of the ladies. What do you say, Fred? How much? What? Thirty cents? Sold to Fred for thirty cents. It's worth the loss, just to get a guy like Fred to learn how to act in public. Be sure and get the money, Charlie. O. K. Here's a gem. I have before me, a skeleton key, which will let you in any front door. Think, gentlemen, how valuable this may be. Why even I, who have been batching for two weeks, could find excellent use for such a treasure. If any lady here will just indicate— Pardon me. What did you say, Charlie? What? My wife on the phone? There's a mistake, somewhere. She's in Chicago. Are you sure? Well, well— Pardon me, folks, my wife has unexpectedly returned. I had better keep this key. It belongs to our front door. Excuse me. Here, Charlie, here is a set of false teeth for you to auction off. Get busy—"

(To appear at ease and not let the audience know you are funning is golden coin for the actor. To keep a crowd alive on the stage for the people in the audience, is a priceless quality. Rapidity of speech is chiefly animation of spirit.)

47. *The Suicide*

An OLD MAN comes into room, strikes match, lights gas, goes to table right, picks up revolver, examines it, comes to table center, writes letter, signs; slowly raises revolver to head. GIRL enters, screams.

GIRL: Father, father, don't. [Knocks revolver from his hand; it drops and explodes. Girl grabs chest in anguish.] [Note: when staged, shot is fired offstage.]

GIRL: Father, father, you've killed me. Why did you do it? You've always been a curse to our family. Your drinking and gambling killed mother and now your recklessness has killed me. Why, oh, why did you do it? Oh, Daddy, Daddy. [She faints in his arms. The OLD MAN gradually awakes from his drunken stupor and recognizes the lifeless girl.]

OLD MAN: Marie, Marie, wake up. Don't die. [Looks at revolver.] I swear to God if you'll live I'll never drink again. Marie, hear me. By the sacred name of your mother, I swear to you I'll never drink again. Don't you hear me? I swear.

GIRL: [Slowly awakens.] Do you mean it? Do you swear by God and mother?

OLD MAN: Yes, Marie, believe me, I mean it. [She slides her arms around him.]

GIRL: Honest, Daddy, honest? [As if dying.]

OLD MAN: Yes, Marie, I swear it. [She gets up quickly, takes the gun and throws it out of the window, after emptying barrel. She is crying with happiness.]

OLD MAN: Aren't you hurt, didn't I—?

GIRL: Yes, Daddy, you did, let's hurry to Dr. Jones and tell him of your promise. Hurry, before it's too late. [She leads him out, both wondering about promises made just that way.]

(Another exercise for practice in transition and resolution. Relaxing in another person's arms is often called for on the stage, but seldom sufficiently practiced to look real. Avoid pointing revolver at audience. When a person acts as if dying, and words are spoken, be sure they are audible. Even though the words may be unimportant, the audience thinks they are.)

48. Nemesis

A young man goes to the safe, opens by touch method; searches papers. Two desired out of the many. Stands and eagerly reads; joy from one letter, disappointment from other. Tears letter. Straightens safe; puts papers back; closes safe. Footsteps; he hides behind the curtains; watches grandfather come in and go to safe, open, and search for missing paper. Grandfather puzzled, looks again, goes to table center and writes, then signs; spasm of pain; falls limply on table. Grandson rushes out, "Grandfather!" Shakes grandfather, but he is dead. Boy unclasps hand and takes paper from it, reads eagerly. "And he was thinking of us all the while." He pleads with grandfather for forgiveness. "Oh, Grandfather, I didn't know." The door bell rings; young man moves slowly to door, but quickly turns and goes back to grandfather; lifts tenderly; carries him to couch. Girl enters. Boy points toward couch, as she hurries over. He goes to safe; pulls out other paper and takes to girl. Takes signed paper from table; lets her read, and tears into bits. Penitent. He goes to telephone and calls, "Morning Heights 7654. Is this the Undertaker's? Come over to 777 North University. My grandfather just died." Slowly hangs up phone and walks to couch.

(An exercise for transition and relaxation. When Irving studied the part of Romeo, he practiced many different ways of carrying a relaxed body, weeks before he was satisfied. One cannot just pick up a dead body, it takes considerable practice in playing dead and as much properly to handle the "dead." The voice is often unnatural when the mind is occupied with too many extraneous matters.)

49. *A Glance of Cupid's Arrow*

Ruth is talking to her fiancé, at her home.

"Please don't go, George. I didn't mean to do it. Had I known that you would have taken such offense I wouldn't have done it for the world. Please don't go. You'll smash both our lives. I'll do anything to prove to you that I love you. I never did love him and you know it. Don't go, George, please." He leaves hurriedly, as the mother enters gently from other door. "Oh, Mother, he has gone. He wouldn't listen. He thinks the worst. What shall I do? I want to die. Mother, Mother, he has —gone."

(To work an emotion to a climax, to a point of exhaustion, and not become hysterical oneself, demands more than ordinary control. This scene demands tears. What George and the mother do in this, is as important as the girl's acting. "Bits" can ruin a great play; they must never be minimized.)

50. Desperate Innocence

Trial scene. Last chance to prove innocence. Girl has saved sister who isn't big enough to admit own guilt. Judge has given her last chance to speak: "Honest, Judge, I didn't do it. I swear on my bended knees I didn't do it. What if he was my lover? That doesn't prove anything. And what if he was seen with me last? Neither does that prove anything. Look at me, Judge—do you think I am lying to you? Oh, God, make him understand. I loved him too much to kill him. We were to have been married this spring. I wasn't even in the house, Judge. We had said good-by for the night and I had gone on the hill to look at the stars. I wanted to be alone with my own happiness and when I came back and saw him—Honest, Judge, oh, oh, you know I didn't do it. I loved him too much. Oh, how I loved him! Oh, Judge, please—"

(To keep good voice, despite emotional pull, is one of greatest strengths of the stage. Work to a climax, until there seems to be no more to be said.)

51. Joyful Excess

(Laughing heartily) "I had the best time I ever had in my life. First I giggled, then I snickered, then we both tee-heed, and then we ha-ha'd, and then I lay down on the grass and just roared. Every time I think of it I just about croak. He had his ha ha and I had my ha! ha! and we both had—oh—" (cry of pain) "Mother, mother, mother, get the doctor. He told me I should be careful. I feel as if blood—were pouring all through my head. I'm getting dizzy. Mother, something—has—I can't see, Mother—"

(Sudden transition from joy to terror is excellent practice for emotional control. Keep in mind, work is done for audience.)

52. *Positive Proof*

A pretty girl has a good-looking caller in the parlor The girl speaks:

"I was hoping for just such a time as this and I thought you never were going to make love to me. You're mine, all mine, and you may put that ring on my finger as proof. There, one more lingering kiss." She suddenly breaks away from his embrace. "If you touch me I'll kill you. You dirty low beast! I knew you were only trifling with my sister. This is the ring you took from her and swore eternal faith. You vile beast. I am Gertrude Collins, your wife's sister. I told her you were nothing but just this. I told her—but why talk any further? I loathe you. I wouldn't waste my spit on you. Get out of the house before the servants drag you out. James, show this worm the door."

(Just as the words change, so does the voice and gesture. The more vital the scene, the more full and long are the lines of gesture. In such a scene, the volume of voice will lessen though the spirit of vehemence does not retard.)

53. *Bad Eyes*

Two people talking. The Man squints and looks over the top of his glasses. The Lady opens but one eye.

Man: How are you to-day?

Lady: Not so well. Have a bad pain in my stomach.

Man: Is that so? Here's a peppermint.

Lady: No, thanks. I'm under the doctor's special care. I am on the way to mother's with this letter. Read it.

Man: Well, what does it say? [Adjusts glasses. Shows surprise.] Is that so?

Lady: Yes, it is.

MAN: I wouldn't stand it under any conditions. Tell him to beat it.

LADY: I can't. He's the only support I have.

MAN: That makes me sore. You're a fool to stand it. [He walks away.]

LADY: Well, that's all the comfort you get out of a man. Tells me to beat it. He knows I'm not well. Every time I confide in men I get more disgusted with them. [She looks up the street where MAN disappeared. Raises her voice for his benefit.] And you can keep your advice to yourself. He's no more a fool than you are, you squintin' fool; can't see straight, anyway. Guess that'll quieten him. Wish I hadn't showed him the letter, anyway. [Going off as she talks muttering to herself.] I know darn well, he's right though. My old man— [She disappears.]

(Gesture is best means of making voice appear louder on the stage. Putting your hand cupshape, near the mouth, is a convention of stage whispering. The voice remains about as loud as in good stage speech. An eccentric character need not have a pinched tone, or harmful throat distortion.)

54. *The Walk of Life*

A young girl applies for work at producing company's studio. The MANAGER is pleasant but very conservative.

MANAGER: Had any experience?

GIRL: Yes, sir. I was a floor-walker.

MANAGER: Floor-walker? Where?

GIRL: At Callaways.

MANAGER: Callaways? What's that got to do with acting?

GIRL: I watched every kind of character there is in the city.

MANAGER: You did? Well, get out there and move around a bit. Walk like a mother eighty years old, asking for a letter at the general delivery.

GIRL: [Walks slowly, deliberately, feet close together,

toes pointing directly in front of her, body a trifle bent. Takes several steps and talks to imaginary post-office employee in a thin, clear voice.] Have you got a letter from my son?

MANAGER: All right. You are in a dance hall reception room. Show that you are the typical flapper girl of to-day.

GIRL: [Goes up to several imaginary friends and claps them on back, as she does a few Charleston steps.] Hot-diggety-dog! Oh, baby, hear that syncopation! Me for the light fantastic! How do you like this little step, Velvet Skin? [Takes hold of skirts and does a few ultra-modern movements and pirouettes daintily. Most of action on balls of her feet.]

MANAGER: Now, you are an old nigger mammy with bunions.

GIRL: Bunions! Well, here goes. [She puts right hand on small of back and the left thumps an imaginary cane. She cautiously shifts weight of body from one foot to the other, toes lifting outwards as weight changes to other foot.] Doggone you painkillah, you ain't doin' yo' dooty. Why is ah buyin' you if you cain't assume some of dis responsibility? Sufferin' steeples. Dem rocks am like razor blades. Ouch!

MANAGER: That will do. You are now a young girl at a dance and shoes are much too small.

GIRL: That's easy. I've watched hundreds of women leave our store in agony. I am now standing with a crowd of girls and fellows. [She walks over to chair with quite a swaying movement, as if she would transfer weight at each step, little movement at knees. She sits.] Oh, Fred, come here a moment. Let's sit this out! [She slips off left shoe and rubs foot against other leg, as two friends come over.] Hello, Bob, how's everybody? What? Oh, I'm sitting this one out. No, wait a minute. Wait, please. This is Fred's dance. [She is struggling to get shoe on as man pulls her up—she is finally successful with the shoe.] Well, if it's all right with you, Fred. [Gives BOB a painful look and as painfully one-steps away.]

MANAGER: Now, Miss Callaway, you are an Italian waitress in a fashionable restaurant.

GIRL: Watta you mean? I worka for Travaligini? Sure, Signor. Dees ees good place to eat vera best in dessa ceety. Please to seeta here. We make a specially Italiano spaghetti and dam' fine raviola. Maybe you don't like Italiano, eh? Maybe corn beefada ca-buge an' hamma da egg? Eh? What—only you want small boula da soup? Say, I bet you some mon, you're name he is Macpherson. Ha. Ha. You theenk I do nota know. Allaright, Signor, soup she is—

MANAGER: Let's see. What if you were a Swedish girl finding your way in a big city and your arms were full of bundles.

GIRL: May I pick up a few things to help?

MANAGER: Go ahead, if you want to.

GIRL: This wastebasket is my valise and this—this letter file will be my bundle. I'll fix my hat. Ready? Val—here go. O meh gracious, ay ban lost un no frant to halp me. Ay skoll faint, ay know. Vait a minute, Mr. Corndoctor, your car go to fest for Lina. Stop da car vile ay ask you ver ay am. Oh, hal, he vont vait. Der ban a polisman. Mister officer, stop dese dem oatmobile till I get to you. Dy splash mud up all my back. Meh gracious!

MANAGER: How old are you, Miss—

GIRL: Carol Condon. Age? Must I tell? To be sure. The truth. I'm twenty.

MANAGER: Report to me at ten in the morning. I wonder if you could introduce a few stars to Callaways? I want to give some of them a little training. See you here to-morrow.

GIRL: We haven't discussed salary yet. Have we?

MANAGER: Salary? Oh, that's unimportant. See you in the morning.

GIRL: That's right. What a joke on me! Toodle-oodle, until to-morrow. [As she goes she laughs, but by the doorway she stops.] I wonder what he meant b-- unimportant?

(Absolute abandon in a part, and keeping conscious of everything done, is possible only when technic is positive and done with knowledge. One cannot guess and be an actor; one must know. Versatility will supplant the type actor, our present stage bugaboo. No player can claim the title of musician if he can play only jazz.)

55. *A Rendezvous*

The young husband has unexpectedly been given a vacation. He is coming home a week earlier than either he or his wife expected. It is the anniversary of their marriage. He buys a bouquet of orchids and hurries home. It is the dinner hour. Instead of ringing the bell, he goes to the living room, but the light is in her room. He will surprise her the more. He opens the heavy curtains and sees —his wife in the arms of his best friend. He stands amazed, as the bouquet drops slowly from his hand. He looks from one to the other, becoming whiter and trembling with suppressed emotion. He is finally able to speak:

"My wife in the arms of my partner and pal. My first impulse is to shoot you like a dog in the street. My companion! You who played with me through boyhood. You, who slept with me all through our school days! Who shared my every dream, hope, and even my clothes. You, who stood up with me a year ago to-day. My best man. My best—hell! Shooting would be too good for you. Get out of my sight and never let me see you again. If you come to the club, return to our bank, or associate with any of my friends, I'll blacklist you from one end of Paris to the other. You will become a hiss and byword among decent people. No—don't come near me. No words. No lies. No further hypocrisy. Out of my life forever."

He watches his friend leave the room. "Oh, Yvonne. How could you? How could you? No, no, don't cringe from me. I will not hurt you. No, I never intend to touch you again. And this is our wedding day. I have tickets to Monte Carlo—another honeymoon, we had promised ourselves. Honeymoon—bah." [Tears the tickets slowly as tears swell his eyes.] "My greatest sin is that I loved you too much. Only you have I lived for, dreamed for, and hoped with. The days we spent in the mountains, the moments in the arbor—and I so conceited that I thought you loved only me—that I could fill your life! How long you have loved another does not matter—that you have loved another at all is enough. Would to God you could kill my love! Yvonne, to the last breath of my life I shall love you—that will be your Nemesis. Do not talk. I have said enough for both. My first words and my last shall be 'I love you.' God knows I love you." [He backs out of the room and curtains slowly close as she falls in a heap.]

(In sustaining two emotions of intensity, be careful not to let one subdue the other. There is even greater strength in pathos than outburst. The very effort to control emotion often makes it stronger than the actual expression of the emotion itself. In this exercise, the girl has as difficult a portrayal as the man. What she does is suggested by the husband's words and actions.)

56. The Race

A Scotchman and an Irishman are in a box at the races. They have bet on two different horses, both favorites. The Scotchman is positive and the Irishman is certain. They quarrel but never fight, they are that kind of friends —each enjoys the spirit of the other.

O'BRIEN: Niver moind yer blarney. Ye are goin' to loose foive dollars to-day, if ye niver did in yer loif bayfore.

MACDONALD: Ha, ha! Would ya hear the mon?

Blowin' aboot a fiver he'll soon ken naught aboot. You can brag on your nag the noo, you willna in a few minutes yon. Canna you see for yoursel'? A broken-doon filly withoot e'en a past. Ha! An' look at the Roan! What a morsel o' flesh for you! Pairfect in every detail, as well as the tail! Ha! An' mine is booked for two to one! Please pass the bottle! [Shows ticket.]

O'BRIEN: Yis, an' moine is booked ayven, which is the more to be feared. Two for one is only for suckers. Oi niver lost a bet in moi whole loife and this one—whurra! They're loinin' for the tape and Shamrock draws the pole. Now for us Oirish! We've fought togither and we can run togither! Oid bate ye if Oi had drawn the back lane, but now—

MACDONALD: Ye needna banter sae cocky, me boy. The Roan is third from pole, which wull gie him a clear field an' nae pickets to dodge, look ye, noo—they're off. They're off! [Both speak more or less together. A woman stands next to O'BRIEN and waves a small flag, and in her excitement, occasionally hits O'BRIEN on his hat.]

O'BRIEN: What did Oi tell yez? Huh, to ye! Shamrock is brushin' the flies aff iv the Roan's nose with his tail alriddy! By the toime they raych the tur-rn, Shamrock will be a black dot in front iv the field. Go it, ye black tail-devil o' Hell. Oi'm proud to be yere counthryman.

MACDONALD: The front parrt o' the race willna last sae lang! Me Roan hasna his oats for nil. Gae ye noo? Dinna ye disrupt my confidence in the whole horse kingdom.

O'BRIEN: Two for wan, is it? Oi'll take me wan for wan as any honest man. Did ye iver see sooch beautiful gainin' in all yer loife? Pardon me, lady, but 'tis moi hat yer celebratin' with. Did ye bet on Shamrock, too? Thin, yer a gintleman. Come on, Shamrock! Foive lengths ahid and only half the race is done. Oirland foriver!

MacDonald: I had me doots aboot racin' as an honorable sport an' noo I'm convinced 'tis nae honest. [Sees lady pound O'Brien upon the head and gives her his umbrella, which she accepts in her joy of winning.] Nae mon can pretend honesty when he takes money under false pretenses. I much prefair merchandisin' with gentlemen than— [Lady hits O'Brien with the umbrella.] Nae sae harrud, lady, 'tis na necessary. Ye may brek it!

O'Brien: [Grabbing hat.] Hurrah! Hurrah! Shamrock in with a canter, an' almost walkin', so far ahead av the whole bunch. If ye had treated animals with generosity, Mack, me boy, they would not av diserted ye in yer hour av adversity— Lady, Oi don't mind me head, but ye have ruined me hat. But 'tis in good cause, the Oirish foriver! [Takes betting ticket and waves at Mack. Notices Mack taking the umbrella from the lady and looks at his hat suspiciously.] Well, onyway, there is no question as to race superiority! 'Tis the fall av the year, onywise, and Oi have the proice of two new hats. An yer umbrella's bent! Come on, Mack, Oi'll treat ye to a schooner. Oirland foriver!

(Dialect needs very careful study and often robs action of its importance in trying to assume sounds. Once acquired, a new power has been added to an actor's talent. But dialect is virtually a study of a foreign language, more or less simplified. The lady's part is suggested by action and words of two men.)

57. *Partnership in the Stock Market*

A husband and wife are just ready for their evening meal. Toby has come home tired and really enjoys the quietness of his home, his pretty wife, and her good cooking. The table is being set by Antonia while Toby finishes the evening paper. Table is in center. Toby is lounging in chair down right and telephone is on tabaret, left, just below kitchen door.

Toby: [Holding his paper at full length.] See where

Scotland has bought a carload of American rubber heels.

TONY: [From kitchen.] Is that so?

TOBY: Yes, they buy rubber heels, because they give a little.

TONY: [Coming in.] You mean the Scotch give so little for the rubber? [She sets food ready for serving.] Well, well.

TOBY: [Looking at her with pity.] Sure, honey, you get it every time. Well, what do you know about this. Scientist has just discovered that fish swim with their gills, and not with their tails or fins. Two thousand years finding that out. Think of a fish putting that over on us for that length of time!

TONY: [Sitting down at table left.] I bet they don't know anything about it. Every fish I ever saw always used its tail. Come on, dear, everything is ready. Good hot tomato soup and hot rolls. Your favorites!

TOBY: [Still lingering over the paper, but rising reluctantly.] See where the Cards are expected to beat the Cubs.

TONY: Well, any bunch that will gamble, gets it sooner or later. Sit down, dear.

TOBY: [Seating himself right and using napkin.] What? Oh, yes, honey. You know that the Braves are nearly down and out, don't you?

TONY: Yes, to be sure; we haven't seen an Indian around here for several years. Like the soup?

TOBY: Just a trifle hot. Will taste it in a minute. [Telephone rings—they look at each other, and he accepts the challenge—goes to phone.] Hello. Yes, Toby speaking. Yes, Mother, she's right here. Tony, your mother wants you. [He puts receiver down.] She always calls at meal times for some reason or other. Make it snappy, honey.

TONY: [Puts her napkin on her chair as she goes to phone.] Yes, she knows we're here at meal times. Hello,

Mother. Why, I think we're going to a picture show if Toby—

TOBY: [Just seating himself.] Why, Tony, I'm too tired to— [Door bell rings; he looks at TONY, puts down his napkin and goes to door right. Lets in insurance collector.] Hello, Mr. Jones, what you doing around at this time of day?

JONES: [Talking as TONY talks.] Missed you last week and can't let it lapse, you know, not as long as Chicago is at war with Great Britain! Couldn't collect while your wife had that party on here, could I? [Gets his book out.]

TONY: [During interim.] Toby is too tired I guess, besides we have company. Yes, they just came in. [Winks at insurance collector as she hears him tell of the party.] Good-by, Mother, will call you in a minute. [Slams phone.] Yes, that party at mother's was quite a bit of fun. [Walks over to MR. JONES and steps on his foot—he looks at her.]

TOBY: [Standing by his chair.] Oh, a party here, eh? [Looks at TONY.] Hadn't heard of that. Big crowd?

TONY: Yes, dear, I left a note for any one to call over at mother's if they wanted me and when he saw the crowd of women there, he didn't stay long. Did you, Mr. Jones?

JONES: I should say not. Well, here's your receipt. Now for the coverage. [TOBY pays him.] Thanks, much. Don't want to raise that policy for your wife, do you?

TOBY: Not to-night, though I might regret it soon. [Looks at wife, who hustles MR. JONES out.]

TONY: Good-night, Mr. Jones; kindly arrange to come in the daytime, next time, as Toby does so dislike being bothered at meal times. Good-night.

JONES: [Looking at her.] Why, you told me to come at the dinner hour [seeing her gesticulate] but, I guess I was mistaken. Good-night and may you enjoy the moonshine!

TONY: [Closing the door and coming back to her

place.] My, this soup is stone cold and it is the best I ever made. Better warm it up. [He watches her take the soup out; she sings unusually loud and gay.] Look at your paper, dear, won't take but a minute.

TOBY: [Stares at kitchen doorway.] Why did you say the grocery bill was ten dollars higher than usual? [Telephone rings—he goes to it.] Hello. Yes, Mother. What? She hurt your ear? Oh, well, we had company. Some of the people who were at your party last week, called on us just now. A fine-looking fellow—what? You didn't—it was at my place? No! Oh, you mean the Bridge Club group. No? Twenty-four! Oh, yes, she told me all about that. Chicken, no? Turkey, pudding, punch and—well, you did have a good time! That's fine! Yes, Tony will call you up soon. [He hangs up receiver and goes back to his chair, thinking.] Tony, oh, Tony. [She comes in with soup, flushed and radiant.] How much does turkey cost a pound?

TONY: Turkey, dear? I don't know. I'll see. [Gets paper and turns to market prices.] Forty-two cents, why? Going to get one?

TOBY: [Wondering.] How did you know where to turn so quickly?

TONY: Why, you goose, every woman looks at the market page, so as to know how to buy. Sit down. [She sits.]

TOBY: [About to deny, but changes his mind.] How many were here to your party last week?

TONY: [Startled.] Eat your soup, Toby. It's your favorite. Can't waste anything now, can we, dear? And to think, in three more months, we'll own our big car.

TOBY: Car be damned. Why did you have two dozen people here last week and feed them turkey and gumdrops when you know very well I borrowed fifty dollars last week to pay off the last grocery bill? Ten dollars higher last week than week before. It's getting raw, I tell you.

TONY: Am I to be denied a few friends occasionally?

Toby: Going through that again, eh? [Rises.] Didn't we agree I was to cut out the club, cigars, new ties, etc., so as to get on our feet once? Have I smoked since? Didn't I keep my part of the bargain? And here you spring a party on me, of twenty-four dames, and feed them avocado preserves!

Tony: [Also rises.] I kept my word, Toby Pilling. It's none of your business, but that party didn't cost you a cent. And it was a good one, too.

Toby: [Picks up a knife and rubs it.] Come, Aladdin! Spread our table. Now put champagne on it for twenty-four. Caviar and capons. [Rubs knife harder.] Now bring on six dancing maidens!

Tony: How did you guess so near, darling; there were four beautiful girls who danced a Godiva for us.

Toby: [Throws knife on table.] And it didn't cost a cent. That's the best lie you ever told me!

Tony: That's enough of that, Toby Pilling. You wouldn't let me spend a cent, so I asked the few friends I have to bring their own victuals.

Toby: Yes, you did!

Tony: [Leans over table.] Yes, I did. Stella Jackson brought the turkey, Mame Devereaux the salad, Carol Schyler the champagne—yes, and it *was* champagne, and Nell Silvers brought the rolls and cakes and—

Toby: Wait a minute. You've said enough. You mean to tell me that Mrs. Jack Devereaux brought salad over to our house for your party?

Tony: [Picking up the soup dishes.] Recognize the truth and weep. None other, cutie.

Toby: I think you're lying now, more than ever. We'll see. [Goes to phone.] I haven't taken out the bankruptcy yet. Furnish their own, will they?

Tony: [With soup dishes in hand.] Toby Pilling, what are you doing? If you phone one of those women and ask them about that party, I've cooked my last meal in your house!

TOBY: [Ignoring her and finding number in book.] North Shore 535.

TONY: Don't you ask Mame Devereaux about that party. Please, Toby. [She goes toward him.]

TOBY: Just as I thought, lying, and can't back out gracefully. [In phone.] Hello. Is this the Devereaux residence? May I talk to Mrs. Devereaux, please?

TONY: You'll regret this all your life, you fool—hang up before—

TOBY: Hello? Mrs. Devereaux? This is Toby Pilling speaking. Yes, Pilling. I have a very funny request to make of you. You'll sure laugh. Huh? Yes. You know that salad you brought over to our house last week—yes—salad. What? You didn't bring any? Oh, I misunderstood. I was going to ask you how you made it. It was the most delicious salad I ever ate. I thought Tony said you brought it over. Well, pardon my calling—what? What? Oh, you *did* bring some over—last week—but you bought it? Oh, well, I am surely disappointed as I did so want to know how it was made. How is Jack? Oh, he's not very well? Too bad. And you—ouch! [As phone is banged in his ear.] Well, of all the nerve, nearly deafened me. Hung up like a shot.

TONY: All right, Toby Pilling. You've humiliated me beyond words. Anything else but what you have just done. Are you satisfied? So am I. We had a party; we've been having parties for the last five months, but not at your expense. Call up Stella and ask her if she brought the turkey and ask her how she got the money. Go ahead while I am packing. [She goes off.]

TOBY: Since when have we been so poor that you have our friends bring in their food? Answer that. [He goes toward the door.] Why don't you answer? [Phone rings—he goes to it.] Hello. Yes, this is Toby Pilling. Yes, she's here. Tony—Mrs. Silvers want to talk to you.

TONY: [Comes in with coat and hat on; does not look at TOBY as she goes to phone.] Hello? Yes—yes—I'm sorry. Yes, he knows. Mother gave him the hint and he wormed it out of Mame. No, don't come over to-night —anyway, not here—I'll be at the Blackstone in half an hour. [TOBY gets back of her and starts taking off her hat—she stops him.] Yes, in half an hour. Can't talk here, too much racket. Will see you later. [Hangs up phone.]

TOBY: [Turning her around.] What's all this ridiculous nonsense? Maybe I was blunt about the party, but a guy likes to share part of the daytime with his wife. What was so terrible in phoning Mame Devereaux? She was here, all right. I apologize. I still don't know why she had to bring her own groceries. Let it pass. But why this tragic pose?

TONY: Pose, you think? All right, old man. Marriage is all right when all adjustments are made within your own walls. You can stand much. But when your affairs are settled and spread outside your own—[Phone rings.] Another one! They'll all know it within ten minutes. [At phone, listlessly.] Hello. Yes, Stella. He knows. Yes. I'm the goat. But for him none would know until we sold. But now—I'm sorry. Good-night. [Puts up phone.] Read this at your leisure, Tobe. [Gives him paper from her purse.] It will tell you how twenty-four women have been playing the market and are way ahead; how we agreed to drop out of the pool as soon as our husbands messed into it in any manner. Only those can remain in the pool who are *trusted* by their husbands. Funny contract, eh? Tobe? And I thought my husband was the safest of the crowd. Yes, he is—the first one in twenty to bawl his wife out to her friends. We bought radio stock and it has more than trebled. What we could save from our own actual living expenses. And they put the stock in my name. [Phone rings.] You answer it—I—I'm not here any more—

TOBY: Why Tony, old girl, what in the hell have I done? I didn't know. I— [Phone rings insistently, but

TONY walks toward door.] You can't go. What do you think I really am? Take off that coat and hat—I'll square it— Do you think that a little thing like a salad can come between us?

TONY: [Going to phone.] Hello. Yes, Carol, it's true. I'll receive my friends at the Blackstone to-morrow. Tell Mrs. Dowling I'll indorse the stock over to her. I saw in the paper to-night that radio had gone up eight more points. Good for you, girls—it will be a good Christmas present for your husbands. Good-night, Carol. Yes, I'm sorry too. [Hangs up phone, walks deliberately to door.] No, don't stop me, Toby. I'm going. Nothing can stop me. Whether it is permanent or not depends—you'll find the soup on the stove, quite hot. The rolls and meat-loaf are in the oven. Everything is just where you expect to find it. When the rest of the girls phone, tell them I am at the Blackstone.

TOBY [Forcibly drawing her to him.] You can't go. [She pushes him away—phone rings again.] All right, you stay and I'll go, if that's the way you feel. [He goes to inner room for his things—TONY leaves quietly, looking at room, in tears. As TOBY enters with suitcase and coat, phone starts ringing.] Damn that phone. [Sees that TONY has gone—goes out calling.] Tony, Tony, Tony!

(A natural use of telephone, dishes, napkins, coats, and hats should be practiced, even on the stage. All business must be definite, but appear spontaneous. Such a scene above demands intensity of feeling, but not loudness of voice.)

58. *Prepare to Shed Your Tears*

A middle-aged person comes to manager's office, and tells the manager he once played Hamlet. That the younger generation had no emotional power.

MANAGER: Let me see some of the work you can do.

VETERAN: Crying was my forte. I would like to show you how to really cry. Suppose you name some situations,

MANAGER: This is your show, not mine. But here goes. Let's see. All right, go over there, and use the corner of the room as stage. Make up your own words, and fit these situations:

(*a*) A soldier reaches his home town and reads in paper his mother is dead.

(*b*) A father is told his only son is a common thief.

(*c*) A husband goes home and finds that his wife has left him a note of her desertion. He had no knowledge of her intentions.

(*d*) A violinist comes out of anæsthetic and learns that his fingers have been cut off in an auto accident.

(*e*) A fond parent watches his girl leave for a distant school, her first trip away.

(*f*) A business partner, who you thought was stealing money from the firm, presents you with a ten-thousand-dollar check as part of his personal winnings.

(*g*) You see the girl you love, married to a worthless clubman.

(*h*) The great boat is bringing you home from Germany, where you were held two years as a prisoner. The flag on Liberty unfolds gently as you pass.

(Laughing and crying are neglected arts. We can cry to nearly every emotion. The above are but suggestive. Nothing is so laughable as poor crying. Tragedy so easily slips to farce if actor is not consistent.)

REVIEW AND QUESTIONS

1. Why must a strong, dramatic scene have perfect harmony of gesture, tone, and words?
2. From laboratory study and empirical knowledge, we know most unpleasant emotions demand greatest visceral response and produce greatest throat restrictions. What problem does this present to the actor who "feels" his part?
3. Good diction is voice gesture—what theory of language bears out this statement?
4. Which is true—gesture is more dependent upon speech

than speech is dependent upon gesture? Is animated speech possible without gesture?

5. Pick out the five consistent combinations of *Crazy-Patch Cross Plots* (39). E.g., a Negro fisherman (without adoration) says "I love you" to a hotel chambermaid.
6. How does that which is visible as agony resolve into normalcy? What is sequence of the resolution?
7. Does sudden transition from one strong emotion to another prove or disprove that acting should be a conscious art? Discuss *The Burglars* (42).
8. How does the actor carry a fast, vital scene and have all words understood? Which is more important, speed of speech or animation of spirit?
9. Why should we avoid the pointing of a revolver towards the audience?
10. In all complete relaxation of body, what dominant principle is evident? Explain by *Nemesis* (48).
11. What is an emotional climax? Discuss from *A Glance of Cupid's Arrow* (49).
12. Which demands greater technical training: the ability to carry an emotional scene to a gripping climax, or the ability to change from one strong emotion to another, equally strong, and quite different? Use *Joyful Excess* (5) as example.
13. How does gesture aid voice in making it sound louder than it really is?
14. Of the characters enacted in *The Walk of Life* (54), which is the most difficult to repeat? Why?
15. What is meant by the "power of controlled emotion"?
16. Why does dialect become a favorable agency for comedy? Which dialect gets the best laughing response to-day? Give reasons for your answer.
17. In what other ways could you logically end the playlet *Partnership in the Stock Market* (57)? Where is the climax?
18. Cry with some ten consecutive emotions dominating your efforts. Which portion of *Prepare to Shed Your Tears* (58) presents biggest problem to you? Why?

CHAPTER X

PANTOMIMES FOR THE INDIVIDUAL

THESE pantomimes are intended to be enacted by one individual. One person may enact several characters or be but one character and show the effect of various associations upon that one character, e.g.: two Irishmen are walking along, when Patrick gives Mike a smoke and Mike gives Patrick an apple. (*a*) If actor were doing two characters, he would first represent Pat giving Mike a smoke and taking one himself and then actor would be Mike receiving the smoke and giving Patrick the apple. (*b*) If actor were to be Patrick alone, he would give Mike the smoke and pantomime his acceptance of the apple from Mike. In this (*b*), the actor would be but one person, showing the effect of his associations on that one person. In (*a*), the actor would be two characters, each showing effect of actions upon the other.

NOTE. Most of the emotions commonly used in drama are depicted in these studies. No actor can intelligently analyze character until he knows the outward and inner manifestations of emotions. Emotions flavor gesture and qualify voice. They must always be servants and never masters.

The first fourteen pantomimes of this group are written to aid actors in establishing character with minimum of time and properties. All are intended to be solos; and more or less elemental.

59. *Around the World in a Classroom*

Object: In one minute establish a character in pantomime, avoiding extremes. Suggestive characters:

1. Child
2. Hollywood slicker
3. Old woman
4. English dude
5. Old maid
6. French waiter
7. Old-time stage villain
8. Alaska miner
9. Flapper
10. Swedish lumberjack
11. City crook
12. East Side vender
13. Irish washerwoman
14. Italian workman
15. Bolshevist
16. Concert maestro
17. Nevada bartender
18. Telephone girl
19. Old man
20. Iowa farmer
21. Negro barber
22. Policeman
23. Tramp
24. Sophomore grind
25. Sing Sing convict
26. Hotel clerk
27. Chauffeur of Rolls-Royce

60. *Saturday Night Movies*

Person goes to movies. Gets ticket. Counts change. House dark. Finds seat. First sits on a person's lap. Apologizes. Removes hat. Eats peanuts. Show by expressions the nature of the performance. Work out own finish.

61. *Letter Technic*

(*a*) Gets letter in one of many ways:

1. From postman
2. Come home and find it on table
3. Mother gives it to you
4. Take it away from little brother or sister
5. From post-office window

(*b*) Read letter. Show ten emotions while reading letter.

(*c*) Finish letter. Work out ending according to the theme of the letter.

1. Disappointed; tear up letter
2. Thrilled
3. Sad
4. Joyful for others, disappointed for self
5. Worried
6. Angry

62. *Sight-seeing in Coney Island*

(*a*) Go to the different concessions:

1. Scenic railway
2. Fun house
3. Negro ducking
4. Merry-go-round
5. Ring throwing
6. Weight guessing
7. Hot-dog stand
8. Bowling
9. Photograph gallery

(*b*) Work out according to the kind of time you had:

1. Good time
2. Disappointed
3. Broke

63. *A Street Car at Five O'clock*

Riding home during rush hours. You are carrying bundles. Dodge an auto. Get on steps of car. Pay fare. Work way to inside of car. Feet stepped on. No seat. Hang on strap. Drop package. Hat is tipped on nose when getting bundles. Sharp curve. Try to get seat but fat lady is stronger. Street is called. Work way through crowd. Get off car. Watch for autos.

64. *In the Cafeteria*

During noon rush. In line with friends. Get tray and silverware. Select food. Get check. Get water. Find table. Put dishes on table. Sit and eat. Show kind of food eaten from four dishes. Use napkin. Pay cashier. Where is hat?

65. *Tillie's Night Home*

Girl prepares to meet boy friend. Gets parlor ready. Sits and reads. Impatience. Bell rings. Last preparations. Unexpected fellow arrives. Embarrassment. Invited in. Bell rings again. Right fellow. Tillie makes it evident. Wrong youth soon goes. Tillie turns on radio. They sit on lounge. Problem.

66. *A Rainy Day*

(*a*) Preparing to leave home, take rain coat, rubbers and umbrella, etc.

(*b*) The experiences: meet friends en route, market, have wind ruin umbrella, drop tomatoes in mud, meet friend, get in auto.

(This type of pantomime is given to develop imagination

in assuming distances within a small scope, such as is used in *The Little Clay Cart.*)

67. *The Family Car*

(*a*) Taking the family on a picnic. Get them into the car. Car won't start. Starter won't turn. Fix gear shift and move car so engine will turn over. Get in and start. Jerks. Tire blows out. Fix same. Start. Arrive at park. Johnnie drops picnic basket. Miniature family quarrel. Lunch.

(*b*) Son takes his girl out for a ride. Call for girl. Help her in car. Get interested in girl. Narrow escape. Slowing down for speed cop. Ice-cream cones. Parking in wrong zone. Ordered on. Fire engine coming down street. Stop and watch. Take girl home. Father meets son at garage. Forebodings.

(You will observe that the eye is the greatest agent of expression to denote distance and change of locality.)

68. *At Church*

(*a*) A character going to church.

1. Young boy or girl
2. Child
3. Elderly person

(*b*) Meeting people. Some liked, others indifferent, and others boring.

(*c*) Entering church. Find seat and locate friends.

(*d*) Services. Reactions, according to character, singing, contribution, sermon.

(*e*) Leaving.

69. *School Again*

Determine age of character. Get ready. Eat hurried breakfast. Leave home. Arrive on campus. Greet classmates. First class bell. Seat in room. First class. Problem.

70. At the Dentist's

Go to the dentist to get tooth pulled. Dread operation. Waiting room. Enter doctor's office. In chair. Point out your sorrows. Doctor calls assistant, whom you watch. Gas. Pantomime your dream. Come out of gas. Discover tooth is gone. Pay with check.

71. The Dressing Room

The first stage performance. Excitement of preparation. Make up. Bells for readiness. Final look at part. Worried. Last look at mirror. Spirit gum and powder on sleeve. Another bell. Pick up part to take out. Director comes in, astonished at make-up. Hurried dabs. Pushed out onto stage. Problem.

72. Preparing a Meal

Set the table for four. Put food on, several dishes, letting us know contents by your management. Seat guests at table. Eat food as demanded by etiquette for kinds shown above. Clear dishes, carrying on pantomime conversation. Bring in the dessert. After-dinner gossip.

(Table management is no small part of modern stage technic and calls for considerable practice.)

73. Two in One

The actor establishes two characters, taking both parts.

1. Lovers on a bench—finally discover eavesdropper.
2. Mother and child at a circus.
3. Nurse and child at a zoo.
4. Mother taking child shopping.
5. Two burglars—one cautious and other indifferent—in a bank vault.
6. A judge and a guilty boy meet in a friend's home.
7. Doctor and patient.
8. Stenographer and business man.
9. Barber and customer.

10. Beauty parlor customer and operator.
11. Father and son in woodshed.
12. Minister and bride.

74. *A Surprise Visit*

An old woman comes slowly into a room (door back), looks around cautiously. Takes out small bottle from large loose pocket, walks to table center and puts bottle down. Goes to desk at the right, and listens, pulls out center drawer and removes revolver. Goes to table at center. Puts revolver by bottle. Sits down and writes. Writing as knock is heard at door. Hurriedly puts bottle and revolver in pocket. Turns paper over, goes to door, and slowly opens. A little girl enters, to old lady's surprised delight, and then consternation. The grandmother stoops down and presses child close to her. In the embrace the grandmother breaks glass in pocket and cuts little girl's leg. The old lady terrified at sight of blood; puts crying child on sofa, when child's mother enters, joyfully. The grandmother surrenders child to her daughter, hurries to telephone, calls for physician, goes to table, tears up sheet of paper, feels revolver in her pocket. Problem.

75. *We've All Been There*

Girl is made to go to the washstand. Rolls up sleeves. Disgruntled, dips fingers in water. Smears over face. Mother jerks towel away. Turns on more water. Fills basin. Lathers all over girl's arms and face. Splashes. Girl is boxed on the head. Gets soap in eyes. Reaches for towel, wipes face, hands. Combs hair in front of glass. Sulks. Goes to get drink. Breaks glass. Problem. What happens?

76. *The Dime Novel*

Gum-chewing boy sits down to read exciting novel. Hero is being chased. Boy swallows gum, nearly chokes.

Gets out package of gumdrops. Starts reading again. Excitement. Shows by pantomime what he is reading. Fist fight, bloody nose, black eye. Reaches for gumdrops. Picks up thimble. Puts in mouth. Throws it on floor. Loses page. Disgusted. Finds page. Reaches for gumdrop. Sack empty. Looks around sadly. Scratches head. Looks around room. Shrugs shoulders. Settles down to read again.

(This pantomime calls for an absorbing interest in the reading, rather than in the business, which must appear incidental.)

77. *Isaac Near Home*

A big brother is quietly fishing from the river bank, as his little brother watches. He pulls large fish to water surface. Excitement. Jerks fish on bank. Scrambles after it. Little brother gets it and drops it in water. He boxes his brother's ears but the little fellow kicks big brother on the shins and runs. Almost loses pole and stubs toe. Can't find worms. Coaxes his little brother back and finds them in little boy's pocket. Orders him home, but he doesn't go. Rebaits hook and throws it in water. Another bite. Warnings to little one. Lands large fish. General enjoyment. Strings fish. Lets little boy carry it. Go off whistling.

(Watch especially the use of eyes to show size and relationship of two boys. Avoid stamping of feet.)

78. *His First Night Alone*

Father is left alone with Snookums. He tries to read with baby on his lap. Child pushes paper and father reads from distance. Baby pulls at his spectacles, which father adjusts. Changes baby to other arm, and baby immediately grabs his pencils and pen, which he throws upon the floor. Father picks them up as baby tears paper. Dad gives up reading, in despair. Bounces baby on knee for few seconds and then tickles him. Stoops down and places

Snookums on the floor. Father picks up magazine and starts to sit down as baby falls on its nose. Father drops magazine and picks up baby. Carries child over shoulder and pats on back. Baby increases his yelling and Dad goes to sideboard and procures milk bottle. Holds baby on lap and tries to feed him. Baby won't be satisfied or take bottle. Father tastes and shows him how good it is; baby is amused and wants father to take more. He does, a few times, and then tries to get baby to take it. Child refuses and yells louder. Dad turns Snookums over his knee and paddles him quite severely. More howls, as father shakes child and walks floor with long strides. Passing a fruit basket, father grabs a bunch of grapes and offers them to Snookums. To his surprise, baby stops crying and takes grapes. Baby puts one in his mouth and quickly swallows same. Wants another and father refuses. More yells from baby. Mother returns unseen by husband. He makes a feint as if to spank Snookums, when his wife screams. Problem.

79. *Driving a Ford*

An old farmer type, with bunch whiskers and beady eyes, gets in front of his rickety Ford and cranks it, rather cranks at it for three times and the engine starts, nearly dislocating his arm. He throws crank into back of his car and climbs on to front seat (for our purpose a chair, all else is imaginary). Puts chewing gum in his mouth. Takes hold of steering wheel, releases brake and steps on his foot gears. Car starts with a jerk, he grabs his hat and speeds. Turns to left and just misses a man on horseback. Shakes fist back at horseman as he avoids a truck on his right. Gesticulates and swears at truck driver and swallows gum. Sees his old sweetheart on the street corner and tips his hat, as he avoids a laundry wagon. Puts hat back on forehead just over his eyes as he grabs at wheel. Straightens his path and then his hat. Is stopped by a traffic cop and argues that he was not driving too fast or carelessly. Reads slip given him and as cop turns to go, farmer raises arm to strike him, but changes gesture to one of scratching head when cop looks askance at him. Starts his car again and climbs in seat and sits on his hat, crushing same. Throws it out of car in angry disgust. Calls to ice-cream boy and buys a cone, which he manipulates with right hand. Freight train stops him. He leans back on his seat and starts to look for all car numbers containing a seven for his right hand and three for his left. As fast as a car has a three in the number he raises a finger of his left hand and a finger for the right for seven. As the numbers glide by—he cancels a three with a seven until a preponderance of sevens overcome him. He has all five fingers of his right hand up and no threes in sight. He is leaning out of car to look down the line of freight cars for a three when a great explosion occurs. His front tire has been punctured, officially reporting its weakness. Farmer John loses count and gets out of car to survey the damage.

(Pseudoserious characterization is a type of comedy which has a greater appeal to the public than broad comedy. It can be cultivated.)

80. The Traffic Cop

On a busy thoroughfare. Whistles for north-south traffic to go and motions accordingly. Cusses truck driver for starting too soon. Fly keeps bothering him and he swats at it. Bells for change. Whistles for east-west traffic and girl nearly hits him on turning and runs into car going north. Takes number of her car and has her wait till he can call another cop. Blows three sharp blasts and hits at fly, trying to kill pesky thing. Traffic mistakes his movements and all start to go. General tie-up. Other cop comes up at bell for turn in traffic. General consternation and girl gets away. He is bumped by drunken driver. Riot call!

(Another example of serio-comedy. Must not be broad farce, as one is easily laughed at, rather than being laughed with. Such a scene, overdone, becomes silly.)

81. The Pedestrian

Timid old lady tries to get across street. Starts and goes back twice. Tries to follow big man, he walks too fast; halfway across, she returns and is jostled by young girl. Starts again and is ordered back by policeman. Starts again, with determination, but drops her umbrella. Tries to pick it up and is bumped by fat man. She procures it in time to strike him heartily. In grim determination she picks up her skirts, knocks on her bonnet and wades across the street.

(The walk of the elderly woman must not be caricatured, though the situation be comic.)

82. An Airplane Passes over the Farm

Sy sees the plane circling over the farm and looks at it in consternation; sees it circle several times and then calls Sarah. She is more dumbfounded and is spellbound. Plane does the loop-the-loop and then the tail spin. Both catch breath—plane comes very close to farm and a note is dropped over the corral. Sy watches the plane soar away and sees Sarah still looking at the spotless space. Sy ambles under fence and looks at paper, picks it up and cautiously opens it. Adjusts specs and reads. Can't believe his eyes. Raises up fist toward disappearing plane. "Confound ye, why didn't ye stop, if it was you? Sarah. Lookee!" He shows her the note, pinned in center of a paper. "By darn, that's his picture and that's his writin' but if that's the way he's been to college, high flyin' like that, he might just as well been milkin' cows. Ol' Brindle could raise him higher than that. I'll be durned." Throws hat down and starts whittling furiously.

(The old type stage-farmer is fast disappearing but his memory is a pleasant one. Words usually help this type of characterization.)

83. The Movie Director

A blustering director has a scene for a lover, his mistress, and a jealous wife. He tells the lover how to approach the couch and declare his affection. He shows the lady how to accept such advances without wilting too soon. The wife he lets go without direction, as she is married and knows. The scene begins. He is disgusted with the man and sarcastic toward the woman. Only the jealous wife pleases, as she takes out her resentment on the woman. What the director intended to be serious, has proved excellent comedy. He finally laughs heartily and commends the three of them.

(A thread-plot to be filled out by actor. The actor must take the general and indefinite and make very specific.)

84. Her First Visit to the Chiropodist

Velma gets in front of door. Looks up street cautiously, assured, she goes in limping. Embarrassed as gentleman appears. Asks if he is the foot doctor and told he is. She sits and puts out her left foot. He removes the shoe and starts to take down her stocking; she rises, turns around, and takes off her own stocking. Blushes as she sits down and puts foot out. He takes her foot in his hand and she jerks away, ticklish. He brings in basin of water and she is offended. She bathed before she left her home! He assures her and bathes foot. She suffers imaginary pain as he works but enjoys the operation. Content, she extends right foot. He removes shoe, she is embarrassed with large hole in toe of stocking. She is more brave, however, and removes stocking while seated. He works again. She puts on stockings and shoes. She pays him, stands and walks out, smiling, and without a limp.

(Blushing is an emotional response with no definite pattern—it diffuses. One cannot assume blushing, but he can assume the other actions that accompany blushing, which is a type of self-suppression.)

85. The Bug Collector

Nervous and nearsighted man throws net over moth. Captures it. Holds it under lens and becomes excited. A rare find. Gets moth under best light when husky friend, passing by, slaps him on the shoulder. Specialist drops bug and coughs. Looks at friend in disgust and then realizes he has lost his find. Greatly perturbed, he begins to search. Frantically looks in all likely places, finally sees bug on old maid's hat. She is reading. He goes to her apologetically and points to her hat and starts to reach for moth. She slaps him on the hand and giggles. He makes another effort and she slaps him again. With inspiration, he sits on bench by her and starts to make love. She moves away but not too far. He follows, gets closer and puts arm around her neck. She closes her eyes expectantly; he looks disgustedly at her, but it is his moment; he carefully captures moth and bows foolishly over scene.

(This exercise for either type of solo pantomime: either to be both characters or show effect of old maid's actions on specialist.)

86. In the Trenches

Soldier drags his way to trench and pulls off helmet. Jumps as bombs break near him. He is nearly a nervous wreck. His body writhes in agony. He pulls letter from pocket and reads slowly. Eyes blurry, but with effort he reads in full. Kisses letter tenderly. Bursting bomb throws mud in his face and on letter. Wipes letter off reverently. Hears guns in violent uproar and sees his own men jumping the trench, shouting. With heroic effort he gets on his feet and reaches ground level. Struck by bullet, grasps his shoulder and crumples in mud. Dies cursing the enemy and pressing letter to his lips.

(Agony is one of our most intense emotions, yet so wonderful is man's complex nature, that he can accompany one great emotion with another, though one must dominate in expression. Controlled tears are part of actor's technic.)

87. *The Great Lottery: The Old Man Wins*

Hundreds of people are standing on the City Square, greeting each other and talking excitedly. An old man joins group and not welcomed by many. Few see his proffered hand. The band is playing and the manager starts talking in distance. Old man is hard of hearing and toothless; struggles for the words. Finally, a little girl is brought to the stand. All strain to see. Manager says few words. Old man pulls out a bulletin and slowly reads. "First prize $50,000." First prize! He takes out his red bandana handkerchief, unwinds it, finds his ticket and reads the number, "13113." Asks neighbor if his number is 13113. Little girl, blindfolded, stands on box and puts hand down in big box. Pulls out ticket. All are breathless. Old man strains to hear. Can't quite hear the number the manager is calling out. He asks those about him, but they tell him to keep quiet. For the third time the number is called, the number must be called for by sundown. Another number is drawn, called, and old man hears great shout. The Mayor's daughter has the second chance to win and nobody is there with number one. Old man thinks he has lost and works his way through crowd to congratulate winner. Gets to her and reaches out rough hand to wish her luck. Says, "Darn, any ticket with a 13 in it couldn't win She asks to see his ticket; he searches several pockets, finally locating it in watch pocket. She reads it and hurries him to stand. Manager is surprised and reads ticket second time to be certain. Calls for attention to crowd. The old man is declared winner of first and greatest prize, $50,000

Everybody greets him now and nearly mob him with friendship. He waves a happy but feeble response and pulls out horseshoe from hip pocket. Spits on it and throws it over his left shoulder. Takes a plug of tobacco from pocket and is about to take bite, sees his little granddaughter and refrains from his chew. Picks little girl up and tenderly kisses her. "It was your ma what picked the number, but you was the one what give me the horseshoe. Half of it all is yourn, honey, half of it."

(Eccentric characters can be comic without being ridiculous. They can also be heard. The eyes and mouth of above old man need special study.)

88. The Puritan

Man has thumbs under the turnscrews. Agony on face. He shakes his head; will not tell name of woman in his London home. Tighter, still refuses—one more turn and he refuses. Again the twist is given, as a woman dashes in and throws herself on his arms. She is the wife of the torturer. Accused looks pleadingly at Puritan persecutor. His broken thumbs are released. He lifts fainting woman and carries her over to persecutor, who grimly turns his back. Slowly, the released prisoner carries the limp woman from the room—never again to see England.

(A good actor must learn to show strong emotional responses with minimum of energy. 'Tis better to show than feel.)

89. The Witness Stand

Young fellow has been brought to court. He is sworn in and takes witness stand. Looks around room nervously, sees his sweetheart, and calms down into reposeful quiet. The Judge speaks to him and he rises. Answers "yes" to each question. Is told to describe shooting scene. Takes step forward and puts chair in front of him. Gets behind it and looks out to side. Describes getting the pistol from his coat pocket and slowly rises over chair.

Takes careful aim and is about to fire when shot is heard back of him—he turns to see who had fired and then sees his rival fall in a heap in front of him. Looks for person who fired and turns around to see himself covered by house servants. Puts up hands slowly. That is all. The Judge motions him to sit down, and then has young boy brought in. Witness sees it is his brother. Starts to go to him, is ordered to remain seated. Young boy stands before the Judge and starts crying, staggers over to his older brother. Witness rises, and lifts face of brother to his, reads truth. His little brother had followed him and came just in time to see arm raised to fire. Had intended hitting his brother's arm, but shot had gone wild and wounded his brother's rival. Witness pleads that he is guilty and not his brother. Wounded rival comes from inner room and asks clemency for witness. Judge lectures all and they leave, arm in arm, as sweetheart joins them.

(This exercise is best adapted for group work, though it offers excellent problems for the actor of many parts. When acted alone, several parts are shown by the enactor, rather than one character trying to reveal all that happens.)

90. *The Awakening*

A young man, looking at store window, moves with palsied motions. Plays childishly with toy gun and shoots imaginary foes. Is jostled by burly workman and cannot adequately resent. Shoots his jostler with play gun in serious manner. Eyes wander in unfocused listlessness. A flower pot is knocked from fourth story above and people hear a scream. Boy looks around foolishly and wonders, as flower pot hits him on the head and he falls to the sidewalk in a lumpish clod. Lies as if dead, then slowly moves his hands and touches his head. Wipes blood from back of head. Slowly raises up and starts to see, then to feel. Sees people about him and a frantic German lady hoping he is not dead. He stands and looks about him; his face is no longer limpid, his eyes are alert and his body is straight. He remembers who he is. Takes German lady in his arms and hugs her ecstatically; assures strange-looking policeman he is all right, and wrapping handkerchief about head, says to policeman, "Tell me how to get to U. S. A., old Chi, and home. What place is this anyway? The War smashed me but Germany has saved me. Thank God for Germany!"

(Timing and rhythm are the soul of good acting. To make a transition from stupidity to mental alertness, reaching climax at proper moment, requires hours of rehearsing.)

91. The Ribbon Counter

Salesgirl behind ribbon counter. Greets little lady who looks at several kinds of ribbons and buys twenty yards of three kinds each. Girl's arm tired as lady leaves with ribbon and change. Wealthy lady arrives and looks at some forty kinds of ribbon, buys a half yard. Salesgirl talks store-language to girl near her, eloquent but inaudible. Her beau comes in and she pretends to sell him ribbon, squeezes his hand, surreptitiously accepts chocolate from him—kisses tip of fingers and looks around before placing finger on his mouth. Slow customer has her match ribbon on little girl's dress. Decides and redecides, finally takes a half yard. Floorwalker comes over and asks her to take perfume counter; she leaves her beau for the next girl clerk but tries to motion him to come to the perfume. Man tips hat and leaves. In a miff, girl walks to perfume counter and the floorwalker wonders.

(Character types offer a variety of studies and the American store girl is already an institution. She is different from our genus flapper and more clever than the dance room habitué.)

92. In a Windstorm

Young lady is standing on corner waiting for bus. It starts to sprinkle. She holds out her hand; then puts up umbrella. Rain comes down quite heavy with slight wind. Little dog comes up and rubs against her leg. She kicks it away and briefly quarrels with old maid owner. More wind and hat almost blows off, she drops bundle. Procures bundle. Rain and wind stronger and umbrella almost out of her hand as skirt flies up to her face; in pulling skirt down, drops bundle. She is now sticky wet and wind blows hat across the street—she grabs frantically but lets it go. Puts skirt down again. Bus pulls up crowded and passes on. She demands it to stop but conductor is heartless. Umbrella turns inside out. Hat is gone and she is dripping wet. She moves down the street, too angry to speak, too wet to be reasonable.

(Very often a representation is more humorous than the reality. It is training with this ability to represent that gives us our best comedians. Plan every gesture until presentation is spontaneous.)

93. *The Chemist*

Aged chemist is working over test tubes in laboratory. He is excited; calm excitement before eve of great discovery. He takes one tube carefully and pours slowly into smaller tube. Takes small tube over to sunlight and is delighted with results. Can hardly wait to perfect his experiment. Pours his precious liquid over tin plate and takes wire from his rheostat and gradually turns on electricity on his tin plate. Small crystals form on tin and burn themselves onto surfaces. He turns off electricity—surface of tin now shines like diamonds and is hard as steel. His decorative art surface at last! He hurries with precious piece to door and calls his son; as he turns around and holds piece up better to see it glisten, he drops it in boiling pot and liquid splashes on his face and in his eyes. An agony of pain and fear. Son hurries to him. Old man stands in anguish but triumphant, and tells his son to write what he dictates. He starts to tell the steps in the experiment and falls in son's arms.

(Another exercise of quick transition from one strong emotion to another. Of such stuff are great actors made. Every action is planned beforehand, until audience sees a reality, but reality under control.)

94. *On the Boat*

Maggie is sitting in steamer chair, reading. The boat is more active than usual and she, uncomfortable, rolls her eyes. Young man comes up and offers her a chocolate. She accepts, is about to eat and decides best not to. Tries to read again as young man leaves her, starts now to feel peculiar. Eyes follow the ups and downs of the boat. She tries to rise but sinks with the effort. Is now visibly affected and looks for aid to escort her to cabin. Calls cabin boy and leans on his shoulder. As she sees her friends approaching, she releases cabin boy and walks in proud isolation and with forced smile and uncertain step. She flicks hand on deck rail as if in caprice—but really for support. Cabin boy walks expectantly behind. Passes friends with a merry wave of handkerchief and staggers toward cabin door. She is leaning helplessly on cabin boy as boat swerves to one side.

(A gradual crescendo in facial climax takes as much practice as a crescendo in music. Each are rewarded in perfected technic. This exercise is helpful to eye and mouth technic.)

95. *The Guardsman at the Bazaar*

A veiled lady tells fortunes with cards. A fat man visits and she takes his hand, reads the lines and verifies with the cards. He will be prosperous and fall in love. Gets five dollars for this information. She tells her neighbor at the candy booth. Old maid comes for advice and the cards predict sudden fortune of unknown value. Twenty-five cents is paid over. A fine looking fellow sits down (her husband). He does not know her! She reads his palm first and is shocked—wishes to corroborate with the cards but he takes her hand, tries to flirt with her.

Kisses her hand and she feigns shyness. He tries to kiss her and she draws back—finally lets him kiss her, then she takes off veil from eyes and bitterly denounces him. He declares he knew her all the time. She is not quite sure and wonders.

(Another exercise for choice of presentation; either as the fortune teller in solo, or as fortune teller and fat man impersonation. When an actor does two or more characters, he must diligently practice proper blending. It must not be evident that he, personally, stands between.)

96. Typist at Telephone

She is writing vigorously. Phone rings and she answers it. Connects with president's office. Starts writing. Phone; connects with president's office and carefully listens in. Writing with right hand. Customer in, she puts phone up and in response to question says president is in. Phone rings, she replies, "No." Vigorously finishes letter, addresses envelope, puts in letter and seals envelope. Phone rings as she starts another letter. She puts chew of gum in mouth and switches call to president. He calls her suddenly and she swallows gum. Gets up to go to him as the phone rings. Switches on to president as another customer in. Twelve o'clock whistle blows. Problem.

(An exercise for hand movements accompanying other activities. Clever uncertainty calls for awkward grace.)

97. Southern Kidnaper

Negro has taken little five-year-old boy from aristocratic home. He steals through bushes and comes upon a marsh. Hesitates as to direction. Hears dogs baying in distance, getting closer very fast. Thinks to cut across marsh and throw dogs off scent and also gain time. Goes few steps and starts to sink. Tries to turn back—he is in quicksand! Terrified, calls for help. Pulls boy out of gunnysack and tells him to go back the way he came. Boy is dazed as Negro pushes him toward the shore. Little fellow starts to sink and Negro finally convinces him of his danger. Boy crawls out on the willows as Negro slowly sinks up to waist. Dogs are closer and men's calls frighten little fellow who would run back. Negro tells him he will kill him if he comes back to him. Boy climbs small willow tree as dogs and men come to mire. Negro now sunk to his neck. Problem.

(Sequential responses to intense climax. Each step leads logically to another, each blending but not omitting another.)

98. Vendetta—with Justice

The old Italian plays hand organ in street and has his monkey dance and take the pennies. Tips his hat each time a gift is made. Suddenly sees well-dressed man passing on sidewalk and he stops playing. He lays organ down carefully, draws knife and dashes toward man. Makes lunge, but his arm is caught by a strong hand, and forced to drop knife. Policeman is called who comes up hurriedly. Well-dressed man pretends to be ignorant of reason for threat on his life but organ grinder accuses him. "He stole my wife in Philedelphia and thees is first time I have fou' heem. He is Antonio Scarati. See how Felipo, he even know him." Monkey on his arm scolding viciously. Scarati hands policeman a card and starts away. Is halted, with the old Italian jabbering at him; both are led away after organ is picked up, Felipo on the organ, scolding.

(A transition pantomime of quick change. Italians are expert in hand movement, vigorous in spirit. The first time I had this assigned, the young man brought in a small boy on his shoulder to represent Felipo. I do not recommend its general practice.)

99. The Speakeasy

A little Irishman stands at the peephole talking to a Loquacious Guest, and opens door to members. Big athletic chap brings two girls, gives countersign and shows card. Door opens. Irishman shows that all are tipsy, as he talks to friend. Offers hip flask to friend, who takes only a sip. Doorkeeper offers guest more but is refused. Puts flask in pocket. Grouchy fellow and his pal present themselves and are admitted, but Irishman examines the card closely, though he knows Grouch is a member. Tells friend that Grouch is very wealthy and also a drinker. Two young fellows try to get in, have no cards, and are closed out. Entertainer is admitted. Chucks her under chin. Two young fellows try to crash door for entrance, but Irishman grabs each by collar and gives them quick exit. Closes door and shows his big muscles. A party is presented at window and Irishman doffs hat, a Johnnyboy brings in a dozen girls and men, tips Irishman a ten spot. Doorkeeper tells his talkative friend that there'll be a live party on to-night. Big burly fellow comes to window and asks to get in. Is refused when Loquacious Guest sticks gun on Irishman and has him back away; door lets in a dozen plain-clothes men. Look of utter contempt shown by Irishman, as handcuffs are slipped on his unwilling hands. He goes over toward door and is about to step on electric button as Loquacious Guest detective backs him out of the door to waiting arms of two policemen. Irishman is too consternated to talk before he is in patrol wagon.

(Eye levels and types of characters as revealed by Irishman, make this pantomime interesting for practice. Best done as solo.)

100. *The Nursery*

Young girl is spending her first hour at the community nursery. She looks hopefully at her dozen charges. She goes around to each of them and does some little cheerful act: to one she gives a comforter, to another a doll, to the third an orange, the fourth she sits up rather than have it on its stomach, the fifth and sixth she separates from hair-pulling, she steps on the seventh's finger in trying to avoid a little colored boy. Special attention to crying babe and gives it piece of peppermint. Number ten sees the candy and cries for a piece, this sets three others going also. The crying of the babies interests a young Airedale pup, who comes to the fence and barks gleefully. The whole dozen is now in a state of unsettled discomfort. The largest screams the loudest that he wants his "mama." That familiar name helps two more to remember such a person and a medley of aching hearts fills the air. Twelve milk bottles are rushed to the rescue, one hour before schedule. This appeases ten—but two are obdurate and only the most weird of gymnastic contortions satisfy their bruised dispositions. Once more there is tranquillity, until little darky pulls Rosetta's hair. The Italian mother is just returning. We must draw the color line and leave the rest to the Chamber of Conflict.

(To pantomime space and direction demands definite angle locations. Each baby must be where it was first located, as if in real flesh. That does not mean that a chair represents a baby. All is in the mind of the actor, as if real in life.)

101. The Dog Fight

Two boys meet. Frank has an Airedale pup and Skinny has a fox terrier. These boys are natural enemies, for they live on opposite sides of the canal. It is evident that the friendly dogs must be taught tribal tradition. Skinny is the villain of this sketch. He walks around Frank with challenging mien. He puts a stick on his dog, Brave, and tells Frank to have his hound dare to take it off. The pup ambles over to Brave and playfully bumps it off. Brave is patient, knowing dog etiquette in respect to ages. Skinny now has his motif. Honor must be avenged. He takes Brave between his legs and starts the avenging by pointing the dog's nose toward the restless pup. Skinny challenges Frank in the name of his dog. Frank holds his dog, but rather in protection. "Sic 'em" is Brave's battle cry and when he lunges at the Airedale the big-legged pup merely lies down on his back and starts to play.

This is too much. Skinny walks menacingly over to his ditch-bank rival. In the manner of his victorious pet, he walks around his watching rival. Without proper parliamentary war, upon Frank's part, he strikes Skinny viciously on the freckled nose. Skinny is unbalanced, surprised and bleeding. The pup puts a muddy paw on Skinny's only clean shirt. A defiant Frank awaits his return. Skinny rises, holds his nose and backs away, too full of evil thoughts adequately to express them.

(For solo or duality of impersonation. The mock-serious attitude of boyhood is one of his chief attributes.)

102. *An Evening Home*

Jones, a tired father, comes home from work. Takes off hat and coat and goes to his wife, whom he kisses indifferently. Pats daughter on cheek; he is not feeling well, shows his tongue and rubs his stomach. Sits in chair and mops brow. Wife and daughter are dressed for evening party, and impatient at father's disinterest. He protests to both of them that he cannot go, but insists on their going. Wife is suspicious, but intends to go any way. Brings husband a tray lunch and leaves him rather worried in conscience. Daughter follows soon after. He watches them through lace curtains and then takes several spry dance steps. Goes to phone and invites fellows to his home. Indicate three are to come. Hangs up phone, goes to servant bell and rings. Orders James to get four quart bottles and glasses and sandwiches. Gets cards from coat pocket, fixes tobacco trays, matches, chips, and chairs. Helps James arrange bottles and goes to fireplace smiling. Door bell and James shows in three club pals. Shake all around. Glasses for beer held out in a toast to good-fellowship and a quiet evening home. He has James clear bottles and they sit around table for games. Jones deals and has a royal flush. He raises the ante cautiously and plays his hand for what it is worth. Two of his pals stick it out; Jones has just about broke his pals on the first deal, when his wife unexpectedly pounces in on him. Men all rise and look sheepish. Husband is chagrined. Wife grabs his cards and throws them on the floor. Takes sandwich tray and hurriedly leaves room. Jones starts to apologize to his pals, but they leave one by one. He follows them to the door. Then he walks slowly to fireplace. Looks at door recently used by his wife, picks up a smiling Cupid statue and smashes it on the fireplace. Grabs hat and coat and hurriedly leaves room.

(For solo or mutual impersonations. Decide exact type of husband before working on his exterior.)

103. At Sister's Toilette

Young miss cautiously enters sister's boudoir, tiptoes to dressing table. Seats herself. Looks at array of cosmetic equipment. Cold cream is used first. Handkerchief used for towel. Eyebrow pencil marks eyes elaborately. Three shades of lip rouge; selects the darkest. Powders face and neck, avoiding work done on brows and lips. Slips off dress and gets sister's best gown from hanger. Puts it on in queenly manner and surveys results. Walks as if she were impersonating Carmen. Puts a big comb in back hair. Starts a tarantella, when sister enters from her bath. Problem.

(A young girl is less conscious than her grown sister. Actions are consequently less reserved and more bodily vital.)

104. At the Piano

A young composer sits at piano, with manuscript on arm of chair. He plays a few chords; then writes a few notes which he plays with pleasure. Gets a melody going and is delighted. Writes the notes down and plays from the manuscript. Has something wrong, after several attempts, finds his error and changes paper. Now satisfied and plays with gusto. Gets up to imaginary audience, bows and seats himself at piano and plays with thrilling excitement. Gets up and bows lavishly. Meets imaginary publisher who offers him check for five thousand for rights for the song. Young man hesitates, and finally hands over the rough manuscript. Bids the purchaser au revoir, looks fondly at imaginary check, rubs stomach, showing he is hungry. Cold reality is upon him and inspiration gone. He grabs his hat from piano and walks gravely out.

(Consistency of property management, as piano cannot change its position or size. While this pantomime is chiefly descriptive, it is the manifestative ending which produces actors.)

105. The Mountain Cabin

A young girl is brought, gagged and bound, to a lonely mountain cabin. Two masked men walk around her and she sees the shorter one draw a knife, lunge, as taller one whirls and shoots him. Short man writhes on floor, then dies. Girl falters, but leans against center pole of cabin. Tall man comes to her and kisses her on neck. Then he takes out gag from mouth and undoes her hands. They are bleeding, but she spurns his offered handkerchief. He comes toward her and takes her in his arms; she tries to beat him off. A knife flies through the air and an Indian stands in doorway. Tall abductor slowly sinks to floor. Girl is horrified, as Indian approaches her. He hands her a letter, which lifts her to extreme joy. The Indian (faithful guide of her host) had followed her, unseen, when she strayed from the path to the lake cabin. Indian stoops and pulls mask from tall abductor. Girl is further surprised to see the dying man is also a guest of the mountain party. She orders Indian to help her lift tall man to couch, picks up a dipper and goes to look for water as she meets her host coming in doorway. She springs to him, throws arm about him and— Problem.

(This pantomime is better done in group, though character of girl is the chief part for acting. When done in solo, have girl show as much emotional change as possible.)

106. *The Initiation*

A young man is led in, blindfolded. He stands expectant. Receives three healthy blows where nature provided. Winces at each blow but does not falter. Holds out arm and is stabbed (with icicle), lets the water drip from his "bleeding" arm. Holds out his hand and is struck seven times by broad paddle. Must not withdraw once, though shows he is pained. His shoes are removed and he is made to walk over a number of marbles on the floor. A ballet skirt is pinned upon him and he is told to dance on his toes for twenty seconds. He pivots heavily. He washes his face from gold basin (which contains chalk water). He suddenly hears girl's subdued laughter. His blindfold is removed and his girl shows him a mirror. He sees himself and some twenty school chums. Looks down at dress and feet—roar of laughter greets his consciousness. He knocks down the mirror and hurries from room.

(By occasionally showing attitudes of his companions, the young man is able to portray the entire process of initiation without words. Blend all transitions carefully.)

107. *A Search in the Library*

Bigler, an elderly man, comes cautiously into a large library and goes to table. Picks up the magazine section of the *Times* and looks through it casually. Servant enters and surprised at man's presence. Bigler smiles at him and walks to large chair and seats himself. Servant leaves, and Bigler quickly goes over to history section of library. Pulls down several large books and looks through them carefully. Pulls out a memo book from his own pocket and glances at a small map. Looks around the room and finds location desired. Puts memo book away and goes nonchalantly across room and starts to read titles of books as two servants appear. Bigler bows and hands one of them his card, turns to reading titles on books. He pretends surprise that servants do not leave. He orders them out and they leave. He now searches hurriedly, finds the volume he wishes, puts it under his vest on side and strolls to table, again picking up magazine. Walks to doorway; he is confronted by owner of library and the two servants. Looks at all three and the owner is the least vicious in appearance. Takes out an insurance prospectus and hands it to owner. At glance from owner, both servants cover the visitor with revolvers. Bigler, now evidently disturbed, raises his arms as ordered. Tries to look offended and protests. A servant searches him and finds the book. Bigler grabs for it and succeeds in getting it. Frantically points to an open page and tries to show the owner what it is. Bigler is questioned and gets little memo book, yellow with years. Compares map and page in open book. Owner and Bigler look at each other and Bigler leads way to center table. They move table slightly to one side and Bigler points to a flat ring on circle where table leg had rested. He takes hold of ring and pulls. A small floor door responds and all are astonished. A box of Spanish doubloons is revealed. Servants pull it to the floor and then the table. Bigler is now weak with joyous anticipation. He shows a little miniature to owner of library, who is more surprised. Owner goes quickly to library drawer and procures duplicate of Bigler's miniature. They look at each other and slowly walk to each other's arms. Bigler had found the fortune long stolen from his island home, and the owner, Johnson, had found the father of his wife, whom he had never seen and thought had drowned at sea. The daughter-wife is called and— Problem.

(A pantomime for group or individual. If individual, it is better done as an impersonation than as solo.)

108. *His Favorite Game*

A large darky walks into an East Side saloon and gets a drink of beer. He looks around the room and picks out a likely group. Ambles over to them and watches as they play cards. Is invited in. He takes three hands and loses each time. Very glum. Casually takes out a pair of dice and fingers them in retrospect as fourth deal is given him. He loses again. Slowly rises from table but throws dice across table and smiles. A small darky comes to the table and invites him over to end of room. As big boy walks we see he is bothered with bunions. They play on long table. Each throw has a limit of ten cents. Big boy loses six consecutive times. More glum. Takes out rabbit foot and brushes his head. Luck turns on next throw. He wins back his sixty cents and lacks ten cents of a dollar when his buxom wife is seen darkening the door. All scramble from table but big boy. He stands defiant, until she reaches the table. He then walks cautiously around as wife pursues. He dodges a glass and breaks into a run out of the door.

(Another example of serio-comedy. Because of the whiteness of the eye against a dark background, the eye of the Negro seems to move more than a Caucasian's. When impersonating a Negro, eye movement must be exaggerated for this purpose.)

109. *Her First Shot*

They have gone to the mountains and all are now ready to shoot. It is her turn. She puts shotgun to shoulder and starts to take aim and drops gun. He assures her and once more she puts gun to shoulder, closes eyes and is about to fire, but, again, desists. He reassures her and helps her put the gun to her shoulder, very snug. She takes courage, closes both eyes, lets gun slip high on shoulder, and pulls trigger. She is knocked backward and she thinks she is shot in her own shoulder. She grabs shoulder in pain—but this is a good story; just as she shot, a deer came bounding out of the woods and received the full charge in the shoulders, jumped high and fell dead. He rushes to deer and drags it to her feet. She is incredulous but there is the evidence. Between tears and laughter she receives congratulations from crowd. She gets up rather loosely, but proud of her first shot.

(Tears in laughter, joy in pain. Emotions offer more of paradox than any other phenomenon. The above exercise is more difficult than its mere reading.)

110. The Addict

A nervous, thin, old man steals into back of drug store. Hides behind boxes as clerk comes into prescription counter. Watches him undo safe, take out some powders and close door of safe, but not tight. Clerk goes out as old man sneaks to safe, picks out a little bottle and hurries back of boxes. Takes paper out of bottle, shakes contents into his mouth and reaches for bottle, procures and drinks. Clerk comes in and sees addict stand in smiling complacence. Stands and waits while clerk phones police. He sinks into a chair and stares dreamily before him, as a policeman comes, tries to arouse him. Old man stands and falls in a paroxysm of pain. Policeman lets him relax in chair—old man puts hand in his pocket and brings out a picture of a beautiful woman and two children. Gives picture and a letter to policeman, smiles serenely and falls asleep, never to awaken.

(Uncertainty — anxiety — exhilaration — repose — coma —pain—serenity—relaxing peace—what a great organ man has to play upon! All the colors, forms, and tones of life. The trained actor knows his instruments and uses them consciously.)

111. Tango at Venice

A crowd of farm boys have come to the California beach. A Japanese runs a gambling game of lotto, which he calls "Tango." Numbers are called as a ball is thrown into a pit. Cards are purchased for ten cents with certain numbers on them. Josh buys a card and awaits the calling of numbers. He must get five in a row, up, down, or crosswise. First number is called and he puts a marker on his card. The second he misses. The third he again places, and the fourth and fifth. Josh is now expectant. The sixth is called and he cannot place, the seventh is his number and—a tango! He is given a slip worth five dollars in trade. He plays once more and wins again. Decides to quit. He is loaded with ham, canned goods, bottled goods, bacon, salt and candy. Struggles out of crowd—and we see him wondering where to put his winnings. He had forgotten that he was a hundred miles from home. He puts goods down and gives them away, piece by piece, to little boys and girls. He retires, in good spirits.

(Action is the genius of drama. This exercise could be done mostly in a quiet, unrevealing manner. The actor must devise means of telling the eye as well as the ear. The above is good practice for eye-pantomime.)

112. The Hunchback

Marco, a little hunchback, comes quietly into a violin workshop. Listens cautiously at doorway and goes to his own bench. Takes out a beautiful instrument which he fondles tenderly. Plays on it for a few measures and lovingly places violin near his own case, then goes to his workmate's bench. Takes the violin from friend's case —looks at it with disgust and pity. Takes it to his own bench and puts it in his own case, then takes his own wonderful instrument and puts it in his rival's case. Perito, his rival, enters and strikes at Marco. Marco responds in looks only and is about to leave, when Camilla, secretly beloved by Marco, enters. She runs to arms of Perito and kisses him. Marco silently watches. Sees Perito take his own violin from case and, thinking it his inferior instrument, goes to Marco's bench and exchanges violins. Marco has done what he can for Perito—and drinking a toast to the winner, he puts his own violin in his own case. The girl and Perito bid the hunchback adieu and go off laughing. Marco takes his beloved instrument out once more, puts it under his arm, pulls a cap well down on his head and limps determinedly out of doorway.

(To create pathos without being pitied is one of the best attainments of an actor. It is power in drama. The above exercise is for solo or impersonation.)

113. His First Badge

Fred, a boy scout, has just come from a court of honor and has received a merit badge. It is evening and a Shriners' parade is passing. He stands on the street curbing to view procession. A companion comes up to him and notices his badge. Fred lets him admire it but stops hand from marring the badge. Two other boys come up and Fred lets them examine his new honor, but this time he is more condescending. He waves to his uncle going by in the parade and points to his badge. A group of men stand by him and one, Fred's neighbor, shakes hands with him. Fred tries to call attention to his new badge without telling about it. He looks at four men, and finally goes up to his neighbor and looks at his Elk pin but gets no response. He takes hold of the Elk pin and the neighbor pats him on the head but does not notice Fred's badge. He borrows a pin from his neighbor and puts in his coat lapel near the badge, but still gets no response. He finally nudges the neighbor, gets his attention and points to his badge. Neighbor glances at it and turns to the parade. Fred is a little chagrined. A merit badge and not noticed! The parade breaks up and a group of girls come up to him, with their kindly chaperon. The prettiest girl sees badge first. Fred is an immediate hero. Girl shows badge to all her friends and Fred goes home with them in triumph.

(More drama will yet come from that period of life which is freest from sorrow and pain, but so innocently sincere in the personal. Young people becoming adult is the world's sweetest study. Is a boy a man delayed, or is a man a boy continually changing? Your viewpoint will show in above pantomime.)

114. Chinatown Courtesy

One Long Hop, proprietor of a Grant Street restaurant, is watching a group of diners at their evening meal. He smiles at various customers as they enter, but he watches rather furtively this one group. He watches a young man pour whisky in a girl's cup as she converses with another friend. Hop calls to a waiter and motions him to watch table carefully. A fellow at table takes a powder and slips it into the girl's teacup. Hop beckons the waiter to go to table and ask girl to come to telephone booth. She does so and Hop goes to her. Back of his fan, he tells her in pantomime that her cup contains more than whisky. She strikes him in the face and goes back to her seat. Hop watches her drink the contents of the cup as she steadily gazes into his eyes. Hop again signals for his waiter, who goes to the telephone booth and asks for a plain-clothes policeman. Hop sees girl gradually slump in chair and fall into arms of male companion, who picks her up and starts to take her to a private room. Others at table laugh and continue eating, unconcerned. Hop steps in front of man with unconscious girl and denies entrace to private room. Fellow tries to bully past Hop, but is stopped. Enraged, the fellow puts the girl down and the diners gather round. Hop claps his hands and several waiters come to him. Fellow suddenly draws pistol and fires at Hop, who is hit. He stands, unsteadily, and points to the rowdy as policeman enters. Fellow is surprised but fires once more before arrested. Hop orders girl to lounge, and falls dead.

(A pantomime for duality of impersonation. When in solo, confine characters to Hop and young man. The Orient shows emotional life less than the Occident, and contrast is good study.)

115. Waiting in the Blind

Bob and Bill are sitting in their boat, surrounded by bulrushes. It is three o'clock in the morning. Bob is cold but moves within himself in his shivering. He chastises Bill for rubbing his hands. They look anxiously toward the east as they see the first faint glow of dawn. A noise is heard to their left and both pick up their guns cautiously. They strain their eyes, Bill almost tips the boat as both grab the sides. Bob again cusses in vehement quietness. A sudden whir to their right and a black line in the skyline. It moves slowly toward them. Both get guns ready and remain motionless, except as they watch line of ducks approach them. Bullfrog hops onto Bill's hand and he lets out a healthy scream. Bob jumps in response and black line of ducks swerve instantly and are soon out of sight. Bill is looking for snake and keeps rocking the boat. Bob grabs gun as if to strike Bill and shows snake was not a yard long, as Bill declared, but only a frog, four inches long. Bob motions for silence and shows his disgust for Bill's babyishness. Like shots from the sky, a flock of mallards hit the water not ten feet away. Both are dumbfounded but Bob recovers first. He slowly gets aim and Bill, now numb, sneezes. Bob fires, but not from his own intentions. Ducks almost bound from water as Bill sneezes again. They fly low. This was the last straw. Bob is now vehement in denunciation. It is getting much lighter. Bob stands in boat and to his great surprise sees three dead ducks and one still struggling. Rows boat few feet, procures all four ducks, holds them up and brags. What he would have done if Bill hadn't sneezed!

(Drama in constrained action is more difficult than in fuller lives, and requires longer practice.)

116. The Connoisseur

An old gray-haired man stands before a table, on which are a dozen rare volumes. He slowly puts on his spectacles and runs his hands caressingly over all the books. He looks at all of them, individually. Picks up each volume and thumbs the pages and lingers over some of the pages of each. He walks from table to his empty cupboard. Gets out breadbox. It is empty. He knew it was, but he looked for a crumb. Yes, there was a small crumb, upon which he nibbles. He is suffering pangs of hunger and his eyes take on a glassy stare. He hurries over to his books and picks up Boccaccio's *Decameron.* Centuries old and the youngest of his collection. He is so weak he nearly faints. Seats himself and again caresses his prizes. Takes out letter from his pocket, reads again slowly. He has been offered a fortune for his dozen books. And the youngest would keep him for five years. Why not sell the book to the big library and do a great number of scholars good? Just as the letter says. He will. He must! He slowly straightens up, takes his Boccaccio and starts for the door; agony marks his countenance. He falls into the chair clutching book to his bosom. He dies, his face brightens and rests in tranquil peace, with the beloved book still clutched to his heart.

(An exercise for face and hands. A person who loves books and lives with them, develops a definite finger technic.)

117. The Tease

Becky, twenty and the life of the party. She is in a boarding school. It is nine o'clock Sunday morning and she goes from room to room. She discovers Teddy asleep, looks around and finds piece of curling tissue. Shapes it into a long tickler and tiptoes over to Teddy's bed. Gently runs tickler over Teddy's face, who hits at it viciously. Tickles again; is very successful the third time as Teddy lands a healthy palm on Becky's nose. As Teddy arouses and laughs at her accurate response, Becky leaves the room nursing a bruised face. She goes to Millicent's room and sees Milly sleeping serenely. Becky gets a glass of water from table and pours a little in

Milly's ear. Screams and terror. Milly jumps from bed and in so doing knocks the water down Becky's shirt front. Matron and other girls respond and fill the room. Becky is made the object of their banters. Cora, the largest girl, grabs her about the waist and two others hold her hands while Cora ties Becky's arms behind her. Girls sprinkle water in her face. One paints cold cream on her for a mustache. As Becky kicks at assailants, her feet are grabbed and tied with her own stockings. The pajama parade marches around her as Becky ignores their celebration. When Hulda brings in a pitcher of ice water, Becky is uneasy. Hulda marches solemnly to Becky, who remonstrates to the Matron. Matron calmly reads near the window. Becky pleads for mercy and with water over her head, takes the oath of morning silence. School banner is taken from wall and she places her hands on it and repeats their oath of social obedience. They undo her hands and feet and leave her to meditate. She sits and stares into great spaces.

(A solo pantomime to practice in showing group activity. Consciously work out emotional responses from each activity, and determine climax.)

118. The Old Cobbler

An old cobbler sits at his bench mending a man's shoe. He finishes the big shoe and picks up a baby's shoe. He touches it tenderly, stops his work to dream of the past. A tear drops from his eye and he slowly starts to work. Cuts a sole for the little shoe as if it were precious gold. Sews carefully around the shoe. Does the same for its mate, and sets the little shoes on a nearby shelf. Takes out a little locket and gets lock of hair, a curl, and holds it closely to his face. Returns the lock to its resting place and picks up another shoe, ready for work. A little girl comes in leading a baby brother by the hand. They have golden curls. Old cobbler stops his work and looks at them. Then gets the little shoes for the baby. He seems unable to touch the little fellow, though yearning to embrace him. He places the shoes in the girl's hands and brings little boy slowly to him. Kisses his forehead tenderly and holds baby closely to him. Brings out toy hammer and puts it in baby's hand. Refuses the money offered him by the girl. Pats cheek of little boy and holds him to him once more. Then watches them out of the door, his eyes on the little one. With distant gaze, slowly gets lock of hair again, and bows his head over the workbench, weeping.

(Pathos has a slower tempo than most comedy. Rhythm is one of greatest studies necessary for good technic. The rate of the stage is consistent with rate of life.)

119. At the Terminal

Beldon, a middle-aged mail clerk, stands before his sorting bags, methodically distributing mail. He is nervous and twice wipes his brow. Looks about furtively and bids an indifferent good-night to depot mail carrier. As last man leaves his section, Beldon goes quickly to light and turns it toward door so as to blind any one coming from the dark. Goes to two of the deep bags and hurriedly feels in each. Finds two packages in each bag. Get a small, flat alcohol lamp from his pocket and lights it. Whistles as he works. Heats flap of first envelope. Disappointed with contents. Seals packet and throws it in bag. Heats other envelope which is slower to respond. Glue melts and he finds five hundred-dollar bills in envelope. Looks around again and whistles louder. Pours some powder over envelope before he seals with heel of hand. Puts envelope in proper bag, starts on third packet as he is confronted with a sawed-off shotgun. A robber orders him to "stick 'em up," which clerk slowly does. Robber takes the money and, with piece of carbon paper, gets imprint of postal clerk's hand. Folds paper and backs to window. Clerk stands stupefied, seeing his money and finger prints disappear in window. Problem.

(Suspense, surprise, and fear are not uncommon to drama, though quite infrequent in prosaic life. Study well the means of their portrayal. It promises better acting.)

120. Discovery

Denman, a wealthy clubman of middle age, has brought to his rooms a nineteen-year-old girl of dashing beauty. She is modern in every respect and independent to a fault. She wants to know life and the wealthy man has fostered her acquaintance. They are at last in his private suite. He closes the door and takes off her coat and throws it over the arm of a big chair near the door. Hangs up his own hat and coat in hallway. Brings her to fireplace. They stand warming their fingers. Togo comes in and sets the supper. Togo is told to go home for the night. Togo gets his hat and coat and leaves by front door. Denman locks the door and places girl at table. He sits opposite, nibbling at the food, watching her eat. He pours champagne and drinks a toast. They laugh heartily. Denman is anxious for the meal to end. He looks at watch, affects surprise at hour, and shows her the time. They rise and go to couch by fireplace. He gives her a diamond pendant and places it about her neck, but in so doing takes off a small amulet she has always worn. She accepts necklace but asks for amulet, which she holds in her hands, letting chain fall from one hand to other. Denman holds her in his arms. He suddenly rises and turns out all lights but the distant hall lamp. Comes back and playfully takes off her slippers. As he kneels, he sees amulet glisten in the firelight. It attracts his attention. He looks at it closely and nearly falls on couch. Slowly rises and goes to hall light. Looks at amulet again. An unmistakable truth. She wears the amulet placed on her just before they were wrecked near Ireland, eighteen years ago. The night he lost his wife and daughter! His daughter! Long thought dead and drowned. How can he reveal himself? What can he say? Let her go and forever lose her friendship? Tell her who he is and remain forever disgraced in her and his own eyes? Become suddenly ill and trust to the future? Problem.

(Such a struggle as is presented in this exercise is the very soul of much modern drama. Cleverness of dénouement is necessary—it challenges your capabilities. So does life.)

121. The Old-Clothes Man

A Jewish peddler is sorting out his old clothes. He finds two good overcoats and is delighted. Most of his collection contains only rags. He picks up one very old coat and is about to throw it on rag pile but notices the weight of one side. He runs his hand over the coat again; in and out of pockets. But all are empty. He throws coat on pile and, in so doing, his eyes catch sight of a hole in inside coat pocket. He picks up the coat again and examines hole. Hurriedly tears off lining. Coat has been sewn with twenty-dollar bills—five, twelve, forty, eighty-six of them. He sinks in weakened excitement. Rises, goes to window blind and pulls it down. Locks door and recounts the bills. Assures himself that money is genuine. Picks up coat again and looks for possible name, finds only place of sale and name of firm making sale. Should he go to them? Tries to rise but is unable. His heart is acting queerly. Leans helplessly on table and pounds it with his hand to attract attention. Calls with what strength he can muster. Struggles slowly, drags himself to door, unlocks and opens it; waves his hand to policeman on opposite corner. Policeman hurries over, helps the old man up and puts him on bundle of old rags. Old-Clothes Man tries to tell him of his discovery, closes his eyes, and—is dead; or would you have him live?

(One is tempted to words in such a situation—control is the keynote to all success. Avoid excesses—even with emotion.)

122. The Barker

A clown is entertaining a crowd before a fun-house. He shows all five fingers of his hand and passes his other hand over the palm. Does this several times and then grabs his thumb and gives a jerk. The thumb has disappeared (back into his palm away from the audience). Takes a feather and balances on his nose. Grabs a coin from a man's hat and gives it to him. Grabs a quarter from a woman's back and presents it to her. Crowd comes closer. He takes a long knife from scabbard and prepares to swallow it. As he is about to start, he sees his wife clinging to arm of handsome stranger. His wife thinks he works at the lighthouse, being rowed out every night and back in the morning. He has been too proud to tell her he makes a fool of himself for their living. He can hardly begin his trick, he is trembling so. Pretends nervousness for crowd's sake and watches his wife. Stranger has wife get on the Giant Coaster and clown watches her snuggle up to the stranger. Clown does his trick while watching the coaster-car ascend its height and start its ride down the curving tracks. As wife and stranger exit from ride, she is still in his arms. Clown throws knife over their heads and it sticks in doorway above. Stranger comes toward clown, menacingly. Clown laughs heartily, sticks tongue at fellow and poses for mock fight. Crowd laughs and wife pulls reluctant stranger away. Clown drops head in supposedly mock sorrow and shuffles on to his dressing room.

(For solo or impersonation. Just how much can the clown show which will reveal what his wife is doing?)

123. At the Ticket Booth

A girl is seated in a picture show ticket booth. It is the rush hour and fifty cents is general admission. Sells to a fat fellow who tries to flirt with her. She gives him the cold and stony reply. A little woman hands out her fifty cents in five-cent and penny pieces. Girl waits patiently while woman recounts it. Telephone rings. She answers in monosyllables and sells tickets as convenience permits, three in number. Fellow gives her hundred-dollar bill. She looks at her change box and finds she can make change, in ten- and five-dollar bills mostly. She accepts a piece of candy from a friend. Sells four more tickets when flashy girl comes up and suddenly throws gun in her face, covering gun from public view with handkerchief. Girl in booth reads piece of paper held up to her by a man at side window. "All you've got or you're a dead sister." Fellow goes to door at back, puts in his hand as door is opened and grabs handful of bills. Both robbers dash through crowd to waiting car and turn corner. Girl in booth screams and points to disappearing couple. Manager of house comes out and she tries to explain in incoherent ejaculations. Shows him the money till and calls upon several customers to witness. Policeman comes up and she tries to tell him; as situation is thoroughly grasped by herself, she does the logical thing, faints. Is there another solution?

(For solo or impersonation. Solo pantomime with this offers the best study. Have girl show what others are doing, by the use of facial expression.)

124. The Sleepy Clerk

It is midnight, and the clerk has been working on a balance for hours. He is so sleepy he can see only the darker figures. He bumps his head with his hands and starts in again. He goes down a column of figures and is startled—now he is out twice as much. Adds it up again and they go back to original result. Drops water down his back, spills more than he intended. Walks around the desk, exercising vigorously. Sits once more and takes book for checking. Cat meows mournfully and disturbs his thinking. Goes to window and motions cat away, meowing in derision at its activities. Takes paper weight and throws at cat—wind flurries through room and blows his papers on floor. Desperate closing of window and gathering of precious sheets. Puts them in order and finds two pieces missing. Sits in meditation, with drooping eyes. Counts sheets again and finds two sheets still missing. Looks sleepily around floor and finally, under desk. He pulls out three sheets of paper. Three, he is sure! Looks at them and is aroused to an awakened excitement. The amount on the third sheet is exactly the amount he needs for a balance. A quick check-up—Eureka! A balance! Some scoundrel had thrown an invoice under the desk. But he had found it. He sings lustily and janitor appears. Offers him a cigar. Grabs his hat. Puts paper away in desk. He can work for finish to-morrow. He has his balance! Kisses desk good-by, and goes out happily.

(A transition from weariness to exhilaration, in graded steps. Analyze to a proper conclusion.)

REVIEW AND QUESTIONS

1. Define monologue—impersonation—acting.
2. What is difference in technic of acting one part in a play, and one person impersonating all the parts of a play?
3. What is meant by "establishing a character"?
4. Which character in *Around the World* (58) is most easy to establish? to recognize?
5. Name some "conventions" of dramatic art?
6. Which is the more effective in pantomime, the use or nonuse of properties? Use pantomimes of this chapter for your conclusions.
7. Why can we present a scene in ten minutes which takes thirty minutes in life? Develop.
8. What is the difference between "being laughed at" and "laughing with you"? Explain.
9. Can two strong emotions be expressed simultaneously? Explain from exercises in this chapter.
10. What factors of impersonation and acting are especially necessary for eccentric characters?

11. What are the chief variations and differences in behavior between the adolescent and the adult? Demonstrate from exercises in this chapter.
12. What factors of exaggeration must be most carefully guarded in all acting and impersonation? How could we ruin the desired effect of *The Addict* (*109*)?
13. Develop "the rate of the stage is the rate of life."

CHAPTER XI

PANTOMIMES FOR THE GROUP

THESE pantomimes have been written to develop such emotional and acting technic as is found necessary for the stage of to-day. The cry of the modern stage is more for good actors than it is for actable, decent plays.

Acting is learnable; acting is teachable. Most of the better actors never cease studying the art. Most of the average actors have never studied it. Every emotion that ever existed in the human race is either patent or latent in each individual. Each emotion has a physiognomic pattern and should be learned by the student and actor, so as to effect an unconscious technic when acting.

Live your character, but always remember *you* are doing it, consciously controlling by the life of the thought. Art is interpretation and revelation, not reality.

125. Teaching Oliver to Steal

An old man stooped, but vigorous, comes into hovel of room and looks cautiously around. Assures himself of secrecy and pulls out small bag from torn coat. Looks at some jewels which he handles with caresses. Noise is heard at door, left. He hurriedly covers jewels on table with lapel of coat and slowly looks around. One of his boys enters, whom he greets with a grunt and returns to his table. He is just putting his jewels in bag when three other boys enter, two born to the street and the other, timid and frightened and well dressed. Timid boy is pushed in front of old man who feels texture of cloth. The old man shows decided interest in newcomer and gives him first lesson in stealing. Has other boy take a handkerchief as he walks by. Teaches newcomer how to get handkerchief without pushing up against him or calling attention to his act. This is accomplished on fourth trial, and old man leaves room, gleefully. Two street urchins strip newcomer of his plush coat and linen shirt. They put on him an old heavy coat and dance around him gleefully.

(Literature offers many examples of good pantomime. This is a suggestive number. This exercise best done without props.)

Old man, 4 boys

126. A Spanish Night

A moonlight night. Two lovers are seated, looking out toward the ocean. He is playing a guitar, a veiled bandit steals behind them and strikes the man with pistol butt. He falls, and bandit grabs girl as she rises. Puts gag over her mouth as she screams and faints. He snatches necklace and rings from girl and lays her upon the bench. He stoops down to the prostrate man and lifts his head against his own body, searching the pockets, belt, and vest. Robber takes ring from man's little finger and leans him against bench, close to girl. He performs a mock marriage over them, pretends to be placing man's ring on girl's finger, as moonbeams flash upon the stone. Bandit is startled and examines ring closely. Compares it with one on his own finger, and finds them identical, even to the monogram on the side. His long lost twin brother! Bandit kneels and lifts up the prostrate figure in his arms. Calls gently, "Roderigo, Roderigo! My brother! Oh, Santa Maria, don't let him die." Buries his head in brother's breast as girl awakens, rises slowly, looks about her, sees the two men and calls for help. Bandit straightens up and lays limp figure on bench, as he speaks. "Señorita. Please do not run. I am his brother. The one he thought dead long ago. He, Roderigo, was stolen by gypsies, when but a boy, and I swore vengeance on all mankind. Even God Himself. But now I have found him. See, our rings are identical. Keep them. For I die with him. I died with our separation and now I live with his death. Oh, Roderigo! My brother! Together!" Bandit slowly raises pistol to his head, when girl calls out. "Look—he revives." She hurries to her lover and raises him gently. Roderigo looks about him dazedly and puts hands to his aching head. He speaks. "Rosita, Rosita, what has happened? Where are you?" Girl holds him closely as bandit kneels and looks into his brother's face. "Roderigo, it is I, Juan. Your brother. Your boyhood brother. The rings, Señorita, the rings!" She unclasps hand and shows them to Roderigo, who recognizes them and pulls his brother's face close to him. As old servant is seen approaching with lantern, Roderigo clasps his brother to his heart. "Oh, Holy Mother [Señorita crosses herself.] I have found my Juan. My brother Juan. Juan, Rosita and I were betrothed just as—" Old servant speaks, "Señor, may I be so bold as to ask if you called?" Roderigo slowly rises. "Yes, Baldo, lay covers for my brother Juan. His coming has quite upset me." Juan starts to speak, "Oh, Roderigo. I—" and he falls at Roderigo's feet. Roderigo totters unsteadily, but lifts Juan to a standing position. He says, "None of that, Juan. To-morrow you may tell us all. I feel much better now. I must have struck my head as I fainted. There—not a word for now. Rosita, my arm. Juan, you may take the other, and I might lean on you for a few steps. Baldo, the guitar, and follow up with a good lusty song." They go off slowly, as Baldo adjusts his lantern, smiles approval and starts singing "In Old Madrid."

(Conversation is written to express their thoughts. The pantomime needs no words to make it very understandable.)

3 men, 1 lady

127. A Busy Street Corner

Saturday night shopping crowds pass by a corner, where stand two beggars. One is blind and sells pencils; he holds them out before him in helpless manner and accepts whatever is paid. The other is crippled and distorted. His hands are clumped, one shoulder is higher than the other and a foot hangs limply and crooked. He holds his hat and looks piteously at passers-by. The cripple gets the more money and even a five-dollar bill. As the crowd thins down, the crippled beggar becomes restless, looks up and down the street and slowly straightens himself and stretches entire body. Takes out his money from pocket and counts to his satisfaction. He is about to leave when he sees a dollar bill in the blind man's hat. Stands looking around, then goes close to the blind man and says: "Here's a quarter, old man. I had a good day." He slyly slips bill from blind man, straightens and starts to leave. As he turns, the blind man puts hand in pocket. He speaks vigorously. "Stick 'em up, Gillins. We've been watching you for a long time. Stick 'em up."

Gillins turns around and sees revolver aimed at him. "Well, I'll be damned, and you ain't blind either."

Blind man, "No, Gilly, old man, and you thought to rob a blind man, eh? Well, the force isn't dead yet. See this little button? Yes? Burns Agency. Mulligan by name. Heard of me?"

"Mulligan—you?"

"Stick 'em out. [Puts handcuffs on Gilly.] They feel cold on a night like this, don't they? So you had a good day? That's fine. So did I. Come on."

2 men and passers-by

128. The North Pole

Two aviators are searching the heavens for the relief plane. One is Italian and the other Swedish. Their words are unintelligible to each other. They are both startled, look at each other, then raise up hopefully. Straining their eyes they look toward the south. They look hopefully but only a stray bird flaps by and they drop again in despair. Each one has written a letter. They have spent days together, but each knows the end can't be far away and, with the same thought dominating them, they rise and shake hands. They are cold and starving to death. Each kisses his own flag fervently and kneels to flag of the other. On a broken wing of airplane, they tie the two flags and pin their letters. The Italian crosses himself and kneels in prayer. The Swede looks out, arms outstretched, and prays for some viking boat to return. The effort is too great, and he sinks to the ground, but by main force of self-power, holds himself in control. As the Italian lifts his eyes to heaven, a distant whir! A speck— Look! The Swede cannot rise, but leans on his arm and waves with the other. The Italian seems to have gained in strength, he waves frantically and calls. The airplane comes nearer. They are saved! The ship circles over them twice and passes on! Despair more acute. They are unseen. They call vehemently. Italian waves fur blanket until he falls exhausted. The stray bird returns, squawks piteously and flaps on.

2 men

129. Rivals

Two old ladies come to a concert. They are to hear a famous singer on his farewell appearance. They sit in seats the usher turns for them. They look askance at each other, and each thinks the other has a familiar "something" about her. They look about the auditorium and recognize a few of their friends. Miss Blonde drops her program and Miss Brunette picks it up, though with some difficulty. They exchange greetings and again scrutinize for possible memories. Miss Blonde offers some peppermints and smiles. Miss Brunette accepts and nudges closer. As she does so, she notices the locket Miss Blonde is wearing—a locket not unlike the one she gave the famous singer years ago, one she hoped he would wear as a watch charm. As the acquaintance grows, she exclaims her interest in the "odd" locket and asks to see it. Miss Blonde hesitates, but takes it off and hands it to Miss Brunette. Brunette takes out her glasses and examines. There is no mistake. The initials, in miniature letters are there. The very locket she had given Mr. Padrones fifty years ago—the afternoon he had sailed for Europe. At last she had discovered the woman who robbed her of her sweetheart. She looks at the picture inside. It is not her own, but one of a young man somewhat resembling the picture of the evening's artist. Brunette, calm and watching for opportunities, returns the locket. She refuses the second helping of peppermints, rather testily. Blonde notices the change of attitude and draws into her own shell. It is about time for the concert to begin. As Blonde sits back in solitary silence, she lets her glance rest upon Brunette's chubby but small hand. There was a peculiar cameo ring on the large finger. Why wear a ring on that finger? Curiosity bent her head a little closer and—no—yes—the identical ring she had given the great singer on the evening of his departure for Europe—it was on this woman's finger. So—there sat the woman who had robbed her of her sweetheart! At last she had found her. Where there was calmness between them a moment ago, there was now a heavy frost. Distance separated their dark dresses. The great singer appeared and all applauded heartily, except the two virgins. Their thoughts were too much occupied in other channels—but what is this? A lady is brought on the platform and introduced as the principal feature of the program, Mrs. Padrones, the life-long companion of the great artist. The two virgins become pale, and almost simultaneously sympathetic. They had been duped. Each had been presented with the personal present of the other. Padrones had left each as his one burning love but had gone to

Europe and married an American over there. They saw a regal beauty stand and bow at the side of their faithless lover. Could they blame him? But he could kiss so gloriously! Each wiped out a surreptitious tear, slid a hand into the grasp of the other, and leaned understandingly against each other. They sighed together and pressed each other's hand when the great artist sang "Love's Old Sweet Song."

2 ladies

130. The Section Boss

A big burly Irishman stands on pile of sand, overlooking a group of Italians as they work on a sidewalk. As they pass near him, he comments to each one of them, ten in number. To one he orders speed, to the following three he suggests more punch in their back, to two others more speed, at the following four he merely looks disgusted. As the first man appears again with a half load of gravel, Mike is very indignant and cuffs Tony on the head. Tony shows fight, but a menacing attitude from Mike cows the Italian and he trudges on. As the next workman follows, expectantly, Mike strikes out again, but misses, as the workman has dodged the blow and strikes back viciously. Hits Mike in the jaw. Mike grabs a club and raises to land promiscuous blows, when the biggest workman flashes a knife and comes forward slowly. Mike grabs a whistle from his pocket and blows lustily, backing from his vendetta. An Irish policeman appears immediately with drawn gun. All workmen recede to a group and all begin to talk at once, drowning all efforts of Mike or policeman to be heard.

12 men

131. Ever the Twain Shall Meet

A psychologist comes to the library and gets a dozen books from the stacks, and goes to a distant table where only a girl is seated. Young man spreads out his books over the table and gets his reference sheet ready. He opens books at respective pages. The girl pays little attention at first; she is interested in her Freudian novel. As the books crowd her elbow ease, she turns her scrutinizing eyes upon the unconscious student. He is writing rapidly. He adjusts his glasses from time to time. Girl leans an elbow on one of his books. He soon needs that very volume, looks around for it, finally sees it. He reaches for it, then withdraws his hand. She is deep in her reading—but he needs that book. Gently he touches girl on her arm. She can't resist the impulse to fuss him—so she touches him back in mock shyness. He smiles but is visibly affected. Girl touches his shoe with one of her own. The dig is now nonplused and starts piling his books. He has forgotten why he touched the girl. She looks flirtingly at him once more and leans her elbow on the same book and starts reading again. He is gradually regaining a little composure. Arranges his books again for study. But that volume—he must have it. He touches the girl again. This time she drops her own book and moves closely to the dig. She leans her head on his shoulder. This is too much. People will see. He moves slowly from the little vamp and stands. He gathers his papers, as in a spell, watching her eyes. She is pretty—he hadn't really noticed before. She moves closer to him; he backs away and breaks into a fast walk out of the room. She laughs heartily, pokes his books from her, gets gum and begins to read.

1 man, 1 lady

132. Bursting Bubbles

A maid comes into her lady's boudoir and hangs up several dresses. She goes to door and looks down hallway, closes door and goes immediately to the dressing table. She uses milady's powder and rouge and decorates her eyelashes and brows. She is not quite satisfied with her appearance—she needs a touch somewhere. She thinks of her lady's jewel case. It is in a secret drawer, which she springs and procures case. Opens it and looks excitedly at fortune in front of her. Takes out an emerald pendant and hangs on her neck. Her dark dress is not appropriate. She slips off her dress and gets her lady's silver bead dress. It clings to her as she surveys the transformation in the mirror. The pendant now adorns her white neck. She puts the diamond eardrops to her ears and sees them glisten in the morning light. In her yellow hair she puts a black Spanish comb. She powders her arms and hands, then puts on the two largest diamond rings. She is now satisfied. Footsteps down the hallway. Could it be? Laughter in front of doorway. Maid stands stupefied. Her hands refuse to obey her promptings. Milady and her friend enter. The mistress is equally surprised as the maid, but in a different manner. Friend looks at both and laughs heartily. Milady comes to the maid, looks contemptuously upon her and slowly takes rings and earrings, tells the maid to take off the pendant. The maid is speechless and trembling. Milady slips party dress from maid and throws maid's dress in her face. The girl is now composed and begs her mistress for opportunity of explanation. Milady orders her from room, the maid goes out protesting but crying. Milady is such a picture of firmness that her friend laughs again, so hard that the mistress gradually sees the humor of the whole scene and laughs unrestrainedly.

3 ladies

133. In Court

There are five prisoners to be tried. The sergeant-at-arms has them stand as the judge enters. The judge is cross and irritable. He is worried. Clerk reads the first case. Chinaman stands up. Clerk shows judge by his actions that Chinaman was drunk. Chinaman shakes his head. Fifty dollars or fifty days. The Chinaman smiles and reaches in his long coat sleeve with its several linings and produces fifty dollars. Goes out gingerly. Next case. A girl is called. Young, pretty, and frightened. She is poorly dressed. The clerk says she accosted two men on the street last night about midnight. She hangs her head. The judge gives her ten dollars or ten days. She cannot pay. A young man jumps up and offers to pay. The Judge looks at him in surprise. It is only a Boy who stayed away from home last night. The first time he had ever done so without the family permission! The Judge rises and asks if the girl was the cause. Boy laughs, shakes his head for "no" and the girl looks at the Judge. She doesn't know the Boy. Judge lets Boy pay the fine, and the grateful girl leaves. The Judge asks the Boy (his own son) why he is there. Clerk answers and tells him that his son is the fifth case, arrested for speeding and fighting. Son smiles with assured ease, and awaits dismissal from his father. The Judge calls for the two other cases. First is there for disturbing the peace. Ten days or ten dollars. Prisoner leaves. The second for stealing a coat. Thirty days. Prisoner accepts situation as one relieved. Judge calls for the fifth case—his own son. Speeding and fighting! Three days! The boy laughs, but the Judge pounds his gavel and repeats: "Three days." Then he walks out, in sorrow. The son is dumbfounded. He is obliged to respond to a new order in his life. He'll see them in hell first, but, he goes to the interior of the building with the insistent sergeant.

7 men, 1 lady

134. A Sister's Dilemma

A cashier of a book and novelty store is standing in line, waiting her turn at the teller's window. The line moves slowly. She reads a magazine between move-ups. A dark handsome young man is in front of her. He glances at her from time to time. He has a check to cash. Young man reaches teller and has to produce letters for identification. Has unsatisfactory proof, so folds the check and thanks the teller sarcastically. Hurries away. Girl steps to window, absorbed in magazine story. Reaches down for hand bag and opens it, closing magazine at same time. Smiles at teller as he waits patiently. Girl searches for her deposit book and contents. It is gone. She researches for it and is convinced; she goes down the line of her approach and finds no trace of book. Besides, the hand bag was almost entirely closed. Some one had to take it. Who? She had shown the book and contents to the guard at the door. It was the biggest deposit for months—the guard is summoned and verifies girl's statement. She looks around, helplessly, almost crying. Nearly three hundred dollars. Who was near her? Workman back of her was still being detained at window. Had he seen any one? He had seen nobody suspicious near her and offers to be searched himself. Guard does so. There is nothing found on him, except a silver flask which workman grabs and hides quickly. The girl remembers handsome man in front of her. Describes him to guard and teller. The teller remembers and picks up piece of paper with gentleman's name. Shows it to the girl. She reads again and staggers. Her brother's name. Was it but a coincidence, or could it be her long-unheard-from brother? A runaway at eight. Should she try to locate him? What if he were the thief? Problem.

(It is profitable to try out several conclusions and effect the strongest drama. Give reasons for criticism or choice, always.)

3 men, 1 lady, supernumeraries

135. Soup for Three

A young couple come to an élite restaurant and are shown a private table. Fellow removes the girl's coat and seats her very solicitously. Seats himself. They both order the regular dinner, as waiter hovers about them. Soup is served and the man spills some on his shirt front, tries to cover up the wiping-off operation. Girl listens to his chatter, as she eats and shyly looks around the restaurant. Discovers her very dearest flame. Starts flirting immediately, though very conservatively. By the time they have finished soup, the man, Fred, comes up to the table, and the girl introduces him to her host, Archibald. Archie rises but is not too enthusiastic. Girl suggests that Fred join them and Archie politely responds with an invitation. Fred eagerly accepts and waiter is summoned to add another order for dinner. Fred and girl sit very closely together and converse intimately. Archie tries several times to break through but remains to roll pills with fancy bread. Soup is brought to Fred and Archie takes the girl's hand to call attention to his existence. She, in turn, takes his hand but hears only Fred. Archie is now a prisoner—every time he moves, the girl squeezes his hand affectionately. He tries to remove his hand, but girl only holds it the tighter and leans closer to Fred. She is almost a full arm's length from Archie when the waiter brings the meat course, but Archie eats alone. He tries to eat his turkey—still being one-handed, and his asparagus is a trifle too long. The affectionate pair are in earnest conversation. Archie takes an asparagus and drops it daintily on the girl's wrist, but she lets it remain a bracelet of gustatorial affection. She is under the spell of love. As she is enfolded in Fred's arms, Archie collapses.

2 men, 1 lady, supers

136. The Reading of the Will

Aunt Jenny has called all her near relations for the reading of her will. She wishes them to understand all the conditions before she dies. Lawyer Jones is ready. Aunt Jenny has her kin come in, one at a time, and sit around her. They are farm-folk. Her drunken brother, now dressed and sober for the occasion, is first to enter. He sits at extreme end. He is followed by a stuttering sister, now in the sixties. A little girl is shown in next and sits next to Aunt Jenny. Aunt squeezes her hand in kindly assurance. These all sit at Aunt's right. A nephew and niece by marriage enter, carrying a six-months baby. The last seat is taken by a crippled teamster. He limps visibly with a crushed foot. He is conscious of his discomfort throughout. The young husband has the baby and remains its nurse during the scene. The brother has taken a chew of tobacco and is distressed because no cuspidor is evident. They are now ready. The lawyer stands before them and looks at each one. He assures Aunt Jenny she is right. He takes out six envelopes and solemnly presents to the respective heirs. They all look at the sealed envelopes and then stare at Aunt Jenny. She wants them to read their own allotments. Each opens his envelope in his own characteristic manner. The stuttering sister is first and she reads in haste—then rereads. Gets up in severe indignation and goes to Aunt Jenny with menacing index finger. Tries to speak and fails. She takes several steps about the room and comes again to Aunt Jenny. Shakes her fist at Aunt and Jenny strikes her gingerly with her cane. Sister goes out in a dudgeon, still trying to talk. Others look on, wondering what might be in their envelope. The wife is next to succumb to curiosity and sits with puzzled mien. She wonders what it means. Shows writing to husband who is bouncing the baby. He reads the letter with attending difficulties but we learn from their expression that they are not exactly satisfied but glad the baby is to benefit when it comes of age. Both shake Aunt's hand and wife takes the baby, lovingly. It will be worth ten thousand some day, soon. They go out concealing their personal pique but glad for baby's sake. Lawyer escorts them to the door. The teamster has opened his letter but cannot understand. Aunt tells lawyer to explain. He is told he is to receive fifty dollars a month until he dies. He goes to Aunt Jenny and bows in gratitude. Aunt Jenny pats his hand and is affected by his response. He leaves tearfully happy. The brother fumbles his envelope and looks askance at his sister. She waves him to proceed. He opens the envelope and sees only a blank piece of paper. Turns it over, looks in envelope again and around the chair. All are watching him. Brother finally bursts out laughing and goes to Aunt Jenny. Shakes her hand in mock ceremony as "Queen," then laughingly goes toward door. Is about to leave, when Aunt Jenny signals lawyer to stop him. Brother returns wonderingly, though still mirthful. His kindly sister also starts laughing. And all join in. Lawyer offers the brother another envelope but he smilingly refuses. Aunt Jenny insists and her brother opens and reads contents of letter. He cannot believe contents of letter. Nor will he accept such generosity. He slowly shakes his head, tears come to his eyes as he tears up his signed portion. Lawyer tries to stop him, but the brother goes over to Jenny and kisses her hand. Pats her cheek and slowly walks out. Aunt Jenny tells Mr. Jones to rewrite the apportionment and mail it to her brother. The little girl, by Aunt's side, looks on in wonderment. Lawyer tells her that the home and ground and all that is on it is hers with money to keep it with. Both Aunt Jenny and girl cry, in each other's arms. Lawyer is leaving. Shakes Aunt Jenny's hand, when she pulls an envelope from back of her and gives it to him. He laughs, opens it and is surprised. A ten-thousand-dollar check. He starts to return to thank her, but with one look from Aunt Jenny, he leaves the room.

4 men, 4 ladies, 1 baby

137. In Location

A mountain cabin has recently been occupied. An old trapper comes sauntering in and throws down his kit and gun. He puts them on the table at center. He gets out his pipe and is ready to strike a match when a pretty, vivacious girl runs in and almost embraces the trapper before she realizes she is not alone. She is followed by a cameraman, who comes in rather sulkily. He is surprised to see the trapper sitting at the table. Almost throws the camera at him. Trapper looks at man and girl and slowly procures his gun. Cameraman orders both girl and trapper over to window and tells trapper to put his gun down. Tells him to hold girl in his arms and kiss her several times, while she pretends to faint. Girl droops limp in trapper's arms as he looks stupefied. Cameraman comes to them and shows trapper how to hold girl and what to do. Girl takes trapper's arm and puts it around her waist and then falls limp. Trapper is about to kiss the girl when a mountaineer comes in. He, too, is surprised. Asks cameraman who the trapper is. Both girl and cameraman look from trapper to mountaineer; then the girl begins laughing. The real actor has just arrived and they are in the cabin of the trapper! All laugh except the trapper. He does not enjoy being laughed at. He picks up his gun and orders them out. They back up, but girl is not to be denied. She goes over to trapper, puts gun down and kisses him and then offers hand. He gradually relents, joins them in their laughter. Offers them the use of the cabin. They are getting set for picture, with trapper looking on, as curtain falls.

(The usual lights required to take an interior are unnecessary in this set, because of the brilliant sunlight flooding the room.)

3 men, 1 lady

138. His First Appearance

Terry, a young high school graduate of the olden days, comes out as a major-domo of senior festivities. The parents have been invited. The program is to be given with all its ribboned frills and thrills. Terry comes to the front of the stage and looks around with confident smiles. Jim, his chum, is nervous. Terry's suspender is hanging loose on one side. Jim writes a little note on the program and sidles to Terry and places it in his palm. Terry is giving welcome to all present when he glances at the note. He colors, looks aside and sees a swinging elastic band. He stands sidewise to the audience. He reads the program, at least he starts to read it, when his little brother climbs up the stage steps and picks up the dangling suspender and holds it out to Terry. Terry takes suspender in his hand and pushes little brother away. Terry pushes him so hard that he falls and it attracts attention of audience to him. Terry whispers to Jim and Jim disappears. Suddenly the lights go out. Brother ceases crying and when Terry says "Please turn the lights on," the lights go on. Little Brother is walking off with a fifty-cent piece and the suspender has disappeared. Terry motions to Miss Sweetface at the piano that now it is her opportunity.

3 men, supers

139. The Model

A beautiful girl is posing for "Carmen" and is tired from the long sitting. The painter comes over to her and raises her chin a little—she has changed the attitude. She is so tired—but she must smile, capriciously. A fly bothers her and she tries to get it off her nose without breaking pose. The artist sees she is restless but does not know real reason. She grabs in front of her and he throws down brush and comes to her again. He is angry—almost enough to strike her, but she defies him. He walks quickly away from her, studies her—is sorry—comes back, hesitates and takes her in his arms—just as her husband comes into the room. Of course he is astonished and furious. He comes in menacingly toward the artist. Painter thinks quickly. Holds out hand to husband who refuses. The artist turns to girl and pushes her into her husband's arms and poses them identically as the husband caught his wife and the artist. The girl comprehends and plays up to the situation. Tells husband that the artist was trying to get her to look as if she adored—now she can look that way. Husband is somewhat mollified and stands hesitant. Artist goes to new easel and hurriedly sketches both, fixing the position of the model. Shows sketch to husband and thanks him for wife's inspiration. She looks at the artist knowingly. She goes to closet and changes clothes. Artist offers money to husband but he refuses it indignantly. He is delighted if he has been able to help. Wife comes out and clings to arm of husband. Artist invites husband to come to-morrow, too, but he won't be able to. The wife can come though. They part merrily.

2 men, 1 lady

140. His Last Stake

The room is dark, save for a dim stand-lamp. The door at back is slowly opened and a young man comes cautiously in. Closes door quietly and locks it. Takes off the handkerchief that covers his face, puts it in his hat and throws it on chair. Goes to table center and stands listening. Satisfied that all is quiet. Takes a bundle of greenbacks from his coat pocket and thumbs them. Takes a handful of checks and currency from another pocket. Sorts out the checks from the currency and goes to fireplace with checks. Pulls out his cigarette lighter and starts pile of crumpled checks to burning. His young wife is standing in the doorway, in a kimono. She realizes for the first time that her husband is a burglar. She watches him burn the checks to the last ashes, separate the charred remains, and sees him give big sigh of relief. Man gets up and turns toward table as he sees his wife. She stands crying, but accusingly. When he is first aware of her presence, he drops his hand to his gun holster, but changes to gesture of wiping off his hands. He goes quickly to her, kisses her and shows her the money on the table. He tells her he won it all at cards, but is now through forever. He has made his pile. Takes pile of greenbacks and puts them in her hands, then he takes them from her. Adds loose bills to pile. Then shows his wife two tickets. They are going west tomorrow! He embraces her, and she puts her arms around him, but lets her hand rest on the revolver. He takes her hand away and tries to get her to go to their room. She asks for the gun and he refuses to show it. She sees his crumpled handkerchief in his hat on the chair. She picks it up and sees it has been tied at the ends, as we do when tying on a mask. She holds it up to him and he takes it quickly, unfolds and wipes his brow. She goes to the fireplace and looks down at paper ashes. Husband comes to her and assures her he got the money playing cards. She goes to table and weeps bitterly. He is trying to get her to go to bed when a sharp ring from the door bell is heard. He instinctively puts his hand on his gun and his wife sees. They both look at each other. He starts for the bedroom, motioning silence. He looks around room as he moves, takes hat from chair. Wife slowly goes to door —as insistent bell rings. She opens the door expecting the police. A messenger boy gives her a telegram. She signs the slip dazedly and walks to armchair, sinking into it. Husband comes carefully from bedroom, over to her, after looking out through the curtains. Takes envelope from her, opens hurriedly by lamp and reads. Face brightens. His brother invites them to use their cottage by the sea, can they come? Husband kneels down by wife and shows her the telegram. She reads indifferently; he is excitedly happy and is leading her on in his dreams of a summer's joy—when a loud knock is heard at the door. Problem.

2 men, 1 lady

141. The Old Ladies' Home

Five sweet old ladies are seated in the Home. Tilda, Bridget, Yvette, Sarah, and Rosita. They all cling somewhat to their Swedish, Irish, French, English, and Spanish rearing. Their clothes and actions would proclaim them. They are sewing, reading, and generally busy. Each thinks herself superior to the others. A bell rings and all look at the door and then at each other. All work ceases. Tilda rises and goes slowly to the door. All arise as Tilda opens the door. They are very surprised to see Jemimah, a buxom old darky, come bouncing into the room with a mouth of assuring smiles. Jemimah puts her bundles down and looks at them all. She smiles and seems to say, "Heah ah is, and heah ah intends to stay." They had never had to solve the color problem before and the Home had nearly been disrupted on race lines only recently. The old ladies all sit down opposite Jemimah. They have never felt so near to each other before. They seem to understand each other now. Rosita and Bridget are the first to express themselves. Rosita begins crying and gathers her sewing materials; Bridget stands up and walks twice across the room. She has words to say but she is too much of a lady. Sarah is the odd one—she is the only one who sleeps alone. Can it be—? It is now her turn for concerned thinking. She rises quickly, goes out and returns triumphant with the news: "Girls, meet the new cook." Jemimah is beamed upon and they all accompany her to the kitchen. Bridget gathers up her parcels and carries them out.

(Each character should endeavor to establish national traits, without use of dialect.)

6 ladies

142. The Stowaway

A sixteen-year-old girl is hiding in the ship's stokehole. She is dressed in overalls and khaki shirt. She has just awakened. It is dark and she is cold. A light slowly enlarges and she is sitting on coal. She sees a large rat. Impulse to scream, but stifles it. Throws a coal at rat and watches it run to darkness. A great beam of light is suddenly thrown on her and a large man stands staring at her. He stoops and grabs her two wrists, standing her up. He raises his arm to strike her, but she pulls off cap and reveals her curls. He is further surpised. Looks at her closely. Convinced she is a girl. He starts away, she pleads with him not to tell of her whereabouts but to help her get to Cuba. He hesitates. They both hear voices. An officer is approaching. He looks in coal hole, as man pushes girl back into the darkness. Officer asks man what he is doing there, man gets bar and starts coal down the chute, smiling. Officer starts away, as girl screams. Man and officer see several rats run through the beam of light. They look at each other. Man grabs girl and brings her out into light. Officer looks at both accusingly. Girl protests man's innocence of any responsibility. Officer orders man to the captain's quarters. Problem.

2 men, 1 lady

143. *The Manicurist*

A pretty girl is in a booth connected with a barber shop. A Hollywood sheik comes in with all his manneristic glory. He sits down and puts out a very effeminate hand. He flirts in his most seductive manner. Girl is patient but sheik-proof. He tries to "en-palm" her, but both hands are kept busy. She hurries the operation and uses the pumice roughly, the file rapidly, and the absorbent daubily. But he is satisfied, he has won another heart—at least to his own satisfaction. She gives him his check in almost a miff. He tips her a dollar bill. That partially mollifies her. A big butter-and-egg man enters, with a standing-broad grin. He is conscious of every gesture and movement. When girl takes his hand, he is almost speechless. There are dirt and callouses and the girl despairs of an artistic job. She washes and powders his hands and paints a little face on each thumb nail. He is delighted. He, too, has made an impression. He tips her ten cents and backs out. A business man enters, unfolds his paper, and reads through entire manicuring. Pays his bill without once seeing girl. Leaves a dollar and goes out reading the sports page. Girl looks at dollar tip, the ten-cent tip and the fifty cents' change. Men are such brutes!

3 men, 1 lady

144. Her First Bob

A young lady seats herself in the barber chair. She sees all kinds of eyes looking at her and thinks they focus upon her. As the barber reaches across her to put on the covering cloth, she thought he came unnecessarily close to her. She was about to mention it, but thought better of it. The barber was endeavoring to choke her, but she suffered that also, and adjusted her neck the best she could. The barber raises the scissors up to her ear—she nearly faints but grabs his hand and shows him a much lower mark. He combs her hair and it reaches down a good distance. She takes her tresses and affectionately fingers their silken thicknesses. A man is looking at her and winks. Men are such crude things. What right had he—but then, he buried his head in a newspaper. She remembered she was in a barber shop. She sat back once more and shut her eyes. The barber cut the first full lock, the next, the next, and then fully across. She opens her eyes and looks up into the mirror. Her first inclination was to grab her skirts, she felt so exposed. The barber laid the long locks over her lap. He trimmed her bangs as she peered through alternate eyes. He recut the ends of her hair. Each cut seemed to rob her more of nature's necessary covering. Her hair was parted, was on one side. She would never like that. But she is told it is the style. Well, leave it then. She got out of the chair, light-headed. The same bold man was laughing at her. How dared he! She was going out defiant, when a strange voice called her back. Everybody was looking. The lady had forgotten to pay. Of course. No, thanks—they could keep the change, but kindly give her her locks of hair. Thanks.

2 men, 1 lady, supers

145. An Old Problem

Two people had been alone on a desert isle for nearly a year. He was handsome and poor; she was pretty and rich. But he had saved their lives, after the shipwreck. He had taught her to cook, to make her clothes, to make fire, to build, to hunt, to find roots and berries. He was good to look at. She was pretty, he admitted, but she had too long spurned his suit and had openly insulted him just before the shipwreck. A year had meant much to both. He stood watching her happiness in honest work. He was worried. He admitted to himself that he loved her, he knew that she loved him. But what would their lives be in a city, should they be rescued? He so poor and she so rich? She is cooking some tubers and rabbits. What a picture she is! From time to time she looks up at him, singing and rapturous in the content of her lot. She puts the meal on wooden platters, comes up to him and leans on his arm. They look out into the sea; each knows what the other is thinking. He puts his arm about her and she raises her face to his. He looks deep into her eyes, but does not trust his love, for fear of the future. The future! Even as he raises his head, he sees a great five-master. He presses her close to his heart; so it almost crushes her and she looks up to see the struggle within him. She sees, too, but places her hands over his eyes. He looks at her, one undecided moment, then dashes at the fire, picks up a brand, and waves it in the doorway. The girl tries to pull it down, but he waves madly. They are seen and a rocket is fired to let them know. He stands waiting, depressed. She sinks to the floor, weeping. Wouldn't he understand? They are both silent for a few minutes. He stoops and slowly raises her to her feet. She looks up at him with a last pleading glance. A sailor is seen coming up the beach. He waves a welcome hand. They both answer, half-heartedly. Sailor comes to the door. He looks for others and is surprised to see no more. Man tells him that he and the girl are all. Sailor shakes hands with both and asks them to follow him. The man starts, but the girl refuses to go. Both men are surprised. Sailor starts back and grabs her by the wrist and starts to pull her with him. Man stops him. Sailor releases girl and looks again at both. Girl steps to sailor and whispers in his ear. Sailor looks at man, smiles, then laughs heartily. He slaps the man on the back and runs down the beach. Man asks what she said but she refuses to tell. He picks the girl up and she fights back at him, as he starts toward the sea. In desperation, she whispers in his ear. He stops, looks at her, smiles, kisses her tenderly and puts her down. They stand and wave the sailor a good-by. They watch him get on the ship and see another rocket burst in air. Was the problem solved?

2 men, 1 lady

146. The Gardener

An old Dutch gardener comes into his little plot of ground and sprinkles the flowers. He goes to his bird-cage and talks with his little dove. He feeds it some cake crumbs, watching to see that he is not seen. He loves his bird and almost caresses it. Two boys with a gun go by and the old man stops to talk with them. He gives each of them a tulip. He touches the gun and playfully cautions them. They laugh and disappear. He stoops down to the violets. A shot is heard. He looks around but can see no one. Trims his rose tree and then comes back to his birdcage. He whistles to his bird, but it remains as if sleeping. He shakes the cage and the little dove falls over on its back, dead. The gardener opens the cage, not daring to believe. But the little bird is lifeless. Tears fill his eyes and he looks off in direction taken by the boys. He shakes his head sadly and under the rose tree digs a little grave. He caresses the little body and reverently covers it with rose petals and new earth. He stands looking at the empty cage as the boys pass on opposite side of street. He starts to call to them. They laugh. But he checks his words. He turns to the little cage and then kneels by the rose tree. He picks some violets and puts them in cage. Tears blur his eyes as he looks down the street where boys have disappeared. He leaves his garden with heavy step.

1 man, 2 boys

147. The Night's Adventure

A mother comes from a table and takes medicine to her sick girl. It is late night and they are alone. Mother lifts up the head of the girl and gives her last of the medicine from a spoon. It is not enough. The child drops her head heavily, looks at mother and smiles. The mother takes her daughter's hand and caresses it, tears are in her eyes, the empty bottle is in her lap. The clock strikes four. There is a footstep at the door and a young man enters. He is surprised to see the woman up. They both stand speechless. He is the druggist of the corner store below. That he should want to rob a widow! The young girl turns her head and sees the druggist. She smiles and looks toward the empty bottle. Mother understands and slowly offers the bottle to him. He backs toward door, uncertain. He, too, comprehends. He grabs the bottle, reads the printed instructions on label, smells the bottle and then hurries over to the girl. He looks into her eyes, then takes up her limp arm and feels her pulse. He looks at the anxious mother, and hurries from the room with a determined look. He puts his cap further over his eyes as he puts the bottle in his pocket. The mother comes back into the room and follows him to the door, watching him down the steps. She goes back to her daughter, as she looks at the clock. The girl is motionless. Mother gets up and goes over to the street-window. Looks down to lamplit street. A person is hurrying up to her doorway, but passes on. Why doesn't the druggist come? As mother leans over her daughter, hurrying feet come up stairway and young druggist enters. He opens and closes door quickly. He stands and listens for a brief time, and comes to the mother and gives her the bottle filled with the precious medicine. The druggist stands near the bed, holding upper arm as if in pain. The mother with eyes only for her child, takes the medicine with trembling hands and pours a teaspoon full and prayerfully gives it to her daughter. The girl arouses sufficiently to swallow but remains motionless. The mother watches intensely, the young man has kept his attention almost entirely on the door. A hurried knock startles both and the druggist cautions mother for silence. He gets down in back of bed; the mother goes to the door and a detective enters. He has gun in hand. Looks around and sees a drop of blood on the carpet floor. Stoops down and pulls out handkerchief, which he rubs over the spot. His kerchief is stained. He sees another drop leading toward the bed and walks in that direction. Mother unconsciously betrays hiding place of druggist. Detective tells the robber to stand up. Druggist does so slowly, but is weak from loss of blood. Detective pulls him closer to light. Surprised to see he is druggist, whom he knows. Robbing his own boss! The girl moves her arm and opens her eyes. Mother goes quickly to her. Detective keeps druggist covered as he puts manacles on him. Mother is almost overcome with joy as her girl revives slowly and regains her smile once more. The crisis is over. As she looks at the men, she sees them moving toward the door. In desperation, she takes the bottle of medicine, shows it to officer and points to her girl. She pleads with officer that the young druggist has saved her daughter's life. He had got the medicine for her! Officer searches druggist and finds no plunder or gun. Sits druggist on chair and takes his coat off, after he has removed the manacles. He asks for water and bandages as the curtain falls.

2 men, 2 ladies

148. The Parlor of Old

Hyrum has called on Tabitha and they are entering the sacred front room. It has a whatnot, a family album, the old red plush sofa and several enlarged pictures in great gold frames hung around the walls. A bioscope, with pictures, is on the oak center table. Hyrum has on a checked suit, high collar, wears long hair parted in the middle. His lapel rose is a large one. Tabitha has rats in her back hair, leg-of-mutton sleeves in her plaid waist and her skirt comes to her ankles. They both are sweetly ill at ease. She takes the farthest side of sofa and arranges skirt for propinquitous company. He sits in center of sofa. He has a do-or-die look. From his spacious side pocket he brings a large package of musks and peppermints. He pours a few of the dainties between them as a common vantage ground. She selects a musk and he honors her selection by doing likewise. She becomes a little bold and puts piece of candy in his mouth. He nearly wilts under such delicious intimacy but is strong enough to reciprocate. For a moment, they are muskily at ease. He piles the peppermints one on the other and she takes the musks for her building. They soon are laying a plan for a house. She blushes, as she catches his idea. They rearrange the plan again and have five rooms, as that is all the candy he has. The close proximity of their hands is such exquisite emotional pleasure! Such sweet association! She opens the house by taking three musks and putting them in her mouth. That was a good joke! He tears down the kitchen and puts several peppermints in his mouth. As he inhales, his throat is cool, so he draws a deep breath. He nearly freezes. She must try it. One by one he places the peppermints in her dainty mouth, then he asks her to inhale. She nearly chokes. Wasn't it fun? just to be pepperminting together. They have disposed of all but the last room when Lizzie comes sidling in and goes to her sister. This is not a welcome interruption, as Hyrum is now just one room away from Tabitha and is really working up to a popping point. Lizzie is insistent. Hyrum gives Lizzie the remaining room of candy and suggests she go out in the dining room to eat them. Tabitha urges her also. Lizzie is uncertain but goes out. The house is no longer between the two and Tabitha moves a little toward Hyrum. There is an awkward silence. Then the family album saves the embarrassing situation. As they turn the pages, their heads almost touch and their hands commingle. They are doing famously until—why do parents take pictures of their babies so devoid of clothing? Tabitha turns that page quickly but Hyrum is only a mortal and turns it back. Is that she? What a pretty back a baby has and—but Tabitha closes the book and puts it aside. That picture almost disrupted a future home. She is chagrined. To think that Hyrum has seen—she turns away from him. As he apologizes for his boldness he comes closer to her. He leans over her shoulder, his hand sinks in the billows of her leg-of-mutton sleeve. Ardently he assures her he wouldn't offend her. She gradually wilts under his pleading and to his joyous surprise she leans herself back into his arms and looks trustingly into his eyes. This is his golden opportunity. He hovers over her lips—as Lizzie comes in for more candy. Problem.

1 man, 2 ladies

149. The Girl and the Ring

The girl, Amita, is a beautiful American type. She is expecting some one. She sits in a large *chaise longue* and reads, but it is fitful reading. Glances at wrist watch. Throws novel down and picks up magazine. A bell is heard in the distant hall. She puts down the magazine and walks casually toward the door. Henry, a young man of handsome mien, enters. They greet as lovers do and walk to lounge. The fellow is apparently nervous. He takes a box from his pocket and gets a platinum ring, with emerald. Amita is vivacious in her excitement. He said he would bring it and he did. He takes her hand and puts the ring on it. They kiss tenderly. The bell rings again. The girl ignores but the man is greatly concerned. John, the ardent suitor of Amita, and employer of Henry, walks familiarly into the room. He is followed by a detective. Amita and Henry rise. Amita goes to John and demands an explanation, why the intimate intrusion? John just looks at her, then goes over to Henry and looks at him. Henry outstares him at first, then drops his head in shame. Amita does not understand. John takes out a check and shows it to her. A forgery. For a thousand dollars. John notices the ring and takes Amita's finger. He looks at her, then Henry. She withdraws her hand and goes to Henry. He takes her hand and looks at forged check in John's hand. John motions detective, who comes forward to Henry. Amita stands in front of Henry, withdraws the ring and gives it to the detective. She orders him out of the house. He looks at John for orders. John tells him to take Henry away. Detective and Henry start to go out as Amita pleads with John. He offers her the ring on his own behalf. She spurns his offer; he presses his offer further. Amita is furious and goes to Henry, weeping on his shoulder. As Henry starts to leave, John stops them, tells detective to go. Detective leaves. John walks over to Henry and tears up the check, giving Henry the torn bits. He offers Henry the ring, which Henry firmly but kindly refuses. John takes Amita's hand and starts to put ring on her finger, but she, too, refuses. John puts ring in his pocket, offers his hand to Amita and she shakes it wholeheartedly. John offers his hand to Henry, who takes it eagerly but avoids the eyes of John. John looks at Amita once more, shakes his head, and leaves hurriedly.

Amita and Henry stand staring at each other, as—Problem.

3 men, 1 lady

150. *Charity*

Two cripples meet. One is also blind. They bump each other. Both are inclined to strike back. Each is too eager to retaliate. The blind man knows where to strike and the lame man straightens up too obviously for consistency. The lame man hobbles away a few feet and the blind man turns around to see his bumpee. The lame man begins laughing and the blind man joins him. They are laughing heartily as the blind man sees a well-dressed lady approaching. He signals his new-found companion. The lame man pitifully leads the helpless blind, a sight sad enough to bruise any heart. The lady approaches and is touched. She gives the blind man a dollar and goes away happy. The blind man reaches into his pocket, gets a fifty-cent piece and gives it to the lame. They both go off, whistling a duet. The combination is successful.

2 men, 1 lady

151. *The Old Lady and the Sheriff's Order*

A weary old lady comes into her little room. It is sparsely furnished with furniture of years ago, but homelike. She has been crying. She sees a letter on the center table. She procures her spectacles from her bag and tremblingly reads. It is an order for eviction. She can't comprehend at first, but gradually understands. She is to be put out of her little home after twenty years. The new landlord needs the room and could she pay for the last five years' rent? She weeps helplessly and sits in her comfortable rocker, as a banging knock is heard on the door. Two men come in, each a burly. The larger one shoves a piece of paper in her face for a few seconds and then starts carrying her furniture out of the door. The old lady sees her two chairs taken and her table about to go. She rouses herself and tries to stop the men from taking the table. They brush her aside. She goes from piece to piece with them, helpless. They take her one big rug, almost tripping her as she stands on it. They take all but her little bed and candlestick. They thrust another piece of paper in her hand. It is a green piece of paper, but her eyes are too blurred to read. She sits on her bed, broken-hearted. She must move—where? A timid knock is heard on the door; she pays no heed. The knock is repeated louder. Still she does not answer. The door is slowly opened and a young girl enters. She puts out both arms, as she cries "Mother." She hastens to her mother and buries her head in her lap. Mother pushes her head back, in order to see the better. Can it be—It is her baby girl, now such a woman! She hugs her closely and cries happily. Girl rises, helps her up, and walks with her from the room.

2 men, 2 ladies

152. An Oriental Mart

A very beautiful girl, accompanied by a young American, enter a Chinese noodle store. The girl, Jane, is vivacious and intensely interested. She goes to a booth and pulls the young man after her. He is interested in her but not in the menu. They seat themselves at the table, opposite each other. The girl is too elaborately dressed and her jewels are expensive. The pendant and rings are especially conspicuous. A Chinese waiter comes to them and shows them the menu. He examines the jewels with more than passing interest. The girl orders noodles and the man repeats the order. The Chinese proprietor enters and asks after their comfort. He takes note of the jewels. The young man quietly takes notice of the scene, while appearing interested only in the girl. As the proprietor leaves, the waiter enters with a teapot and cups. He pours a cup for each and stands watching them. Man looks at him and the waiter leaves. Girl puts sugar in tea, but man wishes none. He takes up his cup and smells the steaming aroma. The waiter enters with bowls of noodles and places one before each. He puts the teacups close to each plate. He goes out. The girls sips her tea and almost immediately becomes faint. She tries to laugh lightly, wondering at the strange feeling coming over her. She tries to fight off the feeling and tries to eat some of the noodles. Her eyes close and she lays her head gently on the table. The man pours his tea into the bowl of noodles and then lays his head on the table—as if they were both in a stupor. The proprietor looks in cautiously and seeing both Americans in stupor, he motions for the waiter. They both come carefully into room and stand over the girl. They ignore the man. The proprietor unclasps the pendant and puts it in his pocket. He has the waiter slip rings off girl's fingers, while he watches the doorway. The girl stirs and the proprietor pulls out a large silk handkerchief, on which he pours some liquid from a vial. As girl relaxes again into heavy stupor, the rings are removed and proprietor puts all the jewels in a small black silk container. This he pins on the inner folds of the booth-curtain, high up against the wall. At a signal, the waiter lies across the one corner of the table, in a very limp condition. Proprietor musses up the table and removes the tea things to the next booth. He scratches the forehead of the waiter with his long finger nails. The stage is set now—everything looks very disheveled. The proprietor suddenly assumes an excited air and hurries to the door, calling for help. A "convenient" officer rushes in with him and is shown the three people. The woman is first straightened out and slowly revives. The proprietor pours her a glass of water. She drinks and looks around. The officer arouses the young man, who is slower in reviving. He looks around in a dazed manner. The girl comes to him, thoroughly frightened. The officer looks at waiter and sees the bleeding forehead. The two Americans stand, waiting for developments. Proprietor offers them every assistance. As Chinese waiter arouses, he staggers about the room and holds his head. His face is drawn in pain. He gesticulates that two big men had come in and smothered the two Americans and then, as he entered the booth, he was overcome and struck a severe blow in the head. Proprietor is dumbfounded and most solicitious. Waiter collapses again, sitting in chair. The girl discovers the loss of her jewels. Both she and the young man are now thoroughly frightened. The officer takes out his book and pencil. Records what he sees, what has been said. He shakes the waiter and gets him on his feet. Is going to take him as witness. Gets to door and asks the two Americans to go with him. They readily comply and young man asks that the proprietor go also. Policeman said he intended to have him all the time. Blows his whistle for the patrol, which is unexpectedly near. As proprietor passes the doorway, the young man goes to the curtain of the booth, unpins the jewel bag and shows it to the Chinese proprietor. As proprietor looks at young man, he notices a detective badge which the American is revealing for the first time. Detective pats the girl on the back and they both draw out revolvers to aid the policeman in his round-up. Proprietor walks out with them with all the dignity of the Orient.

4 men, 1 lady

153. *The Serenade*

Carmencita, a beautiful dancer, is being married to Don Alvaro, a wealthy landowner. Carmen does not love Alvaro, but has given her heart surreptitiously to Manuel, a shepherd. The night is a glorious one and a dance is being given in honor of the nuptials. The domineering father, Alonzo, is seen to welcome four guests, and a servant escorts them to the inner garden. The ladies go left and the gentlemen join a small group near the veranda on the right. The strum of guitar and mandolin is heard in the distance. A courtly couple enter and Alonzo gives them especial welcome. He signals to the house and dispatches a servant to the ladies' group. Don Alvaro has arrived, with his elderly father and mother. The men greet affectionately. A young girl, richly gowned, comes down from crowd and the new arrivals bow to her with deepest respect. Carmen is dressed in white satin, with a black lace shawl over her shoulders. Alvaro steps forward and gracefully takes Carmen's hand and leads her to his mother. The girl bows for the parental blessing, the older lady stoops and kisses her on the forehead. Alvaro's father does likewise. Carmen is courteous but listless in the ceremony. Don Alonzo bows the others in and takes Donna and Don Alvaro senior to the archway center, as Alvaro bows Carmen to the ladies' group and then joins the men. There is a stir among the men as Don Alvaro mingles with them. He is highly respected, because of his power. It is evident he is not popular for himself. The father, Alonzo, enters and bids all welcome to the dance pavilion. The ladies cross stage and with their chaperons, join the gentlemen for the dance. The music strikes up a lively Spanish tune and the couples disappear further through the archway. Save for the occasional glimpses of passing couples, dancing, and the hurrying of a servant bent on some errand, the scene is devoid of people. Manuel, a tall handsome man, attired as a shepherd, appears cautiously at the lower right. He moves as one watched, or unbidden. The servant passes and spies Manuel. He looks quickly about and comes to Manuel and tells him to hurry off as the master had given special orders to forbid him entrance. Manuel pleads with the servant to tell Carmencita of his presence. The servant is given a silver coin, hesitates, is urged again, and doubtfully goes to the merry crowd.

Manuel hurries to a clump of bushes, as a belated couple arrive, go to the archway, and are met by a house servant. Carmencita hurries through the archway, frightened but joyous. Manuel comes from the shrubbery and runs to her. They meet and embrace fervently. Manuel draws her to the side but she urges him to go, fearing violence if he is detected. The faithful servant stands at watch on the dancing side. A waltz is heard and Carmencita begs Manuel to go. But he cannot, he will not, not without one last dance with her. The servant trembles with anxiety and gesticulates for Manuel to leave. But Manuel swings her into the dance and she resigns herself to the joy of one last dance with the man she loves. It is an exotic farewell, a madness of precious moments. Their lips meet as the dance is ending and Manuel presses her once more to his heart, as Don Alvaro pushes the servant aside and stands, challengingly, in the center of the archway. The dancers stand as if paralyzed. Alvaro walks slowly toward them and the crowd is seen to close about the back of the scene. Alvaro looks Carmencita over, from head to foot, with the utmost contempt. At Manuel, he glares in anger, and strikes him, flathanded, across the cheek. The father comes tardily in and sees Manuel. He, too, is enraged and goes toward Carmencita with uplifted arms. Alvaro stands, not intending to interfere, but Manuel, who is still debating his best course to resent the slap of Alvaro, stands in front of Carmen and defies Alonzo. Still further enraged, the father draws a dagger and strikes quickly at Manuel. But the knife does not pierce Manuel, as Carmen throws herself in front of her beloved and is struck to the heart. In a spasm of pain, she throws herself upon Manuel and drops limp in his arms. The crowd is terrified, unbelieving, and some run from the tragedy. The father drops the dripping dagger, dazed, and falls in a kneeling position at Manuel's feet. Alvaro has taken out a small revolver and is getting in a position to shoot Manuel, when two men guests seize his arm. They stand as if fixed, watching the favored lover carry his dead love through the archway.

4 men, 3 ladies, supers

154. Cronies

Two old cronies, Jock Mackaye and Rory O'Brien, are playing checkers in the Golden Gate Park. They are in a quiet portion of the park, though passers-by are not infrequent. Jock has made a move with the red, which delights him and puzzles Rory. Jock sits back for a long session and begins to unfold his paper. This nettles Rory who moves quickly and cockily defies his companion. He pulls out his pipe as if for a prolonged pull. Jock is somewhat nonplused and sits down in a brown study. A fly bothers Jock considerably. It is that specie which continually buzzes in front of nose or eye, without quite lighting. Rory enjoys this and puffs in speculation. A young lady passes by and when Jock starts to notice, Rory points to the board, as if that demanded all of Jock's attention. Rory follows the young lady some distance down the path—with his eyes, more for Jock's benefit. Jock is really puzzled as to his next move. Rory seems to have him cornered. He gets up and turns around three times and with eyes shut, runs his index finger toward the board. Opens his eyes to see if a hunch will follow. Evidently the worst place on the board to look for any inspiration. Rory slowly pulls the paper from Jock's lap, who lets it go reluctantly. Rory turns to the "funnies" and enjoys one especially. Jock asks for silence. Rory laughs, but very restrainedly. Their very mutual friend, Miss Wilkins, comes up to the board. She is all smiles, laces, and little movements. She smells of lavender; that is how Rory knew first that she was coming. Both men are ardent suitors. Both arise, though Miss Wilkins bows graciously and asks them to continue the game. Jock is chagrined at his plight on the board and in offering her his seat, he purposely knocks his coat against the solid park table and swishes most of the men from their places. Rory is indignant, but smiles as Miss Wilkins looks at him. Jock stacks the men, one upon the other and shares the seat with Miss Wilkins. Rory walks off several feet and openly indulges in a contemptuous tirade against Jock. To think that a man could risk his honor, even for a woman. Miss Wilkins realizes that her coming has in some way estranged the friends. She rises and Jock insists that she stay. Rory, too, is interested, but has other things on his mind. Jock offers Miss Wilkins a stick of candy, and has much fun in the presentation. She accepts, but notices that Rory is not offered any. She puts the candy in her vanity bag, which is already a copious carrier. Out of this bag, she takes two snapshots; she smiles admiringly at each man, and gives one to each of them. She has written something on each picture. Before the men can read her message, she bids good-by and scampers off. Both try to stop her but she pays no heed. Jock and Rory look at their pictures. Each smiles triumphantly at the affectionate greeting on his picture. Jock is especially pleased. He has won the maid! Her picture and affectionate greeting is doubly assuring. He straightens his tie and correctly angles his hat. What cares he for checkers? While brushing off his shoes, he lays the picture face up so Rory may see, but not obtain. Rory accepts the opportunity and steals a glance at the picture, then more interestedly at the writing. He looks at his own in comparison and begins to laugh uproariously. Jock is first puzzled, then vexed. Why should Rory laugh at Miss Wilkins because of her choice for Jock! Rory places his picture alongside Jock's. They are identical in pose, finish, and inscription! Jock is embarrassed at his previous jubilance and doesn't enjoy the joke. Rory suddenly stops laughing, points at the checkerboard with all his old-time fire. Why did Jock wipe the men from the board? Because he had lost, lost fairly. So Rory takes out his knife, and cuts one more niche in his pipe bowl—one more victory over Jock Mackaye! Jock is furious and leans over the table, shaking his fist at Rory. Rory shakes back; their faces almost touch. Jock grabs Rory by the coat collar and shakes Rory vigorously. Rory knocks his hand off and gets Jock by the nose. He intends to tweak it with malicious vigor, but Jock frees his facial appendage and raises both arms with clenched fists, as to strike. But his face suddenly convulses in pain. He grabs at his heart and with no sound wilts down onto the table. Rory looks at him wonderingly, then realizes his checker friend has taken a stroke. Jock lies lifeless-like on the table. Rory takes off his hat and begins to fan his friend lovingly, but in a hopeless manner. He tries to arouse Jock. The arm he lifts falls back limp. Rory pats Jock's face and looks about for aid. He is about to call for help, when Jock opens one eye and sees that Rory is concerned. Jock moves his arm and slowly opens both eyes. Rory is on one knee, chafing Jock's limp hand. Jock, without warning, leans over and embraces Rory and holds his face. Rory looks up and gradually comprehends. There was not a doubt now of their understanding each other. They look at the pictures on the table. Jock picks them up and tears his across. Rory does the same. No woman can ever separate this Jonathan and David. They lock arms about each other, and go off whistling a cross between an Irish and Scotch jig

2 men, 1 lady

155. Love-Making

A class in acting technic has reached that place in its work when all its members are personally interested. The director has assigned "national love-making." The term is a little ambiguous until we see a young fellow respond. He gets up, procures a blanket of Navajo pattern, puts the blanket over his shoulders, puts an orange ribbon around his head, after parting his long hair in the middle. For atmosphere, a pal seats himself, cross-legged, on the floor;

a young girl is offstage, under a shawl—this represents a wikiup. The transformed buck walks solemnly before the father and bows even with his hips, holding his palms face down in front of him. Father motions a welcome to him, which is done with a hand gesture, palm facing suitor, turned to horizontal position—above a clean space on the ground. The young buck kneels in front of the father. The young fellow tells the father he wants a wife—he points to his heart, then head, and then the wikiup, concluding his request by showing five levels from the ground, meaning he wants a wife who will bear him five children, all boys. The latter idea he conveys, by having each of these five levels use a bow and arrow to represent the boy. The father looks indifferently at the suitor, who takes this as a good omen. The suitor then pantomimes that he has killed ten deer, five bear, four wolves and many geese since last winter. For the deer he uses quick movements and places his fingers apart on each side of his head. For the bears, he stands and walks with loose forearms, as does a bear when in captivity. For the wolf he shows his teeth and snarls viciously. All these skins he has for the big chief for his daughter. Father still just looks at him. The suitor pulls out a full plug of Star chewing tobacco. This interests the father who rubs his chin in contemplation. As a last item, the young buck shows a quart of whisky. The father is now interested. He reaches for the whisky, but the suitor withholds. He wants the girl first. The father claps his hands and the young girl appears. She sees the young buck and seems to understand. She walks slowly toward her father. He tells her she is to be the mother of five children and there stands the father. Her lip trembles, though she does not flinch. The young buck walks around her and looks at her teeth, then feels her back and legs. He is satisfied. He gives the father the bottle of whisky and tells him he will return in two moons for his bride. Suitor does not look again at his bride-to-be. But accepts the good wishes of the father as he goes off.

2 men, 1 lady

A modern type of American next takes the stage. A girl of nineteen sits on a couch reading *College Humor* and chewing gum. A hand is seen to come in the doorway and flick out the lights, all except the reading light. A young chap with glossed hair and bell trousers, in pseudo-cat steps comes over to the lounge and grabs the girl by the neck and, villain-like, almost strangles her with kisses. She comes up for air by sitting on his lap and looking in his pockets for candy. She finds a small box, pulls his ear and gets off his lap. She is peeved that so many kisses should compensate for so small a box. He tries to pull her on his lap again, but she is not that cheap. Laughingly, the young gallant goes over to the side table where he had put his hat and cane, and, under his hat, a two-pound box of chocolates. He brings them in humble supplication to his mate and she, in turn, almost smothers him with kisses. They sit on the lounge and eat chocolates. He gets a ring from his pocket and slips it on her finger. She looks at it, surprised, pleased, and gives him an extra hug for good measure. They are engaged. The father comes in, turns on the light, goes to the youth with a sickly smile. Evidently the father has seen the boy twice before. The father puts on his specs and unfolds his evening paper. The daughter gets up, takes her father by the ear and gently leads him to the door. He turns and scowls at the boy who is grinning with experienced assurance. The girl kisses the bald spot on her father's head with dutiful devotion and pushes him out. She closes the door, turns out the light and, in two bounds, lands on the lap of her future husband. They are engaged. They will discuss finances later. They read *Humor* together. She gets off his lap long enough for him to properly crease his trousers. She is reseated and they assume their evening of education in jokes.

2 men, 1 lady

The third scene of this class is portrayed by the Japanese. Sumato loves Geisha Muri. He has told his father and mother. Father and Mother Sumato are seen coming into the bamboo office of Nakado, the marriage broker. The Nakado is old, wise and wonderfully polite. He bows welcome to each and they all kneel on floor mats. The Nakado offers some tea and each takes the little cup's contents. The father produces a long piece of paper, which itemizes his wealth and gives his ancestry. The mother does likewise; though hers is not so very long. The Nakado runs over each list, makes some notations. He then rings a little bell on his floor desk and a young servant enters. Nakado tells him to show in the prospective suitor, son of the parents Sumatos. Young man comes in, all dignity and kimono. He inhales deeply, holds his breath for a minute, pounds his chest. He is sound of body. He takes the elbows of his seated father and lifts him from the floor. Surely the suitor is strong and healthy. His kimono is expensive, there are his parents. What else? Nakado looks at him critically, and dismisses him politely. Young Sumato retires with his parents. The servant ushers in Mr. and Mrs. Muri from the other doorway. They kneel and drink their tea. The father shows his list of properties. The mother has no list. The Nakado points to item on list. Mr. Muri produces a bag full of money. This he deposits on the little table. The Nakado smiles. With ring of bell, the servant shows in the Geisha Muri. She is beautiful and truly a "sha" girl, as she knows the art of make-up. She turns around several times, stands on one leg, then another. Bends over and touches the floor with her flat palms, without bending her knees. Shows her hands, they are not calloused. Nakado is more pleased. The girl is sent out.

The servant ushers in Mr. and Mrs. Sumato. The Muris and Sumatos bow in pleasant recognition. They drink tea again, kneeling on friendly mats. Each father scans the list of the other house. Sumato weighs the money in his palm. The Nakado verifies amount as correct. Both men turn to their wives and get their approval, which is done by a nod of the head. The men turn to the Nakado, who rises and returns each list to the respective owners. A screen is brought down by the servant and separates the two families. The servant ushers in the young Sumato and then Miss Muri. Mr. and Mrs. Sumato pass from behind the screen and view Miss Muri. She poses again. They are satisfied. They return to their former places. The screen is removed and Sumato stands poised for further inspection. Geisha Muri goes over to him and kneels before Sumato, with her veil over her face. Sumato withdraws the veil and looks upon Muri. She blushes and drops her eyes. Sumato junior is satisfied. Young Sumato leaves the room. Geisha Muri goes back of her parents. The Nakado gives Senior Sumato the bag of money. The Sumatos bow to the Nakado, sign a commission sheet for him and they leave the room. They are followed by the Muris, Geisha in the rear. They are leaving for their temple.

4 men, 3 ladies

156. The Cave

A Girl and Man have found their way to a dark cave. She is calm and positive. He is timid and, at times, frightened. They both have flashlights and pour the light around the cobwebbed room. The Girl goes to an old chest in center of cave and the Man follows. He stumbles over a large chain and stands, chattering. She tries to open chest and lid is too heavy. She motions him to open chest. He puts flash in his pocket and takes hold. As he stoops, weird shadows play on back wall, green lights, moving, look like a dragon. Man stops working at chest and falls on his knees. He comes close to the Girl, who stands unafraid. Man takes courage from her and rises trembling. Girl again tries to open the chest and Man helps. The top opens and they push it back. Out of the chest come vapor fumes and green lights play on them. The Man is terrified. The Girl and Man cling together, though the Man does most of the clinging. Two large men come swiftly from back of cave and seize the Man. He cowers before them and they carry him off bodily. The Girl closes the chest and looks around, goes to a door right, listens cautiously and then lies on the chest. She signals to back of cave and one of the big men comes in sight and unlocks the door. He hurries off. A pounding is heard on the door and it gives way. A well-built young man in chauffeur's uniform comes in as one outraged. In the dim light he sees the Girl on the chest. He comes to her and sees that she is living. Picks her up and kisses her tenderly. Girl remains limp. Chauffeur carries her around room, looking for outlet. Goes back to door, and, for first time, notices it is locked. Kicks on doorway. Puts Girl down gently in old armchair and looks for some sort of weapon. The two big men seize him from the back and he fights furiously. He downs one and almost has the other helpless, when the Girl sits up, alert and smiling. She sees the condition of her helpers and hurries over to Chauffeur. He stops his wrestling and looks at her in astonishment. The big servant floods the "cave" with light. The first Man is seen bound and gagged, and still scared, as he leans against the wall. The Girl tells servants to undo the Man. She goes close to Chauffeur and puts her arms about him. He hesitatingly responds and wonders what it is all about. The Man remonstrates. The big servant hurries the Man off, .as he opens the door. The other servant is arousing, feeling his jaw. He gets up and comes over to the couple. Offers his hand as he grins.

Both Girl and Chauffeur laugh. Servant goes out. Girl has found the man she wants to marry.

4 men, 1 lady

157. Her Own

A darkened room shows a little crib, in which lies a little child. A veiled woman comes cautiously through the nursery door. She closes the door noiselessly. She pulls cord of a floor lamp near the crib. A curly-headed girl is sleeping. The woman, who has been divorced by her husband, has stolen her way into the house to hold her baby. She stands over the beautiful child and, with her hands and eyes, acts as if she could devour the little daughter. She stands crying, feeding with her eyes a love-hunger that calls for embraces. Footsteps at door and handle moves. The mother drops back of a large rocker as nurse comes in. The nurse is surprised to see the light in stand lamp, looks around the room and goes to crib. Snuggles the baby in, turns out the light and leaves, closing the door. Only the light through the curtained window near the street remains. The mother, seeing the indifference of the nurse, desires more than ever to feel her child close to her. She stoops over the little bed and lifts the babe to her arms. A soft breathing of content, as the little girl nestles to her mother. The mother turns on the lamp again, better to enjoy her few moments of bliss. Child and mother are rocking, as the baby wakes up and sees her mother. She remembers her mother, and as in a dream, smiling peacefully, slides a little arm about her mother's neck. The mother gently rocks and cries happily. The father comes to kiss his child good-night. He stands at door, at first speechless, then viciously resentful. He strides over to the babe and almost snatches it from the frightened woman. As the mother rises, the child awakens, and cries for her. The father rings the servant bell and turns on full light. The child and mother are crying. Nurse appears, excitedly, and surprised at the presence of her former mistress. As father puts the child in nurse's arms, the mother comes to them and desires one last embrace. The husband stands before babe and nurse with folded arms, endeavoring to cow the mother. The mother at first pleads for one last kiss from her child, the nurse would comply, but the father is obdurate. He orders the nurse to take babe from the room; as they are leaving the mother runs to her babe and starts to take her. The father seizes the mother and hurls her back—the nurse leaves hurriedly, the little child holding out her hands helplessly and crying for her mother. The mother rises and stands up to a queenly height. Looks at her former husband with pity. Puts veil over her face and starts to leave. Husband comes to her and holds out his arms; she looks at him as one would a mangy dog and, head held high, she leaves the room.

1 man, 2 ladies, 1 child

158. The Employment Agency

A poorly furnished room on the East Side. A desk is seen at center of room. A bespectacled old man, nearsighted and anæmic, works back of the desk. A long bench is on the side and one at back of room. It is the employment agency for the deaf. A Swedish laborer is the first to be seen by the desk. A helper, a small active fellow, keeps a certain kind of order and ushers the prospects to their respective seats. As one leaves the end seat, all move up a seat nearer. The morning sun plays through the worn blind. The Swede shades his eyes from the sun and reads a questionnaire. All is done in action. He tells that he can shovel, has strong muscles, can hammer with sledge hammer, has big strong hands. He is looking around for something to break when clerk stops him and has him write his name and address on questionnaire. The Swede is given a ticket, looks at it, smiles, and offers to shake hands. Clerk puts out an indifferent hand and almost loses it in the vise of friendship. Clerk winces with pain and seizes inkwell as if to throw. Swede hurries out, but not until his exuberance has caused him to push back row of men off the bench. Some smile, some are peeved, and others wake up. Swede goes out laughing and the clerk also smiles at this; though he is still nursing a hand. An Italian is next to leave his seat, and all move up. The son of Italy is short and stare-eyed. He fumbles his cap. He cannot read the questionnaire given him. He takes out a flask from his pocket and offers to the clerk, who refuses. Two Irishmen and a Mexican come to him quickly and Tony shows them the label which is marked "poison." They all go back to their seats and the Mexican is shoved to end of line—but not without a small scuffle with the attendant. Mexican tries to explain that seat six was his. The Italian shows the clerk that he is a barber. Strops a razor, cuts a hair in two, cuts head of hair, all in pantomime. He can also clean finger nails. Clerk gives him an address and Italian knows numbers but attendant has to tell him how many blocks straight, right, and left before prospective job is reached. Italian pulls out a sandwich from inner pocket and goes off eating. He can afford to eat now that a job is in sight. Two Irish, partially intoxicated, come to the desk. They are good pals, and whatever the one does, pleases the other. The desk clerk looks them over and hands them the yellow sheets. Both look at the paper and laugh. The attendant asks them what they can do. They laugh again, and each shows that he could drink again. The clerk orders them out and looks toward the line. The Irish go out, arm in arm, waving their caps to occupants of the room. One pulls out a green handkerchief and they both salute, as they pass through the door. A dapper fellow shows he can typewrite, in fact he is expert. The clerk smiles and phones. The answer is agreeable. Clerk gives the stenographer an address and smiles patronizingly. Steno tips his hat and looks at card and smiles joyously. Goes out quickly. A Chinaman, still wearing pigtails, is next. He hops over with a good old Chinese swing and smiles voluminously. Clerk has nothing but Wong is not to be denied. He can wash windows. He can wash anything. He can iron, all kinds of clothes. The attendant is told to take him out to kitchen. Wong smiles continually as he goes off to employment interior. The Mexican breaks line and comes up to desk as a large Arkansas hillsman is getting up courage. The Mexican jumps in front of the hillsman and begins to gesticulate wildly. It is his turn by law of appearance. He must have a job, he is hungry, he is—the clerk looks at his watch, it is just twelve noon. He takes out a toothpick, puts it in his mouth and turns a sign over on his desk. It reads, "Gone to lunch. Back at two." He stretches, pulls out a little mirror, combs his few hairs and goes off into the interior. Attendant goes to desk, opens up a pink-sheet newspaper and puts his feet on desk—the Mexican gesticulates in vain and finally leaves in disgust. The Arkansan tries to tell the attendant that he can work, when a Negro comes in. He comes to the desk immediately and the Arkansan draws the color line and withdraws. The attendant points to sign. "Take your Turn." The Negro goes over to it and pretends to read. He leans against the wall awaiting developments. They soon happen, as a policeman swings in, gives one look at the colored boy, who immediately turns, smiles at cop, whistles and walks off in front of cop. The others stare in amazement—a crook in their domain!

12 men

159. Crumbs for Esau

Son comes dashing into his father's room all radiant and happy. He is bringing a basket of food for his father, Esau, who has sent word of his failing health. The boy, now nineteen, puts the basket down and goes toward the kitchen door. He calls and looks around. He goes toward the big chair in front of the fireplace. There is his father, sound asleep. The boy takes off his hat and puts it on the sideboard. He gets the basket of food and spreads the more tempting articles on the table, then tiptoes to his father. Blows gently in his ear and hides behind the chair. The father does not move and the boy tries again, this time squeezing Esau's arm. Still no response. The son raises his father's hand and puts in it a large apple. The arm and apple fall ominously to the side of the chair. The boy shakes the father and finally realizes he is dead. The son falls on his knees and caresses the lifeless hands; offers food as if to call back the dead. It is hard to realize the futility of his efforts. The boy goes slowly to the phone and calls for a doctor. He picks up the food near Esau and puts it in the basket on the table. He goes again to his father and pleads with him to live again; see, he has enough money for all of them. The doctor enters, makes a hasty examination, but thorough in its finality. He takes the son by the arm and persuades him to leave. The son puts his father in a comfortable position and reluctantly goes out with the doctor.

3 men

160. Another Paolo

We see the beautiful interior of a Canadian home. Through the large center window, the distant mountains rise to majestic heights, snow-capped and glistening. A handsome young man is reading the supplement of the London *Times.* He is nervous; seems to be fighting with himself. When the young wife of his brother comes into the room, he is startled. Starts to rise but changes his mind. Remains seated and appears very interested in his reading. The wife wears a velvet gown, clinging tightly to her body. She comes to the back of his chair and runs her hands across his chest and rests her head on his heavy hair. He takes her hands from him, and rises quickly. He walks toward the window and looks out, without glancing at his sister-in-law. She follows him, quizzically, and again puts her arms about him. He turns around quickly and kisses her passionately, then dashes from the room, at the left. The wife is happy; her eyes dance with her conquest. She goes to the lounging chair and picks up the supplement. She caresses it, because he had just held it. She sits, dreamily, when her rough and hearty husband comes in from the right. He is dressed for the mountains, in neat attire. His hair is thin and gray and all his manner is dominant with successful business. As he enters, she jumps as one caught in guilt. She catches herself quickly and rises as the lumberman walks to her. He stands off a little and genuinely admires her. She is beautiful. He holds out his arms. He is a good old husband, but so cold and so engrossed. He kisses her tenderly, pats her cheek, and releases her. He takes out a letter and hands it to her. As she reads, he goes over to the window and admires the glorious view. He does have a paradise to live in! He goes to the library table and dashes off a brief note, addresses and seals it. Goes back to his wife and takes the letter, giving her hand a squeeze as he leaves her. The husband goes toward the door left and nearly reaches it, when the young brother opens the door. He has suitcase, coat, and hat—he is prepared and determined to go. The husband is surprised and the younger brother is discomfited. He had intended to leave, unseen by his generous brother. The wife is more surprised. This will demand an explanation and perhaps she will be—but the husband takes the suitcase and coat from his brother and wants to know the reason of his sudden departure. The young fellow is about to speak when he catches sight of the wife, who motions silence. The husband suddenly thinks of the letter which demands his immediate presence at his lumber camp. He hands the letter to his younger brother and awaits his reaction. The wife goes to her husband and joins him in her desire that the brother be longer detained. The young brother reads the letter and cannot form an answer quickly. The wife takes his hat from him, but he grabs it back and asks the brother to go with him. The lumberman laughs at the idea and takes hold of his younger brother's hands and compares with his own. A pianist working on a log-jam! Both wife and husband laugh, but the younger man desires to go. The brother demands a reason, which the pianist cannot give. The husband takes the belongings of his brother and carries them back to his room. He goes to his wife and takes her over to the younger man and tells his brother that he must remain to protect his wife. He rings a bell and an Indian servant enters. The husband gives the Indian his letter and orders it sent. The Indian bows and leaves. The husband shows his brother that his wife must not be left alone, she must be protected from neighboring Indians and wild animals. He slaps his brother on the back and laughs. The wife clings to the brother in mock terror and walks away to the door. Husband puts his arm around brother and demands a promise of him that he will not leave while the lumberman is away. The young man again asks to accompany his older brother, but the refusal is very positive. Finally the promise is given and the two men shake hands. The husband walks quickly to door, kisses his wife once more and hurries out. She follows him out, while the young man walks to the window. He sees the big lumberman get on his horse and start riding away. The trap is set—he cannot get away. He waves his hand in farewell. The wife reappears, radiant, and joins the brother at the window. They both stand there waving their hands to the distant husband. The brother leaves the window first and goes to the easy-chair. He sits on the edge. The wife waves hand once more, blows a kiss in final farewell, and with a sigh of relief turns and walks toward the library table. She faces the brother and smiles. He does not look at her. She walks toward him and sits in the easy chair. She takes his hand. He rises and starts to move away. She rises and follows him. He turns and looks at her for a minute, then draws her to the window and points in direction where husband has disappeared. She shrugs her shoulders and points to the deer head, the bear rugs, the wild goat horns, all the hunter's trophies. These and business are the life of her husband, while she— She goes closer to brother, her arms steal up around his neck, then she kisses him passionately. He puts his arms on her shoulders and looks deep into her eyes. What can he do? What must he do? His hands slide slowly down her body as—the door opens and the Indian comes in to prepare the stove for the evening. Poor Paolo.

3 men, 1 lady

161. Speakeasy Action

A short Italian stands near a door through which he peers from time to time. Two couples are let in and all recognize Varesi. He is playing solitaire. He has just dealt a new game. The couples go over to a table left and a waiter comes up to them and takes their order. Nick, the proprietor, saunters to them and they exchange greetings. A party of six are stopped by Varesi, until he satisfies himself the party is acceptable. Three men and their girls come in laughingly. Lucile and Fred are the youngest of the group. It is their first venture in such a place. All are at ease, save these two. But they are good sports and join at the table for six. Varesi watches Fred carefully. The waiter brings in ginger ale and the two men produce hip flasks, intending to "doctor" the six glasses. Fred remonstrates lightly and laughs with Lucile at this sudden daring. Cards are brought to each of the tables and Nick stands by Fred's table. Straight poker is dealt. Nick helps Lucile to play her hand. They are having a good lark, to be sure. The two girls at the first table stage a real thriller, when the blonde accuses the brunette of cheating. They are separated by Nick and their partners. Nick orders drinks for them and tries to laugh off their misunderstanding. The blonde keeps a bottle by her chair for ready action. Fred and Lucile have been winning consistently. They are both getting on. Varesi signals Nick, who goes over to him. He motions that a "dick" is outside. Nick goes quickly to each of the tables and the cards and chips are dumped into drawers and fruit put on each table. One of the men turns on the dance record of the radio and they all begin dancing. Fred and Lucile do as urged by the others and join them, Varesi looks through the peephole and smiles fatuously. He opens the door and a big detective comes in and walks around. He refuses Nick's hand, who pretends indifference to the affront. The detective runs his hands on one of the men's hips and stops the couple dancing. He reaches back of man's coat and pulls out an automatic. The fellow is cool in his anger but merely winks at Nick. The "dick" holds out a pair of manacles, and Reddo, the Slick, puts his hands in. The detective starts walking Reddo away, when his girl partner gets a small revolver from her stocking and shoots the detective, who falls on the floor. Nick grabs Fred and hurries him from the room. All escape, except Lucile, who finds all doors barred and the detective stunned. Lucile again tries the doors and realizes she is a prisoner. The detective is recovering from his scalp wound. He sits up—Lucile goes to him and assists him in rising. He staggers a few paces and leans on table. He looks at Lucile and sees her as in a blur. She clings to him and looks at door Fred has been led through. She is crying. The detective goes to the street door and lifts the peephole cover. Door is locked and key removed. He takes revolver from his vest-strap and shoots twice at roof through peephole. He motions Lucile to side of door and they both stoop near table used by Varesi. The back door opens and Nick comes cautiously in, revolver in hand. Door is closed and locked again. He looks around, but does not observe the figures back of table. He goes quickly to peephole and looks out. As he does this, the detective quickly covers him and plants his revolver against his back. Nick is ordered to release hold of his gun as Lucile takes hold of it. She is frightened of the man and the gun. The detective puts Nick's gun against him and tells Lucile to shoot if he moves. Detective goes to back door and opens it. A plain-clothes man reënters, directing the two couples of first table in front of him. Reddo still has the manacles on. Nick turns quickly, grabs revolver from Lucile's hand, holds her around the waist and begins to back slowly toward street door. He covers the two detectives. As Nick leans against door, a gun is pushed against his head and he slowly drops the revolver. Lucile is released and falls in a heap on the floor. Nick stands with his hands raised. Detective goes to him, picks up gun and searches Nick. He finds keys and opens the front door. A burly policeman enters and takes Nick away. Detective picks up Lucile, holds her as the four men and women file in front with second officer. Detective looks at Lucile and begins to walk out with her. Fred comes staggering in from back door. He is a sorry sight with disheveled hair and clothes. An eye is eloquently black. He looks pitifully at detective, goes up to him and offers a handkerchief to wipe his grazed brow. Propping up the head of Lucile, he goes out with them. This scene does not necessarily have to be located in Chicago.

6 men, 5 ladies, supers

162. Hunger

A group of American prisoners have been brought in to the enemy dugout. The night is black and the low walls glimmer with shaded candlelight. Six of the prisoners are huddled on a dirty mattress and two are carried to a cleaner bunk. These two are wounded and are almost lifeless. An enemy orderly kneels by the wounded men and puts bandages on; on the head of the youngest and the arm of the older. A burlap flap moves in the wind at the door and falls heavily as the men enter and go out. A burly soldier enters with three small tin plates, on each of which is a cup of coffee and a meat sandwich. The three guards take plates eagerly and begin to eat hurriedly. The blond American stands up and waits for his portion, but the burly attendant leaves, giving food only to the enemy guards. The six prisoners look at each other and all rise. They want food. The blond holds out his hand to the first guard and all Americans show they are ravenously hungry. The larger guard strikes the blond prisoner across his face with a flat-handed blow. Guards all laugh. When the Yanks show fight, huddling together for strength, the two smaller guards hold their bayonets and strike menacingly at their prisoners. The burly guard holds the last piece of his sandwich poised between his thumb and finger and extends his arm before putting the food to his mouth. A Yiddish Yank grabs the tempting portion and swallows it instanter. None of the Yanks laugh, but the two smaller guards enjoy the turn on their sergeant companion, and laugh heartily. This provokes the burly officer to a frenzy and he strikes the Yiddish boy and knocks him to the ground. Too weak to fight, the Americans stand huddled together. An enemy commandant comes in, looks over the prisoners and the sergeant tells him of the Americans' hunger. Commandant gives an order to one of the guards, who leaves immediately. He soon returns with a tray filled with bread and corned beef. The guards are told to help themselves and each breaks pieces of bread and sandwich meat between. They stand around eating insolently before the Yanks. Unable to withstand his desire further, a Nebraska farm boy lurches forward and grabs a handful of the meat. The commandant calmly shoots him. Farmer boy grabs at his breast and falls in a heap on the two wounded Yanks.

This revives the one whose head is bandaged. He arouses, smells the food and gets up blindly. Goes toward the commandant, who pushes him brutally backward. The blind Yank strikes the officer with his helmet and temporarily stuns him. The Yiddish boy grabs the easily procured pistol and shoots the two guards before they can raise their guns. The burly sergeant starts to run to the opening as a Yankee lieutenant stands at the door, automatic in hand, ready for any emergency. The Yanks have captured the line. The two enemies, on command, raise their hands. They are marched out by the lieutenant. The Yankee prisoners, now freed, fall savagely upon the tray of food. One remembers and gives the wounded men a bite each. All are looking for bits of food on the ground as Yankee Red Cross aide comes into the dugout. All the soldiers look at him as a messenger of mercy. The aide stoops to the wounded and shakes his head. Three of the soldiers are still looking for crumbs of food, when the aide shows them out of the dugout. It had not occurred to any that their way of exit was now free. The other men are lying on the mattress as in a drunken orgy. They had eaten for the first time in five days—heavy meat. The aide picks up one of the wounded soldiers as the sun breaks and lights up the dugout.

12 men, supers

163. Thirst

Five English girls have been cut off from their party, on a sight-seeing expedition to the pyramids. They have been made prisoners in a desert tent. It is the fifth day of their captivity and for three days they have been deprived of water. The bandit chief has invited them to be voluntary members of his harem. A peculiar sense of honor has this chief. No women are in his harem who do not "voluntarily" come. For the white girls, he prescribes the denial of water, and to the darker skinned, he forbids food. The five new captives vary in ages from eighteen to twenty-five, and their skins shine white against the dark tent. A dusky guard, with bayonet on carbine, paces past the open passageway. Two dusky women sit on either side of the door; one is asleep and the other drowsily awaiting the command or wish of any of the white women. Pillows are thrown promiscuously about the carpeted sand floor. Basins of dry food are seen near the center on short-legged tables. One of the girls, driven to desperation, picks up a piece of date bread and starts to put it to her mouth, but it is stringy dry and stings her lips. She throws it in a desperate rage and falls, full length on the floor. She lies there, quivering and weak. The oldest girl, with her arms about two of her country-women, sits staring out into space; all three are waiting for delivery or death. The fifth girl, young and pretty, but almost crazed by thirst, rocks mechanically on a pile of pillows. She holds a golden cup in her hands, and is pouring imaginary water from it. A back curtain is suddenly opened and three girls, dancing happily to a dulcet accompaniment, entertain the swarthy Chief. A great Negro pours wine in the several cups. He holds the container high so that sparkling fluid falls plashing in the goblets. Water drips from an overflowing basin as a slave girl carries it to the feet of the Chief's favorite. The slave girl wipes the water from the favorite's feet. The Chief is paying little attention to the three dancing girls, or to the several girls reclining on the cushions, but looks beyond into the prison tent. He claps his hands and the dance stops. He orders all his girls to drink. The great Negro pours pure water into crystal goblets which the dancing girls procure and they drink slowly with the Chief. One of them pours a little of the water on the back of a companion, who returns half her goblet. This starts a playful water fight, which extends to all the girls, the Chief seeming to enjoy immensely. Such an orgy of water waste is more than Goldie (the youngest captive) can stand. She jumps suddenly to her feet and dashes into the dancing room. Her four companions protest, feebly, remaining in their original places. Goldie grabs a half-filled goblet and drains it with convulsive swallows. She grabs at another cup but it is jerked away. The dancing girls, trained in their technic, group on one side of the Chief and leave Goldie a figure alone, before the Chief. She looks, frightened, from one face to another. There is naught but smiles and derision from the girls and the Chief is looking at his new "bride" with unfeigned admiration. She had come of her own choice! The English girls watch breathlessly. The great Negro brings a small cup of red wine and holds it out to Goldie. She grabs at the cup and starts to drink, but sees the triumph of the Chief's looks and throws the cup on the floor and starts to run to the prison tent. Two slave women meet her with arms folded and the guard with the carbine stops in the center of the outer doorway. The great Negro puts down his long pitcher and goes to Goldie. He turns and looks at his Chief, who motions that the girl be brought before him. Goldie is picked up in his arms and stood before the Chief. As the Chief touches her shoulder, she swoons. The Negro catches her and carries her to an inner compartment, and is followed by two dancing girls. The harem girls all laugh as Goldie swoons. The dancing is commenced again. Wine is poured by two Arabian girls, as the Chief requires. The four English girls are whispering together. The older of the four, Diana of the dark hair and fair skin, rises from the group and walks slowly toward the Chief. Again the music and dancing stop. The English girl is almost as tall as the Chief, as she stands in the center of the inner sanctum. She cannot speak the language of the desert, but she makes it plain to the Chief that she will remain in his harem if he will free her four companions. He is interested. This is, truly, voluntary. He sends a dancing girl off to the inner room and Goldie is immediately led in by the two attendants. She sees Diana in front of the Chief, but is too weak to go to her. The Chief rises and comes to Diana. He asks her if he understood aright, that she would remain as his bride if he freed the remaining four. Diana again asserts her willingness to comply with such a bargain. The Chief looks at the other four; two lying on the rugs and the other two cowering at his glance. The Arabian girls bring a tabaret and place goblets of water near the anguished maids and Viola, the darkest of the group, unable to refrain any longer, drinks from two of the cups and would take another but her arm is held by one of the Arabian girls. It is a sympathetic touch and Viola looks at her. Viola is surreptitiously offered a small dagger, which she hesitates to take, but looks around and then accepts, hiding the dagger in her belt. The Chief has satisfied himself with the examination and consents to Diana's proposal. Viola stands near Diana, with a look strangely different. The Arabian girl watches her every movement and whispers to her companion. Both Arabian girls back away to crowd of dancing girls. The Chief stands, for a moment, hesitating just what his exact course should be, how he can liberate the four and keep his rendezvous a secret? He claps his hands, and the guard with the carbine comes to his side. A few hurried words and the guard disappears. The Chief contemplates Diana with unfeigned admiration. Diana sits on the tabaret proudly erect but weakening every minute. Viola stands, trembling. The Chief comes over to Diana and proffers her a cushion near dais. He holds out his hand, which she refuses. As the Chief bows in mock courtesy, Viola plunges the dagger into his back. The dancing girls are terrified, all save the Arabians. They hurry the four girls off to the prison tent and signal two men, who come in quickly—pick up the two weaker English girls, and carry them to the outer door. The Chief, staggering, reaches to his belt and falteringly procures a revolver. He unsteadily aims at Diana, and a Grecian girl throws herself upon him, grabs the revolver and holds it menacingly at his head. Diana is urged to flee, as the Arabian girls take her arms. They hurry her to the doorway. The Chief falls to his knees, gesticulates wildly, as none offer aid. He falls prone on his face and the Grecian girls motion the dancing girls desperately off. All flee for the opportunity of freedom. The guard enters with large turbans, which he intended to bind over the eyes of the four English girls. He sees the fallen Chief, goes to him and turns him over. The Grecian girl, unnoticed by the guard, keeps him covered. The guard sees the Chief is dying, hesitates, then gives an exultant shout and is about to jab the bayonet in the Chief, but thinks better of it and spits at him in contempt. Tyranny is dying. Nearly all the girls have disappeared. An Egyptian beauty comes slowly to the Chief and enfolds him tenderly. The Grecian girl wishes her good luck and with guard backs slowly from the inner tent, the Chief helplessly watching. Diana, weakened to a point of exhaustion, sinks tremblingly to the sand. The Grecian girl, remembering, hurries to the water jug and pours a goblet of water. She hurries to the prostrate Diana, and slowly pours the water down her throat. The guard picks Diana up, gives the Grecian girl his gun and they walk out of the tent. The Egyptian maid, weeping, holding her Chief to her bosom, watches him slowly close his eyes and sees his head fall limp against her. The sunset breeze flaps the tent cover lazily.

3 men, 15 ladies, supers

164. Revolution

The scene is laid in the palace of the Count Koranoff on the eve of the revolution. Luxury is evident on all sides. The large reception room is bright with lights and the Count and Countess are receiving, in honor of their son's betrothal. There is a happy informality about their reception, but grace and ease are generally apparent. The long gowns with beads and jewels add to the richness of the scene. The Countess is wearing the great diamond tiara and pearls of the Koranoffs. The ladies vie with each other in exposition of their jeweled wealth. Rare tapestries are on the walls and tables. Cut glass is seen upon the refreshment table, where punch and dainty cakes are placed in profusion. Liveried attendants move easily among the guests, offering aid when necessary and inconspicuous when no occasion is given for service. A little group is laughing around the refreshments, the Count is talking to four men of military mien and the Countess has a group of several women about her, as they openly admire the dazzling tiara. Near the center door are seen three couples, in attitudes of felicitation and greeting. The bride-to-be, Ilyana, comes through the center door and all turn to her. She is a radiant beauty and worthy of the attention. She moves as a queen among her admiring friends and is met by the Countess. Ilyana curtsies before the Countess and is raised by the hand. The Countess kisses each cheek and takes her over to the Count, who kisses her fingers and places her hand upon his arm. The Count takes her about the salon, greeting their intimate friends. In the midst of this felicitation, young Ivan, heir to the Koranoff estates, enters. He is as handsome as Ilyana is beautiful. He pauses a second in the arched doorway, in his white military uniform. Back of him are two grizzled officers of the army. Ivan proceeds immediately to the Count and Ilyana, who are now in the deep center of the hall. He salutes the Count and kisses the hand of Ilyana. They are a willing couple for betrothal. The Count relinquishes the hand of Ilyana and puts it on the arm of Ivan. The merry group are happy for the young couple. The Countess comes to them, and takes from her head the Koranoff tiara, and places it on the head of Ilyana. All are astonished at this gesture and but few try to conceal their response to such generosity. Ivan kisses his mother, gratefully, and shakes the hand of his father. Ilyana is almost staggered at the amount of attention she is receiving. She has not quite grasped the magnitude of the gift, when a great explosion is heard through the hallway and a huge volume of smoke rolls ominously in the back doorway. As at a signal, all the servants, save one old nurse of the Countess, grab guns from various places of concealment and level at the assembled guests and owners. Ivan laughs at first, but sees the assembling of the servants on the window side of the hall. A window is opened, and four grimy-faced soldiers step into the room, further to augment the rebellious servants. A band of citizens, workmen, and soldiers come through the big hallway with guns and clubs upraised. A short, stocky man, middle-aged and spectacled, heads the crowd. He has no weapon visible. The Count and his guests are now aroused to the seriousness of the situation and have collected into a group near the refreshment tables. Ivan steps up to the leader of the mob and demands an explanation. Two citizens quickly grab Ivan's arms and there is a brief struggle. Keznieff, the leader, laughs at Ivan's futility. The Count goes to Keznieff and strikes him with his glove. A shot rings out and the Count drops lifeless at Keznieff's feet. The women are terrified. The Countess runs to her husband and falls by his body, not daring to believe what she saw. The citizens' crowd now occupies a third of the room and the twenty-odd guests are huddled together. Keznieff satisfies himself that Koranoff is dead. A soldier gives a signal for the women to be separated from the men. Several beautifully gowned aristocrats are seized and rudely moved to center of the salon. A grizzled-haired old servitor of the government involuntarily raised his hand to his scabbard, forgetting that he, as well as the others, left their arms at home. Keznieff notices the gesture for the pistol and smiles ironically at the old gallant. When a rough hand is laid on the veteran, the old man stands erect; with full force, he strikes his assailant to the floor. There is a general movement of intended violence on the part of the mob, but Keznieff stops them. He salutes the veteran for his gallantry. The women have been segregated and stand in different attitudes of aloofness. As by a common understanding, the aristocrats grab for guns from the citizens and the two aides with Ivan begin striking viciously with their swords. This momentarily disconcerts the mob and several shots are fired. Two of the aristocrats fall and a citizen writhes on the floor. The Countess rises and calls for silence. Keznieff bows and demands silence. The Countess takes the pearls from her neck and the bracelets from her arm and throws them at Keznieff's feet and then orders him and the mob from the room. Keznieff bows again and smiles at the beautiful madame. The mob joins with him and all laugh heartily but impatient for results. Keznieff's affability suddenly changes, and at a command, two of the citizens grab the jewels from the women's necks and heads, strip their fingers of their rings. Guns are leveled at the men and pockets are rifled. The men are made to put their arms in air. A younger fellow, unable longer to stand the insults, fights madly at his assailants and dashes from the room. But no shot is fired at him, as Keznieff gestures that he will be met at the stairway. Keznieff gives another command. The Count and others fallen are lifted and carried from the room. The Countess starts to follow and all the women are herded with her. A group of motley soldiers partially surround the women and go off jauntily, as mock courtiers. All the women are led out except Ilyana. She is detained by Keznieff and stands defiantly near the refreshment tables. The remaining mob has surrounded the men, but Ivan is told to stand apart. The aristocrats are banded together and the mob jab at them threateningly as they go out, some protesting, some offering bribes, all wondering about their destination. The great room is a wreck of its former self. The tables are devoid of all their silver and accouterments; chairs are overturned, draperies are gone. Ivan has walked over to Ilyana and puts his arms about her. Keznieff contemplates them and walks slowly toward them. Two guards are seen intermittently to cross the back hallway. Keznieff takes wrist of Ilyana and pulls her toward him. She jerks away and clings to Ivan. As Ivan puts her back of him, Keizneff draws a pistol from his coat and waves Ivan away. Ivan does not move. Keznieff, smiling, raises his pistol and slowly lowers it to the level of Ivan's heart. Ilyana dashes from Ivan and goes to Keznieff, pulling his arm down. Keznieff puts his arm around Ilyana and starts to walk away with her, as Ivan springs toward him. The gun is knocked to the floor and a sharp knife sinks deep in Keznieff's back; he crumples on the floor without a sound. Ivan grabs Keznieff and sets him up in a golden chair and Ilyana sits on his lap as the guards go by. Ivan stands at attention and the guards laugh and go their way. Ivan quickly pulls cap and coat from Keznieff, puts on his glasses and puts his own coat over Keznieff, now laid on the floor. Ilyana pretends to be dragged by lover as they reach the center door. The guards appear, Ivan shoots toward the dead Keznieff and the guards laugh heartily and bow Ivan out to the inner room prepared for Keznieff. Ivan drags Ilyana from view.

9 men, 7 ladies, supers

MAN, ANIMATE AND INANIMATE OBJECTS [1]

165. A Friendly Call

(2 Ladies, a Cat, a Puppy)

Miss Highbrow calls on city relative. Miss Highbrow takes her Pomeranian Pup and is greeted by Miss City and her Angora Cat. Greeting goes from distrust, inquisitiveness, apprehension, challenge, to fight. Hasty retreat.

4 people

[1] These pantomimes are for fun and imagination, to combine the body and appropriate noises. For the person, pantomime only; for objects use body and voice.

166. Woman and Three Flies

(1 Lady, 3 Flies)

A woman is keeping house. The flies buzz around. Woman chases them with fly swatter and misses. Finally thinks of fly paper. Gets the paper and catches the flies on it. Flies light on it eventually, in different ways; with both legs, one leg, four legs, and in different attitudes, making characteristic noises.

4 people

167. The Housewife at Work

(Woman, Telephone, Telephone Book, Vacuum Cleaner)

Telephone rings, woman answers it. Pantomime conversation. She calls number. Business of looking up number in Book; use arms outstretched for pages. Noise of book when pages are turned. Woman dials number on Phone. Noise. Line busy. Noise. Dials again. Line busy. Noise of hanging up receiver. Next time gets number. Happy with result. Gets Vacuum Cleaner and cleans rugs. Noise of cleaner as it starts, runs, and stops. Goes to refrigerator to get the ice.

4 people

168. A Boy and His Dog

(Boy, Tree, Gate, Dog, Flipper)

Boy goes out the gate. (Gate made by extended arms to swing, opens, closes, and squeaks consistently.) Dog follows Boy and is taken back by Boy, who locks the Gate. Dog stands by Gate and barks. Boy shoots Flipper and does distant damage. (The flipper is made by arms as fork.)

5 people

169. The Hunter

(Hunter, Tree, Dog, Flower, Bird)

The Hunter arrives in the forest and stands under the shade of the Tree. Breaks down a Flower which wilts.

Hunter picks up part of Flower and smells, doesn't like its fragrance. Throws it away. Shoots Bird on Tree. Bird falls with broken wing. Dog gets Bird.

5 people

170. *A Miss and Her Music*

(Girl, Piano, Victrola, Radio)

Girl practices the Piano. Gets tired. Turns on Victrola, winds up and dances. Surprised with message from Radio. Tries different stations. Bedtime story.

4 people

171. *Smanthe in Her Solarium*

(Housemaid, 2 Love Birds, Parrot, Canary)

The Maid feeds the Canary some lettuce and seeds. Hears it sing. Watches the Love Birds wistfully. Gives the Parrot a cracker and sees it around the cages; hears the Parrot talk unusual language.

5 people

172. *Cy at Home*

(Farmer, 2 Pigs, Horse, Cow, 2 Sheep)

The Farmer feeds his barnyard pets, each their respective repast and with consistent results. Pets the horse and cow. Have ground distances consistent.

7 people.

173. *The Fowl Farmer*

(Farmer's Wife, Turkey Gobbler, 2 Ducks, Goose, Chicks)

The Wife feeds her pets. Turkey is all ruffled and is not friendly with the Gander. All others are busy eating, though some get in the way of others. A medley of content.

9 people

174. *Nimrod and Honey*

(English Hunter, Honey, Bear, Numerous Bees, Tree)

Hunter stands by a large stump of a Tree. A Bear is about to open a honey deposit, when he notices the

Hunter. Bear's paw slips and strikes nest of Bees. Hunter is made innocent victim, along with Bear, and is too busy to shoot, too scared to run. Victory for Bees.

7 plus people

Review and Questions

1. Does the individual possess the ability to portray any emotion consciously? Whether he has experienced such emotion, or not? Develop.
2. How does strong emotion affect the voice?
3. What emotions "tighten" the throat? How should they be governed by the actor?
4. Is it "natural" for Hamlet to speak in soliloquy, loud enough to be heard by two thousand present? How does the boy in the top row of the gallery know that Hamlet is thinking to himself?
5. What are some of the ways of a "small part" actor which may ruin a beautiful ensemble?
6. Is a "small part" ever unimportant? In what manner?
7. What is meant by "grouping"?
8. How can a group maintain a "climax"?
9. What determines the size of a stage crowd?
10. Which character in this chapter offers you, personally, the best opportunity to develop dramatically? Why?
11. Write a pantomime of six or more characters, wherein all contribute to one major climax.

CHAPTER XII

SCENES FROM SOME OF THE GREATER PLAYS AND SELECTIONS FROM SHAKESPEARE

AN actor (or class) may not be able to afford the time to master all the plays suggested, but they may have the opportunity to study some of the best scenes from such plays.

In this chapter are included suggestive studies from seventy plays and some sixty scenes from the plays of Shakespeare. In each instance, the scene is chosen for its possible acting power, or character delineation. The *best* actors are well informed in dramatic literature, though we have to admit *some* good acting has been done by poorly informed actors.

A perusal of scenes here suggested will prove that the genius of drama is action, and that the best action is motivated by controlled emotion.

These scenes must be read aloud, as well as acted out. The great actor is he who interprets words with a trained body and adequate voice. *Dramatic art for the individual is the intelligent harmonizing of words, voice, and body.* And all dependent upon proper emotional evaluation.

Fragments of plays will aid in dramatic studies, but the entire play must be read to appreciate thoroughly the spirit of play production.

N.B. The pantomimes which follow these scenes are suggestive of what may be done with many of the other plays. It is the pantomime outline which determines the actual conversation. That play which does not "pantomime" well seldom becomes an actable, or even a popular play.

As these few pantomimes are taken from copyright

plays, they must not be presented in any public performance without permission from owners of copyright in the individual plays, nor, without such permission, may they be reprinted in part, or in whole in any form.

Lists of Plays other than Shakespeare

These plays, modern and classic, are listed alphabetically for ready reference. For those who wish *specific study of the various emotions, gesture situations, and scene problems, adequate references are to be found in the index.*

The choice of plays in each group is necessarily arbitrary. In the classic, such plays as "The King's Henchman" and "Paolo and Francesca" are by modern writers, but in beautiful language of accepted classic style. "She Stoops to Conquer," in prose, is one of the greatest of classics, though possessing no exalted style. Its place in literature is secure. We use classic in the liberal sense, rather than a limitation to poetry or age.

Modern Plays

"Abraham Lincoln," John Drinkwater (Houghton Mifflin, Boston, 1921). In *Chief Contemporary Dramatists.*

"Beau Brummell," Clyde Fitch (Harcourt Brace, New York, 1922). In *Longer Plays.*

"Bonds of Interest," Jacinto Benavente (Scribner's, New York, 1917).

"Broadway," Philip Dunning and George Abbott (Doran, New York, 1927).

"Concert, The," Hermann Bahr (Houghton Mifflin, Boston, 1921). In *Chief Contemporary Dramatists.*

"Copperhead, The," Augustus Thomas (Harcourt Brace, New York, 1922).

"Coquette," George Abbott and Ann Preston Bridgers (Longmans Green, New York, 1928).

"Cyrano de Bergerac," Edmond Rostand (Prentice Hall, New York, 1928). In *Types of Romantic Drama.*

"Darling of the Gods, The," David Belasco and J. Luther Long (Little Brown, Boston, 1928).

"Daughter of Jorio," Gabriele D'Annunzio (Little Brown, Boston, 1925).

"Devil's Disciple, The," G. Bernard Shaw (Brentano's, New York, 1915).

"Doll's House, A," Henrik Ibsen (Scribner's, New York, 1911).

"Du Barry," David Belasco (Little Brown, Boston, 1928).

"Easiest Way, The," Eugene Walters (Houghton Mifflin, Boston, 1921). In *Chief Contemporary Dramatists.*

"Emperor Jones," Eugene O'Neill (Boni & Liveright, New York, 1925).

"Escape," John Galsworthy (Scribner's, New York, 1928).

"Famous Mrs. Fair, The," James Forbes (Doran, New York, 1920).

"Fires of St. John, The," Hermann Sudermann (Little Brown, Boston, 1925). In *Representative Contemporary Dramatists.*

"Fool, The," Channing Pollock (Brentano's, New York, 1922).

"Ghosts," Henrik Ibsen (Scribner's, New York, 1911).

"Gioconda, La," Gabriele D'Annunzio (Houghton Mifflin, Boston, 1921). In *Chief Contemporary Dramatists.*

"Girl of the Golden West, The," David Belasco (Little Brown, Boston, 1928).

"Great Divide, The," William Vaughn Moody (Houghton Mifflin, Boston, 1915). In *Chief Contemporary Dramatists.*

"Great Galeoto, The," José Echegaray (Doubleday Page, New York, 1914).

"Hedda Gabler," Henrik Ibsen (Scribner's, New York, 1914).

"If I Were King," Justin H. McCarthy (French, New York, 1922).

"It Pays to Advertise," Roi C. Megrue and W. Hackett (French, New York, 1914).

"John Ferguson," St. John Ervine (Macmillan, New York, 1915).

"Juno and the Paycock," Sean O'Casey (Macmillan, New York, 1925).

"King's Henchman, The," Edna St. Vincent Millay (Harper's, New York, 1927).

"Lady Windermere's Fan," Oscar Wilde (Century, New York, 1916). In *Representative English Plays.*

"Madame Butterfly," David Belasco and J. Luther Long (Little Brown, Boston, 1928).

"Man from Home, The," Booth Tarkington and H. Leon Wilson (Harper's, New York, 1908).

"Marco Millions," Eugene O'Neill (Boni & Liveright, New York, 1927).

"Master Builder, The," Henrik Ibsen (Scribner's, New York, 1914).

"Michael and His Lost Angel," Henry A. Jones (Houghton Mifflin, Boston, 1915). In *Chief Contemporary Dramatists.*

"Milestones," Arnold Bennett and Edward Knaubloch (Doran, New York, 1912).

"Monna Vanna," Maurice Maeterlinck (Little Brown, Boston, 1925). In *Representative Contemporary Dramatists.*

"Mrs. Warren's Profession," G. Bernard Shaw (Brentano's, New York, 1914).

"Ned McCobb's Daughter," Sidney Howard (Scribner's, New York, 1927).

"Old English," John Galsworthy (Scribner's, New York, 1925).

"Old Lady 31," Rachel Crothers (Brentano's, New York, 1923).

"Old Man Minick," Edna Ferber and George S. Kaufman (Doubleday Page, New York, 1924).

"Porgy," Dorothy and DuBose Heyward (Doubleday, Doran, New York, 1928).

"Pretenders, The," Henrik Ibsen (Prentice Hall, New York, 1928). In *Types of Historical Drama.*

"Return of Peter Grimm, The," David Belasco (Little Brown, Boston, 1928).

"Saturday's Children," Maxwell Anderson (Longmans Green, New York, 1927).

"Scarecrow," Percy Mackaye (Houghton Mifflin, Boston, 1915). In *Chief Contemporary Dramatists.*

"Second Mrs. Tanqueray, The," Arthur W. Pinero (Houghton Mifflin, Boston, 1915). In *Chief Contemporary Dramatists.*

"Show Off, The," George Kelly (Little Brown, Boston, 1925).

"Strange Interlude," Eugene O'Neill (Boni & Liveright, New York, 1928).

"Strife," John Galsworthy (Houghton Mifflin, Boston, 1915). In *Chief Contemporary Dramatists.*

"Sun Up," Lulu Vollmer (Brentano's, New York, 1924).

"Three Wise Fools," Austin Strong (French, New York, 1919).

"Truth, The," Clyde Fitch (Houghton Mifflin, Boston, 1915). *Chief Contemporary Dramatists.*

"Wild Duck, The," Henrik Ibsen (Little Brown, Boston, 1925). *Representative Contemporary Dramatists.*

"Witching Hour, The," Augustus Thomas (Houghton Mifflin, Boston, 1915). In *Chief Contemporary Dramatists.*

"Yellow Sands," A. and Eden Phillpotts (French, New York, 1927).

Classic Plays

"All for Love," John Dryden (Prentice Hall, New York, 1928). In *Types of Romantic Drama.*

"Becket," Alfred Tennyson (Prentice Hall, New York, 1928). In *Types of Historical Drama.*

"Cenci, The," Percy B. Shelley (Century, New York, 1916). In *Representative English Plays.*

"Cid, The," Pierre Corneille (Prentice Hall, New York, 1928). In *Types of Romantic Drama.*

"Œdipus Rex," Sophocles (Prentice Hall, New York, 1928). In *Types of World Tragedy.*

"Paolo and Francesca," Stephen Phillips (Houghton Mifflin, Boston, 1925). In *Contemporary Plays.*

"Richelieu," Bulwer-Lytton (Little Brown, Boston, 1918). In *Representative British Dramas.*

"She Stoops to Conquer," Oliver Goldsmith (Century, New York City, 1916). In *Representative English Plays.*

"Sunken Bell, The," Gerhardt Hauptmann (Little Brown, Boston, 1925).

"Tartuffe," Molière (Prentice Hall, New York, 1928). In *Social Comedy.*

"Virginius," J. Sheridan Knowles (Little Brown, Boston, 1918). In *Representative British Dramas.*

"William Tell," Friedrich Schiller (Prentice Hall, New York, 1928). In *Types of Historical Drama.*

MODERN PLAYS

175. "Abraham Lincoln," John Drinkwater

Lincoln has told his Cabinet and friends that slavery must be abolished. He has told the colored preacher, Custes, that his people will be free. The famous cabinet meeting has been held (Scene 2) and in 1865, in a small farmhouse, we see Grant in his temporary headquarters. Lincoln visits these headquarters.

Scene V (pp. 119-123).

Lincoln is the type which has quiet power, in contrast to Grant, with his nervous power. This scene is especially good when Lincoln meets the young soldier who was court-martialed because he fell asleep on guard duty. Sentimentalism would ruin this scene.

176. "Beau Brummell," Clyde Fitch

Beau and his faithful Mortimer, in the attic of the grand dandy's decline. When the Beau awakes from a hunger stupor, he sees about him the King, Mariana, Mrs. St. Aubyn and Reginald. This is one of the great acting scenes in American drama.

Act IV, Scene 2 (pp. 80-84).

The pathetic Beau would entertain on Thursday and Mortimer carries the scene as a reality. Mock pantomime of golden days, turned into a beautiful truth. Pathos of touching beauty makes this scene a great acting part.

177. "Bonds of Interest," Jacinto Benavente

Two merry adventurers are Crispin and Leander. They go to a city, and Crispin conceives a plan to carry Leander on his back, as if ill. They knock at the inn door and Crispin, as servant, calls for immediate aid to his master, Leander. Innkeeper is impressed with Leander's manner and listens to the many lies of Crispin, regarding his master's secret mission and wealth. The imposters, through Crispin, have the inn entertain the Captain, and Harlequin, with the very best. Crispin also lies his way for himself and master into Doña Sirena's fête. There Leander and Silvia meet and fall in love, to the great discomfiture of Polichinelle, who is the wealthy father of Silvia.

Start scene in Act III (pp. 630-634), a room in LEANDER'S *house.* LEANDER *desires to leave entire affair, despite his love for* SILVIA. HARLEQUIN *and* CAPTAIN *leave* LEANDER *and* CRISPIN *to themselves.* LEANDER: *"What is this, Crispin?" Take to entrance of* POLICHINELLE.

This play is good satire, good buffoonery. The pseudoserious calls for the best of acting, the greatest care for details. Contrast "Tartuffe" with "Crispin" for enlightening analysis. Many of the expected situations of Commédia dell'arte are in this play.

178. "Broadway," Philip Dunning and George Abbott

Roy Lane, dancer, works for the Paradise Night Club, and loves one of the new girls, Billie Moore. Nick gets his bootleg from Scar Edwards, but Steve Crandall has come into the Bronx territory. In a quarrel, Scar is killed and spirited away. Roy and Billie saw a "drunken" man being led off by Steve and Dolph. Detective Dan McCorn is close on the scent.

Act II (pp. 167-178). Start: STEVE (*to* LANE) : *"Now you lousy little bum, I got you where I want you." Take to the end of the act.*

Porky has just led the girls from the room. Steve and the gang have Roy at their mercy. This scene is excellent for suspense. Every person adds to the accumulation of dramatic climax. Loudness must not dominate.

179. "The Concert," Hermann Bahr

Gustave Hein, concert pianist, is a handsome fellow of magnetic power and charm. His wife, Marie, is well informed of his charm and popularity. One of his many admirers has been somewhat indiscreet. Hein retires to the log cabin in the country. Delphinia Jura accompanies him. Later we see them with Mr. Jura.

Act II (pp. 539-548). Start scene with seventeen-year-old DELPHINIA *returning to* HEIN. DELPHINIA : *"Here I am." Take to the end of act.*

Few girls of seventeen could play the part of Delphinia, yet this character must positively be fresh, unsophisticated, and trusting. Must have all the beauty of youth. The meeting of Hein and Jura affords excellent contrast in mood.

180. "The Copperhead," Augustus Thomas

The war of '61 is over and Milt Shanks, who had been ordered by President Lincoln to stay in the state and work for the government as special government agent in the ranks of the Knights of the Golden Circle (sympathizers with the South), is more or less of an outcast. We now see Shanks (an old man) and he tells his story.

Scene in Act IV (pp. 158-162). Start: SHANKS: *"Come in, Colonel Hardy, come in, sir. Sit down, Mrs. Manning." Take to end of the play.*

The telling of Shanks' story is a character unfoldment, not given to most monologue developments. We can see Lincoln through the Copperhead's story. And his triumph of retrieved friendships give the finale of this play a real joy for the trained actor.

181. "Coquette," George Abbott and Ann Preston Bridgers

Norma Besant is somewhat of a coquette. She does not take to Stanley Wentworth and displeases her father, Doctor Besant, by entertaining Duke Gaston and Michael Jeffery. Her brother, Jimmie, holds women in same degree of respect as his southern father. Norma has given her love to Michael and they are confronted by a possible obligatory marriage, when Michael is ordered out of the house by Dr. Besant. Michael, in a fit of anger, tells the Doctor the true status of affairs.

Scene in Act II (pp. 91-106). MICHAEL: *"If you'll allow me, sir . . ."* DR. BESANT: *"I'll allow you to leave the house, Mr. Jeffery." Take to end of act, wherein* MICHAEL *is shot by* DR. BESANT *and* NORMA *refuses to aid her father.*

There are some people who attend theaters who have a reverence for God. Swearing is necessary for realism but it need not be used to bolster drama. We may offend with use of blasphemy and swearing is not missed in a real dramatic scene. The talking picture of the play exemplified this. What is climax of this scene?

182. "Cyrano de Bergerac," Edmond Rostand

This excellent drama is filled with good pantomime. A very interesting scene takes place in Ragueneau's cook shop. The cadets have assembled and Cyrano has been prevailed upon to tell the story of his fight at the bridge. All France knows of his sensitiveness to his very long nose.

Act II (pp. 398-401). Cyrano: *"My adventure? I was marching to meet them—" and so on through the scene. He is interrupted by the newcomer,* Christian, *who is the favored gentleman of* Roxane's *affection.* Cyrano *spares him because of his love for* Roxane.

The audacity of Christian, in publicly referring to Cyrano's nose, is a choice dramatic bit. The young cadet is more insolent than brave, but not boisterous. The reaction on the crowd is dynamic drama, as Cyrano tells his story. One character in the crowd could rob greatly the desired effect. Suppressed action dominates.

183. "Cyrano de Bergerac," Edmond Rostand

Act III. The famous balcony scene, where Cyrano, *unseen by* Roxane, *aids* Christian *in his love making (pp. 416-420).* Christian *climbs to balcony and calls "Roxane."* Cyrano: *"Wait, a few pebbles . . ." and on through the scene to:* Cyrano: *"Some one is coming."* Roxane *closes the window.*

The bold Christian of the cook shop is now the timid lover under the balcony. An improbable situation made to seem most feasible by the very ease of Cyrano's directions and speech. The sincerity of Cyrano's love is more apparent as the scene progresses, his voice is chief means of portraying character, as actor is in semidarkness.

184. "The Darling of the Gods," David Belasco and Luther Long

Zakkuri has defied Prince Kara to enter his house. Hassebe has told Zakkuri that Kara will be present at nine. The bell tolls nine. Zakkuri is talking to Prince of Tosan; Yosan is successful in spiriting Kara away by means of her shoji.

Start with Act I, Scene 2 (pp. 164-169). Zakkuri: *"The moment passes—the bell ceases— He is not here. Coward." On to end of scene.*

A beautiful pageantal scene of intense emotion and much action. Each person lends to the dramatic focus as well as theatric presentation. The agonizing pain of Kara is best of restrained acting. The oriental carriage and walk demand hours of study.

185. "The Daughter of Jorio," Gabriele D'Annunzio

Mila, the daughter of Jorio, a sorcerer, comes to the happy home of Lazaro Di Roio and Candia Della Leonessa. All are preparing for the marriage of Aligi, the artist shepherd son, and Vienda Di Giave, when Mila Di Codra arrives. She is pursued by a pack of men and runs to the very hearth of the home, opposite the bridal couple. Mila begs for protection, as the mob of men clamor for her. Mila directs her imprecations to Aligi. The men outside the door raise their voices, demanding Mila.

Act I (pp. 285-290). Mila: *"O innocence, O innocence, of all these young maidens here, you have heard not . . ." To end of act.*

Aligi, in presence of the bride, the mother, and many maidens, is urged to thrust the bewitching Mila back upon the lustful mob. Ages of tradition fight with present needs. This scene is powerful in stage management of two groups; the men on the outside and the women indoors, each wishing the ejection of Mila. This play may well have been included in the classic, but its modern theme permits its present placing.

186. "The Devil's Disciple," G. Bernard Shaw

The reading of the Dudgeon will is one of the best character studies we have in literature. The family has been notified, the lawyer will soon arrive and Judith Anderson, the minister's wife, has proffered aid in fixing up the house.

Act I, (pp. 16-27). JUDITH: *"They are beginning to come. Now remember your aunt's directions, Essie, and be a good girl." To end of the act.*

Compare the will scene in "Yellow Sands" with this one. Shaw gives minute directions and exacting descriptions for his characters. His scenes are written for just these people. In this, Shaw injects the religious note as a major issue and William further shocks the pious faces when he comes as a beneficiary, chief beneficiary. Sham and hypocrisy are met by honesty and fearlessness.

187. "The Devil's Disciple," G. Bernard Shaw

Act III. From the beginning of act to point where SERGEANT *takes* RICHARD *and* JUDITH *from the British Headquarters waiting room.* JUDITH *tells* RICHARD *of her love (pp. 50-55).*

Judith's confession of love is a beautiful unfoldment of character. From anxiety through expression to resignation, with Richard the constant and consistent. The flexibility of love pitted against the stability of self-responsibility.

188. "A Doll's House," Henrik Ibsen

Nora has kept the great secret of her life from her husband, Torvald Helmer. A blackmailing friend has brought to a climax what should have remained her secret. Nora has expected a letter for her husband from the betrayer, Nils Krogstad. She plans to get the letter she knows is in the box, to which her husband has the only key. As she is discussing the situation with her confidante, Mrs. Linden, Helmer and Dr. Rank knock at the door.

Act II (pp. 101-109). HELMER: *"Nora."* NORA: *(With terror.) "Oh, what is it? What do you want?" To end of the act.*

As Helmer knocks, Nora is frightened but lets him and Rank in. The full charm of Nora is used on Helmer to keep him from opening his mail box. She has sent Mrs. Linden away in hopes of reaching Krogstad. The dance goes on to a tarantella, when Helmer stops her. Mrs. Linden returns and reports that Krogstad is out of town. This scene is a severe tax upon restraint in emotional acting.

189. "Du Barry," David Belasco

Du Barry has just promised to leave with Cossé when Richelieu enters excitedly.

Act II (pp. 75-80). RICHELIEU: *"Quick—lights in your halls. A mad impulse has taken his Majesty—he follows me now, incognito—" To end of the act.*

The whimsical Jeanette is preparing to leave with her Cossé when Richelieu hurriedly enters and demands audience for the King's messenger. The King, incognito, is shown in, as Richelieu hurries Cossé into another room. Court dignity must dominate and not court buffoonery. Utter simplicity is keynote of Jeanette's character. Her disappointment at Cossé's leaving is one of the highlights of character portrayal. That she should look for the King's ring is a natural sequence. The throwing of the ring is a vital part of practiced technic, and has an integral part in the learned play.

190. "Du Barry," David Belasco

Du Barry is living in Louveciennes, at height of the Revolution. Jean Du Barry, always the parasite, has returned, wearing the tri-color, to give Du Barry the decree of death. Cossé, the real love of her life, has been sent by the Revolution to arrest Du Barry.

Act V, Scene 1 (pp. 127-130). JEAN: *"Announce me, Jarni. Then I'll announce myself." To end of the act.*

Cossé, the real love of Du Barry, has been sent to arrest the one love of his life. Two souls, standing in the threshold of death, must hear the heartless enthusiasm of the Revolution. The crowd ensemble, the quick adjustment of Jeanette to the edict of her being a tyrant, the enforced reading of her doom by Cossé—these are Belasco moments of throbbing drama. A good study of tempo.

191. "The Easiest Way," Eugene Walters

Laura Murdock is an actress who has met a man in Colorado, one whom she loves. But the stage has taken Laura to New York and she finds herself in desperate circumstances. Her friend, Elfie St. Clair, calls on her and is surprised at her humble surroundings. Urges Laura to make friends again with the wealthy Will Brockton. Laura rebukes Elfie for her suggestions and Elfie is leaving in a huff as Laura calls her back.

Act II (pp. 196-200). LAURA: *"Elfie! Elfie! Don't go now. Don't leave me now. I can't stand it." To end of the act.* Laura agrees to go back to Brockton and tell Madison of her decision.

To appear "natural" and avoid the maudlin, is the real test of an actor or actress, in such a scene as this. Laura writes a letter to the man she loves as dictated by her paramour. The burning of the letter, after Brockton leaves, is a gripping piece, when properly enacted. This struggle between love and necessity is a tense scene.

192. "Emperor Jones," Eugene O'Neill

Any one of the eight scenes in this remarkable play serve excellently to portray true dramatic power. Emperor Jones, a convict Negro from the United States, has gained control of a Negro island, but is challenged by a native son, Lem. Revolution is brooding and the distant rumble of the ominous drum warns Jones that the present is the best time for his exit. He has stored food at various intervals throughout the great forest he must traverse in order to get to the other side of the island and his cache.

Scene V in its entirety, carries the portent of the whole play (pp. 40-43).

All of the eight scenes are chiefly pantomimic. This scene in the forest is where Jones turns to divine help for aid, after a complete confession of his life. Prayer seems to have strengthened him until figures enter and he becomes the center of a Negro auction scene. A great struggle to reach the awareness of reality.

193. "Escape," John Galsworthy

The prologue to this play is rattling good drama and starts out on high. A girl is in Hyde Park, waiting a chance acquaintance for the evening. Matt Denant passes and she carefully attracts his attention.

Start Prologue (pp. 5-13). MATT: *"Do you come here often?" On to the end of Prologue when the* POLICEMAN *calls ambulance.*

Two good transitions in this scene; when the officer accosts the girl, and again, when the blow from Matt's fist accidentally kills the officer. The serious tranquillity of Matt is one of best bits of character delineation in the dramatic index. Flippancy would ruin the part.

194. "The Famous Mrs. Fair," James Forbes

Nancy Fair has gone to the War and returned a famous woman. Her own set is delighted with her and she receives many invitations to talk for lecture bureaus. To the dislike of her family, Mrs. Fair goes on with the public work. Her husband, Jeffrey, has taken companionship with a pretty widow. The daughter, Sylvia, is enamored of an older man, Gillette, and Alan, the son, has taken his confidences to any one but his mother.

Act II. ALAN *comes into room and surprises* SYLVIA (*pp. 245-255*). ALAN: *"Now where's Mother?" To end of the act.*

The delightful conversation between Peggy and Alan, and the follow-up with Peggy and the father, offer good contrast in modern youth and parental response. The mother's reception of the news of Alan's engagement affords another dramatic situation of contrasting power, preceding, as it does, the quarrel between the mother and the father. Contending elements in each scene.

195. "The Fires of St. John," Hermann Sudermann

George von Harten, nephew of Mr. Brauer, loves Marie, the foster daughter. Mr. Brauer wishes George to marry his young daughter, Gertrude. The real mother of Marie, a gypsy, steals to the country home, and asks Marie for money and arouses Marie's curiosity as to her real parentage.

Act II (pp. 125-126). GEORGE: *"Here she is." Down to* MARIE: *"Take this key and lock the garden gate after her, so she'll not return."*

The gypsy woman comes through the garden and Marie is confronted with one she surmises to be her mother. The knowledge that her mother is a thief further wrings her heart. In three presentations of this show, the gypsy mother "stole" the show. Was that a fault of production, the strength of one part over the other, or composition? This is excellent in portraying popular appeal of a plausible eccentric.

196. "The Fool," Channing Pollock

Daniel Gilchrist, wealthy scion, has a high-minded idea of right and wrong in life and starts to put some of his ethics into practice. He loses his best friends, refuses some of the dividends of his money because it is improperly earned, and goes to the poorer part of town to aid those who need help the most. We see him in Overcoat Hall. Even the people Gilchrist helps, think he is crazy. Gilchrist's fiancée turns against him and marries a rotter, Jerry Goodkind. A gang of men, led by Joe, are coming to the Hall to get Gilchrist, saying he is living off the women he helps. Pearl Hening enters to warn him of his danger.

Act III (pp. 149-160). PEARL: *"Mr. Gilchrist." To end of the act.*

Gang scenes are often more noisy than artistic—but noise is seldom the objective of drama. In this scene, the conflict between right and error must stand out, nor must Daniel ever appear sentimental. The miracle at end of act makes good theater as well as good drama.

197. "Ghosts," Henrik Ibsen

Oswald, only son of Mrs. Alving, has been to Paris and returns in a terrible dilemma. He has learned that his own health is forever impaired because of the indiscretions of his father. Regina, the one bright spot in Oswald's life, is concerned about his health. The three are alone.

Act III (pp. 275-295). MRS. ALVING: *"Close the doors, Regina— There now, I am going to sit beside you." To the end of play.*

Regina learns of her paternity and Oswald tells his mother of his discovery about his father. The bitterness of Regina is the more poignant when she leaves Oswald, whom she so secretly loved. Oswald's gradual dissolution of fortitude gives the scene great possibilities.

198. "La Gioconda," Gabriele D'Annunzio

The fiery passion of the Italian poet is seen to good advantage in this play. Lucio Settala has fallen into the wiles of Gioconda Dianti. The wife, Silvia Settala, determines to seek Gioconda and tell her that her husband no longer loves his model. Lucio has again told Silvia of his eternal love for her. Francesca Doni, sister of Silvia, accompanies Silvia to the studio. They arrive and find the place deserted. Silvia is about to gaze upon the great statue of Lucio. As she nears the curtain, Francesca and Silvia become conscious of the presence of Gioconda. Francesca is pushed out of side door by Silvia and Gioconda appears.

Act III (pp. 594-598). SILVIA: *"I am Silvia Settala. And you?" To end of the act.*

The conflict between two strong women, who love from different motives, makes this scene a memorable one. The long speeches must move as freely as passion itself. The outburst of Gioconda, when she hears Silvia's lie, is the real test of an actress to act this part. Silvia's saving of the masterpiece at the expense of her own hands, gives her an opportunity for a most gripping presentation.

199. "The Girl of the Golden West," David Belasco

Johnson, the road agent, has called on the Girl at her cabin, past midnight. Woukle has gone. Johnson tells the Girl of his love and she reciprocates. He starts to go and sees terrific snowstorm. They prepare for the night. Posse comes and Girl lets them in as Johnson hides.

Act II (pp. 363-381). GIRL: *"But it ain't for long you're goin'?" To end of the act.*

The sheriff reveals Johnson as the road agent and finds him hiding in loft of Girl's cabin. The struggle of conscience in the better Johnson, is decided by the ominous shots in the snowstorm. The posse arrives and the Girl lets them in. The cold must be shown but not to dominate over the suspense in the search for Ramerrez (Johnson). The careful manner of playing on the Girl's jealousy adds greatly to dramatic suspense. The great and sudden change in the Girl and daring to risk her lover's life when she gambles with the sheriff, are melodramatic high spots but must not be ruined by overacting.

200. "The Great Divide," William Vaughn Moody

Philip and Polly Jordan, accompanied by Winthrop Newbury, have just left the Arizona ranch. It is dusk, and Ruth Jordan is preparing for bed. She sings and looks out upon the moonlight. All have gone save Ruth.

Act I (pp. 291-295). RUTH: *"What a scandal the moon is making, out there in that great crazy world." The three drunken men enter and bargain for Ruth. Take to end of the act.*

201. "The Great Divide," William Vaughn Moody

On top of the world, in Arizona, Ruth is living with Ghent. Polly and Philip and Dr. Newbury have visited them and Ghent is taking them to other views. Philip remains to talk to Ruth.

Act II (pp. 302-307). PHILIP: *"No, we must have a word together, before the gabble begins again." To end of the act.*

The serious Philip and the earnest Ruth meet. The scene is intensified when Ruth gives Ghent his chain of nuggets. Suspense has certain physical limitations, to maintain dramatic values, but Moody has given to this play and these scenes some of our best American drama. Violence is never so strong as intelligent conflict.

202. "The Great Galeoto," José Echegaray

Feodora, the faithful wife of Don Julian, is seen in company of Ernest, guest and relative. Don Severo and his wife, Mercedes, suspect the platonic friendships of Feodora and Ernest, and these are scenes for the culmination of the Hydra-headed monster, gossip, as it undoes the happiness of a household and drives Feodora to do what could not have previously entered her mind. Excellent pantomime for emotional expression.

Act III, Scene 7 to end of Scene 9 (pp. 120-137).

The continental style of acting is necessary for success

of this scene. A high state of emotional vitality throughout, reaching from climax to climax, as one suspensive scene. The blindness of jealousy and suspicion, evident in all but Feodora and Ernest.

203. "Hedda Gabler," Henrik Ibsen

Hedda has loved Eilert Lövborg and he comes to see her and her husband, George Tesman. Hedda has received the confidence of Mrs. Elvsted, who is the inspiration of Lövborg's latest book. When Lövborg calls on the Tesmans he lets Hedda know that he still loves her. The men go to Judge Brack's party, while Mrs. Elvsted waits, with Hedda, the return of Lövborg. The women have waited up all night, and as morning comes, Hedda induces Mrs. Elvsted to go and rest on Hedda's bed. At this time, Tesman, tired and serious, returns, but soon leaves for a visit to a dying aunt. Presently Judge Brack enters.

Act III (pp. 131-152). HEDDA: *"You seem to have made a particularly lively night of it at your rooms, Judge Brack." To the end of act, where Hedda gives Lövborg the pistol.*

As we find in most of Ibsen, his scenes are slow in development and each conversation builds to an accumulating effect. The contrast between Hedda and Mrs. Elvsted is excellent. Lövborg is a typical Ibsenesque portrait. An intense passion of the snow country.

204. "If I Were King," Justin Huntly McCarthy

François Villon has written verses about what he would do if he were king. Louis, the King, has heard of these verses and in disguise, with Tristan, goes to the Tavern, a certain low rendezvous. Katherine de Vaucelles is loved by Thibaut D'Aussigny, traitor, in league with the Burgundians. Katherine also goes to the Tavern, confronts Villon with some of his love verses written to her and challenges him to make good. Thibaut soon comes into the Tavern, as a common soldier. In this scene the disguised King sees his favorite, Katherine, going up to the lusty Villon.

Act I (pp. 26-33). KATHERINE: *"A word with you." To end of the act.*

Romance ever gladdens the youthful heart and the very essence of romance permeates this scene. The lively ensemble, the vivacity of a popular tavern, the suspense of Villon's meeting with Thibaut and the King's incognito all add to the glamour of this quick moving scene.

205. "It Pays to Advertise," Roi C. Megrue and Walter Hackett

Rodney Martin, son of Cyrus Martin, desires to show his father that the son can earn more than five dollars a week. He gets the coöperation of Mary Grayson, his girl, and Ambrose Peale, advertising expert. They are planning on starting a new soap factory to compete with Rodney's father. They are to keep the real names of the owners of the new company a secret. The three are sitting around the table of Martin's library. They are looking for a name.

Act I (pp. 34-49). PEALE: *"We need something that's universally appealing. What is it? What is it?" To end of the act.*

A delightful scene of sprightly conversation, with the lighter emotions bubbling over with each new idea. Rodney's attempt at French gives opportunity for clowning without being a fool. Speed dominates as climax is reached, speed which remains under control.

206. "John Ferguson," St. John Ervine

John Ferguson, invalid, sits near his Bible most of the day, getting comfort from its verses. He must meet a mortgage, owned by Witherow, on the morrow. Witherow offers to annul the obligation if the daughter,

Hannah, will marry him. She accepts James Cæsar, in desperation. She goes out in the evening, to tell Witherow of their decision to let the house go, as the uncle from America hadn't replied to their request for the loan of the money. Jimmie is waiting for Hannah's return, when Clutie John, half-wit, starts excitedly from his seat.

Act II (pp. 51-68). CLUTIE JOHN: *"Wheesht!" To end of the scene.*

SARAH: *"What is it, Clutie?"*

CLUTIE: *"Wheesht! Wheesht!" Hannah comes running in and tells of Witherow's perfidy and scene ends when Andrew, the brother, takes gun from rack and leaves the house.*

A study of character contrasts. The mysticism of Clutie John, the unsuspecting selfishnes of the mother, the quiet religious fanaticism of the father, Jimmie Cæsar's inability to measure his own values, Andrew's heroic attempt to master fate, and the noble daughter, a magnanimous soul living in enforced suppressions—these are most excellent studies to challenge your acting technic. The suspense we feel for Hannah's fate parallels the outcome of Witherow's destiny. Two great dramatic themes riding side by side.

207. "Juno and the Paycock," Sean O'Casey

The Boyle home, a tenement in Dublin, is the scene of an excellent comedy drama. Captain Boyle and Joxer are cronies; Mrs. June Boyle forbids Joxer a welcome in their home, but the promise of a "cup o tae" causes Joxer to go to Boyle during Mrs. Boyle's absence. Jerry and Mary have just left the room.

Act I (pp. 25-44). BOYLE: *"Childers don't care a damn now, about their parents." To end of the act.*

There is considerable difference between an eccentric character and a character of national type. An Irishman may be eccentric but an actor has to appear and act Irish if he is to act the part of Boyle. The reminiscences and philosophy of the old friends is excellent comedy if not made maudlin. An excellent transition in this scene, when Boyle hears he is heir to some money.

208. "The King's Henchman," Edna St. Vincent Millay

The lords and ladies discuss the future bride of King Eadgar, and also comment upon the shyness of his dearest friend, Æthelwold. The King sends Æthelwold to Devonshire, to procure the beautiful Ælfrida for England's future queen. Maccus and Æthelwold are lost in the forest on Halloween. When Æthelwold awakes from his sleep, he is confronted by the beautiful Ælfrida.

Act II (pp. 39-68). Start from beginning of act to where ASE, *the nurse, returns, calling: "My Lady."*

Eliminate most of the verses of the Halloween song. These scenes are rich in wonder, surprise, and suspense, in controlled action. Contrast the clumsy comedy of Maccus with the dainty movements of Ælfrida. Haze dominates the scene and action must correspond.

209. "Lady Windermere's Fan," Oscar Wilde

Lady Windermere is in Lord Darlington's apartment. She is joined by Mrs. Erlynne, to the consternation of Lady Windermere. Take scene to entrance of Windermere, Darlington and Augustus.

Act III (pp. 822-825).

The contrast of the two women affords excellent opportunities for histrionic development in the wife, who despises the unknown mother, and the mother, who would save her daughter at the expense of her own happiness. The soliloquy of Lady Windermere at the beginning of the scene is a real test. The ultimate acceptance of help from Mrs. Erlynne further challenges ability in character resolution. The part of Mrs. Erlynne is one of the best character studies in the English language.

210. "Lady Windermere's Fan," Oscar Wilde

The men are in Darlington's room. They have been discussing women in general and Mrs. Erlynne in particular.

Act III (pp. 826-828). LORD DARLINGTON: *"The woman I love is not free, or thinks she isn't." To end of the act.*

The fan is discovered by Cecil, after Darlington has been moralizing about the purity of love. Lord Windermere recognizes it as his wife's fan. The friendly party is suddenly turned into an ominous struggle of jealousy and disgust, astonishment and anger. This is a wonderful group scene. Each character contributes to the powerful climax.

211. "Madame Butterfly," David Belasco

Madame Butterfly chases Nakado from her house with her father's sword. Carry the scene to end of play. Butterfly prepares room for Pinkerton after seeing his ship, *Connecticut,* in the bay. Suzuki in forced haste. Butterfly's toilette; rocks baby to sleep, singing an American song—then waits, as night advances. Next morning Pinkerton and Sharpless appear (leave the Nakado out in this scene). Pinkerton sees baby and leaves just before Butterfly enters. Kate appears and offers aid, but is refused. There is but one course for Butterfly!

(Pp. 25-32). BUTTERFLY: *"Lies, lies. Say again, I kill. Go."*

Cho-Cho-San is forced to realize that Pinkerton has another and very beautiful wife. The pantomime wherein she draws her dagger and ends a life so easily made glad and so noble in bitter sorrow, is one of great power. This scene is a good example of the difference in emotional responses between the actor and the audience. Cho-Cho-San has only forgiveness for Pinkerton and ends her own life for his happiness. The audience feels contempt for

Pinkerton and profound sorrow for Butterfly. Her beautiful nobility and trustfulness intensifies our sympathy for her. If part is spoken, dialect should be as perfect as possible.

212. "The Man from Home," Tarkington and Wilson

Daniel Vorhees Pike has come from Indiana to Italy, to look into the affairs of his wards, Horace and Ethel Granger Simpson. He learns that Ethel is enamored of a certain English dandy, Almeric St. Aubyn. On his way to the villa, Pike helps the Grand Duke Vasili Vasilivitch with his car. Vasili is incognito, though the servants know his identity. Lord Hawcastle, father of Almeric, is a scheming adventurer, interested in the American fortune.

Act I (pp. 53-71). VASILI *enters from the hotel, and has just given* PIKE *some vodka.* PIKE: *"I never had any business to leave Indiana!" To end of the act.*

A good ensemble of eccentric types, each easily recognized as being something known as "national." As Royall Tyler years ago wrote in "The Contrast," so we have, in this scene, the New and the Old World standards in conflict. The so-called "dry" humor of Pike, is quite generally accepted in Europe as best representing the American species. The eccentric may amuse, the abnormal can but arouse our pity or our disgust. The chief purpose of drama is to entertain.

213. "Marco Millions," Eugene O'Neill

Marco Polo has gone to China with his uncle and father. He is concerned with making a fortune. While in this oriental splendor, Kukuchin, beautiful princess, falls desperately in love with him. She is pledged to marry the Arghun Khan, and the party is entrusted, en route, to Marco. Kukuchin has made no impression on Marco, who is the most gullible of innocents.

Act II, Scene 3 (pp. 129-140). MARCO: *"Your high-*

ness, or I suppose I'd better say Majesty"—to MARCO: *"The future Mrs. Marco Polo."*

Marco tells the princess that her proposed husband is dead. Her love for him has been intensified by his many heroic deeds in her behalf. But he is duty incarnate. Subtle comedy built on a thread of sparkling satire calls for hours of preparation. The despair of the princess and the constant balance of duty for Polo fight their ways to a beautiful dénouement. Never loud, sudden only once: when Maffeo clangs the stack of coins as Marco is about to kiss Kukuchin.

214. "The Master Builder," Henrik Ibsen

The home of Solness had burned down, and Solness was building another. Mrs. Solness mourned the loss of her twin babes, indirectly caused by the burning of their home. Mrs. Solness has become morose and has no joy in the building of the new home. Solness has become selfish and ambitious, in matters away from the home, the feeling that his entire life was an indebtedness to his wife. It is for Mrs. Solness he is building the new house, knowing that it can never be a home for her.

Act II (pp. 261-288). MRS. SOLNESS: *"The home that used to be father's and mother's, and that was burned to the ground," through scene with* HILDA *and* SOLNESS, *to entrance of* RAGNAR BROVIK.

This scene is dependent upon ability to animate conversation with little action. Ibsen drama is chiefly concerned with greatest action outside of the enacted scene —it is talked about. The power of the things suggested constitute much of Ibsen. Only the best of acting can interpret Ibsen and hold the average audience.

215. "Michael and His Lost Angel," Henry Arthur Jones

Michael Feversham has seen and loves the dashing Audrie Lesden. Being sworn to the ministry, he conquers his personal desires and feels quite secure in his fortitude.

He has gone to the Shrine on Saint Decuman's Island. He has a letter from Audrie, which he struggles against reading, but eventually reads. He is alone, as Father Hilary and Withycombe have been rowed away. He watches the letter burn in the fire. "I've conquered. Now I shall be at peace."

Act II (pp. 88-92). AUDRIE *taps his window and says: "May I come in? You are busy—I'll go—" To the end of scene.*

Which is the stronger drama? A struggle with oneself or a struggle with outside forces? Michael meets both, and the loving Audrie tasks him to the uttermost. The drama of silence is often more powerful than with speech.

216. "Milestones," Arnold Bennett and Edward Knaubloch

John Rhead has married Rose Sibley and has taken charge of the ironworks. He lives now, the kind of life which fretted him so much when twenty-one. He is planning to marry his daughter to Lord Monkhurst, much against her desire. Aunt Gertrude does not want Emily to make a mess of her life, as she has of her own. She asks her old friend, Sam Sibley, to help John and Rose see the virtues of young Arthur Preece.

Act II (pp. 74-87). GERTRUDE: *"Sam, I'm so glad you've come. There's going to be another tragedy in this house." To end of the act.*

The talking of a person, making him a very important part of the scene, and his later introduction into actual dialogue, demands careful details and preconceived study. Ned is the unwitting crux to the whole situation.

217. "Monna Vanna," Maurice Maeterlinck

Pisa is about to be besieged by her enemy and the Florentine general, Prinzivalle, has made a condition whereby he can render aid. Marco Colonna, father of

Guido, has just been released from the Florentine camp and brings the news that Pisa can be saved only if Monna Vanna, Guido's wife, will go alone to Prinzivalle's tent. Thirty thousand lives depend on her decision. Guido is astounded at her decision, better for her to be dishonored than for a town of people to be destroyed. When she arrives at Prinzivalle's tent, she learns that he is a childhood companion. Through her coming, food and ammunition have been sent to Pisa. Doing her no harm, Prinzivalle takes her back to Pisa.

Act III, Scene 1 (pp. 621-625). Entrance of Vanna and Prinzivalle.

A powerful scene of love and hate, suspicion and conjugal distrust, rabid patriotism and glorified sacrifice, sanctified trust. Emotions in plays, as well as life, can be so overdone, that we cease to have responsive interest in the enactor. But emotions such as these in this scene, when direct responses to a logical situation in the play, can pull and move as much as real life. The characters move from one high tension to another and reach a climax of intense interest, whose real solution carries well beyond the final curtain.

218. "Mrs. Warren's Profession," G. Bernard Shaw

Toward the end of the act, the minister gardener is introduced, as he comes in through the gate of the garden. His son, Frank, has met Vivie, the daughter of Mrs. Warren, and wants the minister to meet her. Begin when the minister enters.

Act I (pp. 180-183). REV. SAMUEL GORDON: *"Well, sir. Who are your friends here, if I may ask?" To end of the act.*

The pompous minister is a character too often presented in drama as a ridicule to the church. Drama may teach, but it need not offend. Modern drama has given considerable attention to the clergy and few receive their just due. Shaw is no exception and rather overplays his ministerial characters. In this scene, it is the character which interests us, rather than a representative of the church. This is a scene in which situation offers an opportunity for comedy.

219. "Mrs. Warren's Profession," G. Bernard Shaw

The proposal between Crofts and Vivie; Crofts tells Frank that Vivie is his half-sister.

Act III (pp. 216-223). CROFTS: *"Pleasing young fellow, that, Miss Vivie. Pity he has no money, isn't it?" Continue to where* CROFTS *leaves* FRANK *and* VIVIE *together.*

The rather blasé manner of proposing is not uncommon on the stage, but this scene gives us a different ending to such proposals. The bitterness of Vivie makes this a strong character part, but the theme is too unpopular to be used extensively. The fact of relationship between Vivie and Frank is not so unusual as the brutality of its exposition. Shaw is loquacious, his characters are never "flip."

220. "Ned McCobb's Daughter," Sidney Howard

Carrie McCobb has married a good-for-nothing, George Callahan. George has absconded with two thousand dollars from his company's earnings, but Lawyer Grover promises that directors will not prosecute for honor of McCobb name, if money is raised by the morrow. Lawyer Grover tells Ned McCobb that he is partly responsible, because he had recommended Callahan, coming directly from prison.

Act I (pp. 55-73). LAWYER GROVER: *"Straight from a year on Deer Island, Ned. Served for his part in a hold-up in Boston." To end of the act.*

The captain learns of the duplicity of his son-in-law, George. They all plan means of raising the necessary two thousand dollars to save George from prison. The way each has of looking at life makes the first two acts of the play intensely interesting. The father is a sterling fellow, too seldom met in life or on the stage.

221. "Old English," John Galsworthy

Old Heythorp, with the aid of Molly, is able to reach the liqueurs and bring his premature death. This is one of the greatest pantomimes in modern drama.

Act III, Scene 2, toward end of scene (pp. 113-115). Adela: *"If it weren't for Temperance I wouldn't—I won't have liquor in the house." She goes out; carry to the end of the scene.*

Old age with grace; power in determination to conquer the physical; an unconquerable soul, defeated only by sheer incapacity to move. Definite tempo and rhythm must mark the action of this slow-moving scene.

222. "Old Lady 31," Rachel Crothers

Abe has gone to "The Home" with his aged wife, Angie. They have lost the home of their happiest years. Abe is having a hard time adjusting his wife to the demands of a Woman's Home. His old-time chum, Samuel Darby, has come to visit him. Abe is not well and all the ladies are concerned about him. Abe is all bundled up, all eyes watching him.

Act II (pp. 159-170). Nancy: *"Girls, let me tell you something. Angie's blind as a bat." To end of the act.*

Blossy pays attention to poor old Abe and sets the tongues to wagging. Excellent old lady types make this scene a delightful vehicle for character study. The speeches are revelatory of each person.

223. "Old Man Minick," Edna Ferber, George S. Kaufman

One of the cleverest club meetings ever depicted is found in this play. Fred and Nettie Minick have had their father, Old Man Minick, come to live with them. He has adjusted himself quite well, with the aid of two newfound cronies, Mr. Dietenhoffer and Mr. Price. Nettie and Lil Corey are entertaining an important club group in their home. But before father gets his two partners out of the way, the ladies arrive.

Act II (pp. 161-202). NETTIE: *"Please, Father. The meeting'll be starting." Down to*—MINICK: *"Say, here's the sandwiches, the ladies forgot to eat the sandwiches."*

This scene is chosen to show how much acting is necessary when but one person is speaking. Constant attention to central theme and speaking character is vitally important. Not for a second does any character get out of the scene of this club meeting. Each character is distinctly a type, each contributing a share to the general effect. Nettie's toleration, working up to exasperation, and the quiet interest of Minick, until his social soul can stand the strain no longer, are highlights in part analysis. Comedy dominates—it is enriched with pathos.

224. "Porgy," Dorothy and DuBose Heyward

Porgy is a crippled Negro of Charleston and joins his friends in crap shooting in Catfish Row. Robbins and Crown get into a quarrel. Robbins is killed. Bess, Crown's associate, seeks cover with Porgy, as a place least apt to be looked into. Lawyer Frazier comes to Porgy and is ready to get Bess a divorce from Crown.

Act II. FRAZIER: *"Ef de 'oman goin' stay wid yo' she's got to hab divorce from Crown or else it ain't legal." On to the point where Bess goes to the picnic.*

The Negro is fast proving his ability to act. Emotions are race habits in body response. These two statements may seem far from being a comment on above scene, but are in truth closely akin. The Negro has always been capable of excellent acting; it is opportunity which is proving it. No actor can surpass the Negro in making an intense moment seem so simple, so much a part of actual life. Compare this scene with any in "All God's Chilluns Got Wings" and "The Green Pastures."

225. "The Pretenders," Henrik Ibsen

The people are to choose between Håkon and Earl Skule, who is to be their King. The great crowd is assembled in the King's Hall. The two ladies, Lady Ragnhild and Margrete, her daughter, are in a hall in the Palace, awaiting results. Lady Ragnhild favors her husband, Skule, and Margrete favors Håkon.

Act I, Scene 2 (pp. 516-521). Start scene at beginning and take through the choosing of HÅKON, *to his speech. "She is too dear to me, Earl—a king must have none about him whom he loves too well."*

This scene is excellent for its possibilities of two characters on the stage, in revealing what takes place off the stage. The triumph of Håkon is good study as it elaborates the triumph of people rather than the kingdom.

226. "The Return of Peter Grimm," David Belasco

Frederick and Catherine are to be married on the morrow. Peter has died and James is leaving the florist establishment. Little William is ill and concerns all but Frederick. Peter returns and remains half in shadow.

Act II (pp. 456-489). CATHERINE: *"Did some one call me?" To end of the act.*

This pantomime is strongest with words, though much of scene needs no words. This play is good theater as well as good drama. The scene herein depicted starts where the kindly old Peter has come back to earth to visit his beloved kinsmen. The play is never loud—its key and movement are reverential, as one would try and appease the dead. The dilemma of Peter when none can hear him, until he influences Frederick to recognize the paternity of William, to be again thwarted by Frederick in the burning of the letter; the final message to the little boy, a most clever management and so easily developed that credulity does not enter into the unfoldment. The staging is as important as the acting.

227. *"Saturday's Children," Maxwell Anderson*

Aided by expert advice from her sister, Florrie, Bobbie Halevy lays proper plans to procure marriage with Rims O'Neil. Their marriage is handicapped with insufficient funds and a desire on Bobbie's part to have more money to enjoy life. The family does not greatly help matters. A breaking point seems inevitable, when the father accounts himself quite unable to give good advice about marriage.

Act II (pp. 105-128). Halevy: *"Now, don't ask me to talk seriously on this topic, my dear. After all, I'm your father." To end of the act.*

Two young people, not helped very much by a bitter father; Bobbie is sincere in her hopes for the future, as Rims is weighted down by the worries of the present. Realism may be art, but vulgarity is never artistic. Conversation dominates this scene, with characters trying to find themselves.

228. *"Scarecrow," Percy Mackaye*

Justice Merton is living in snug complacency. He loves his niece, Rachel, who is betrothed to Richard Talbot. Lord Ravensbane has appeared on the scene with his tutor, Dickon. Dickon is described as a Yankee improvisation of the Prince of Darkness. Seeing Lord Ravensbane, hypothetical son, has greatly disturbed Justice Merton. Rachel has fallen in love with Lord Ravensbane and has just departed.

Act II (pp. 378-380). Rachel: *"Till we—meet—again!" To end of the act.*

The hypocritical Ravensbane takes a pseudofainting spell and Rachel shows her concern for his welfare. With Dickon at hand, Ravensbane revives quickly and replies to Richard's challenge by blowing smoke in his face. To portray villainy of the Mephistophlean type demands positive assurance, graceful body, and manners. Dickon's power is his ability to reveal what he may do as well as what he does.

229. "The Second Mrs. Tanqueray," Arthur Wing Pinero

The inability of Paula Tanqueray to gain the love of Ellean, daughter of the first Mrs. Tanqueray, leads to a scene which calls for powerful reserve to reach a forceful climax.

Act II (pp. 47-48). Ellean *has just left the morning room.* Paula: *"Well, have you and Ellean had your little confidence?" Down to* Servant: *"Mrs. Drummle, ma'am."*

Paula's attempt to win the respect and love of Ellean for her own sake, to have her affections reciprocated, make her supersensitive of every affection which Ellean receives from her father. The real struggle Paula undergoes is her own fight with self-respect. Jealousy with a cause is stronger drama than jealousy without a cause.

230. "The Show Off," George Kelly

Aubrey has married Amy Fisher, and spends most of his time with Pa and Ma Fisher. Aubrey borrowed his brother-in-law's car, ran into a traffic officer and is out on bail, furnished by his brother-in-law. Aubrey is at the Fisher home with his head well bandaged. A telephone call takes Ma Fisher, her son Joe, and daughter Clara, to the hospital, where Pa Fisher has been taken, following a stroke.

Act II (pp. 72-86). Joe: *"Are you ready, Mom?* Clara: *"Yes, we're ready," through the scene where they learn of* Pa's *death, to end of the act.*

The unconscious braggart has always been good foil for comedy. Aubrey must not overdo his brusqueness and audience must be made to know he is quite human, through it all. We must be interested in him throughout play. Note how the death of the father in this scene affects the characters and compare this to the effect of the death of the officer in "Escape."

231. "Strange Interlude," Eugene O'Neill

The present is the strange interlude; the past we know and the future is all that matters. Nina, daughter of Professor Leeds, has given her love to an aviator-hero, Gordon Shaw. The Professor dies, after the tragic death of Gordon. Nina has decided she can compensate for her lost love only in a sacrificing manner. The elderly friend, Marsden; the dynamic Doctor Darrell; and the kindly friend, Sam Evans; these three claim her attention. She marries Evans, gives her love to Darrell, and is befriended by Marsden.

Act VI (pp. 225-236). DARRELL: *"Nina—I—I've come back to you—do you—do you still care—Nina?" To end of the act.*

Darrell returns to Nina, torn with respect for his friend, Evans, and the desire to acknowledge the paternity of Gordon, Nina's son. Nina's joy in the knowledge that she has her three men about her again—and each finding in her the great happiness of his life. Her saying "Good-night" to the three men is one of the most exquisite bits of modern drama.

232. "Strife," John Galsworthy

John Anthony, chairman of the Trenatha Tin Plate Works is seventy-six years old, and has dominated the company for over thirty years. His policy is now challenged and his son, Edgar, is sympathetic with the strikers. A meeting has been called and the directors are to meet in Underwood's drawing-room. Mrs. Roberts, wife of a striker, has just died of hunger. The news is brought to Enid, daughter of John Anthony. The directors, in angry mood, gather one at a time.

Act III (pp. 142-145). EDGAR: *"Have you heard this, sir? Mrs. Roberts is dead. Enid saw her this afternoon, she has no coal, or food, or anything. It's enough." Down to* ANTHONY: *"Before I put this amendment to the Board"—to the conclusion of this speech—"bring in the men."*

An intense scene of varied emotions, growing stronger as the various characters speak. Protest, anger, scorn, disdain, incredulity, paternal and filial love, defeat, triumph, pity, and scorn, all have their moments of intense registration—but above all, anger dominates. A great group scene, in which Galsworthy is so powerfully expressive.

233. "Sun Up," Lulu Vollmer

The Stranger has been hiding in the house, when the Sheriff returns to tell Widow Cagle that the man she is hiding is the son of her feud enemy, Turner.

Act III, Scene 2 (pp. 68-75). SHERIFF: *"No use for gun play, Miss Cagle." Down to* MRS. CAGLE: *"No, I reckon my love went on—I reckon you better go, Stranger."*

As the Sheriff tells Mrs. Cagle that she is protecting a Turner all the stored-up hate of a revengeful feudist rises within her. She accepts no hearsay evidence but must have the truth from his own lips, that he is the son of Zeb Turner. Cold, calculating, keeping to the letter of the feud, she gives the Stranger a chance to fight or run. Only a miracle could divert a hate so strong as this, so controlled as Mrs. Cagle. A resolution of a strong, unpleasant emotion into an uplifting, pleasant response.

234. "Three Wise Fools," Austin Strong

Judge Trumbull, Dr. Gaunt, and Mr. Finley, are three confirmed bachelors, suddenly given the responsibility of a beautiful young girl, Sidney Fairchild. She changes their lives and brings them out of their ruts. Gordon Schuyler, nephew of Finley, comes to the house of the three Musketeers, meets Sidney and falls in love with her. Sidney's father is a criminal and Sidney is befriending Benny, the Duck, who is out to revenge his jail sentence, given by Judge Trumbull. Gordon is kissing Sidney good-night, as she is going to the opera with her three guardians.

Act II (pp. 66-80). SIDNEY: *"Please go now—you promised." Through scene where the servant,* GRAY, *is put out by* BENNY *and escapes through fireplace. End scene:* FINLEY: *"Now are you satisfied? You've been tried and found innocent."*

A fast-moving scene of quick changing suspense. Stage rhythm must be carefully watched in this scene, and timing of entrance is imperative. Stage business is often as important as character development. This is true in "Three Wise Fools," being a situation play.

235. "The Truth," Clyde Fitch

Against the wishes of her husband, Becky Warder has sent for Fred Lindon, her paramour. Lindon meets Warder, who informs Lindon that Becky is out, but Servant enters and tells them that Mrs. Warder is at home. Lindon shows Warder a letter, stating that Becky would act as intermediary between Mrs. Lindon and himself. Warder excuses himself and Lindon is alone in the drawing-room. The meeting of Becky and Lindon—wherein Lindon kisses Becky, to her amazement and disgust. Lindon is sent out and Warder returns, serious and calm. He cannot believe the truth.

Act II (pp. 265-268). LINDON: *"Well, she did send for you, Freddy, old son. Now's your chance." To end of the act.*

As Mrs. Warder tells lie after lie to her husband, his anger increases, and her own duplicity is the more punishing. When he leaves, she realizes the futility of truth coming upon the foundation of lies. A climax built upon defeat of an individual and the clarification of a situation.

236. *"The Wild Duck," Henrik Ibsen*

Gregers Werle has gone walking with Hialmer Ekdal and has been told that the copy work done by Gina Ekdal, Hialmer's wife, and the aged father, Old Ekdal, is given to them by Werle, the wealthy merchant, because of a certain favor granted Werle some fifteen years previous. Hialmer returns to the house a changed man. His half-blind daughter, Hedwig, is his only concern. This scene takes place in the Ekdal photograph studio.

Act IV (pp. 40-44). HEDWIG: *"Father! Oh, what a time we've been waiting for you." Take scene to entrance of Mrs. Sorby.*

This play, dealing with the happiness of illusion and the bitterness of reality, is brought to a dramatic climax with Relling and Gregers viewing their philosophy before the saddened wife and miserable husband. Action is seldom dominant in Ibsen and this scene is no exception. The conflict is intellectual and social.

237. *"The Witching Hour," Augustus Thomas*

Tom Denning, half drunk, has offended Clay Whipple, and Whipple has told Denning he didn't like his cat's-eye scarf pin. Tom insists upon tormenting Clay. Tragedy of unexpected nature occurs in the following scene.

Act I (pp. 332-333). HARMUTH: *"What was that?" To end of the act.*

The drunken Tom pursues the sensitive Whipple and drives him to desperation. A paper knife, wildly swung, strikes vitally and a happy party is thrown tragically into the face of death. Incredulity is brought quickly to stern reality. An excellent scene for sudden group transition.

238. *"Yellow Sands," Eden and Adelaide Phillpotts*

Aunt Jenifer Varwell recently died. Every one is anxious about his legacy except Richard, brother and philosopher. Joe, young and active, is against all capital and capitalists, and unconsciously interested in Lydia, working girl for Aunt Jenifer. Mary Varwell is most ambitious for her Arthur. All are present for the reading of the will, even to the twins of duplicate thoughts, Minnie and Nellie. Lawyer Boslow is to arrive soon; Koko, the parrot, is also present, among the other heirlooms.

Act III (pp. 105-122). DICK: *"Mr. Boslow not come?" Down to end of will reading.*

The expectancy of each relative, as the will is read, is a delightful bit of comedy. The sureness of Mary and her ultimate humiliation in disappointment, the easy adjustment of Dick, are delightful studies in contrast. Comedy, stalking in the rooms of death, affords the actor opportunity of portraying character with subtle care.

CLASSIC PLAYS

239. *"All for Love," John Dryden*

The meeting of Cleopatra and Octavia is a scene not usually given by most dramatists who treat this well-known theme. An Egyptian Hall is the meeting place of Antony and Cleopatra. They are interrupted by the faithful Ventidius, who reports a major victory. Octavia and her two daughters enter.

Act III (pp. 227-236). ANTONY: *"Where?—Octavia there!" To end of the act.*

In the first part of this scene, you will note the scarcity of action. Dialogue is paramount though the greeting of the children is very dramatic. Antony's final surrender to the ties of home is well conceived. The meeting of Cleopatra and Octavia is excellent drama, calling for direct conversation and an unforced dénouement. Queen must be sincere.

240. *"Becket," Alfred, Lord Tennyson*

The Bower scene from this play was a great favorite. Elinor has learned the secret abode of the trusting Rosamund and follows young Geoffrey to the very door. An excellent scene for group action. The Queen wants Rosamund to deny her marriage to the King. Fitzurse enters and offers to take Rosamund away with him. Rosamund is saved by the powerful Becket, statesman and priest.

Scene in Act IV, Scene 2 (pp. 470-476). Begin with first of scene, end with:

BECKET: *"And lamed and maimed to dislocation, better*
Than raised to take a life which Henry bade me
Guard from the stroke that dooms thee after death."

Excellent contrast in character is found in the four persons of this scene, both in pantomime and voice. Four types of the old stage are clearly defined. Two good people contending against the "bad" people. A scene so easily overdone, both in actions and sentimentalism.

241. "The Cenci," Percy B. Shelley

Count Cenci has assembled some guests in his magnificent palace. They are being entertained at a banquet. He tells his guests, in the presence of his wife and daughter, that his two sons have been murdered at the University by his command. Beatrice asks the guests assembled to arrest her father, but none dare defy his power.

Act I, Scene 3 (pp. 721-723). To end of scene.

This play makes better reading than acting, but in this scene we have a very strong dramatic situation. The merriment of a feast is suddenly turned into impotent desire to avenge unjust murder. Each part is rich with possible experience for an actor or actress. The struggle is mental rather than physical.

242. "The Cid," Pierre Corneille

Roderick, suitor of Chimène, is obligated by the code of his fatherland to avenge the insult upon his father, by taking the life of Chimène's father, Gomez. Chimène, in her love, is also confronted by an obligation to kill the father of Roderick. The invading Moors call for the attention of the King and the valiant arm of Roderick. He becomes a national hero, though he reaps little personal glory because of his honor obligation. The King helps the situation.

Act IV (pp. 159-162). Start where Chimène *and* Elvira *enter, on to end of the act.*

The bitter struggle of Chimène with her love for Roderick and custom's demand that she kill his father, give this part real significance. Another emotional transition is when the King orders her to wed the victor of the duel. Again the long speech of the classic is a challenge to histrionic training.

243. "Œdipus Rex," Sophocles

Laios, King of Thebes, wishes a son. But the oracle told him should Jocasta and he have a son, he would suffer death at his son's hands. When Jocasta bore a son, the parents had him taken to the hills to live as a shepherd and thus avoid the threat of the oracle. When the Sphinx harassed Thebes, Œdipus came, solved the riddle and slew the Sphinx. As the King was slain, Œdipus was chosen King and he married Jocasta. Œdipus suspects his own identity.

Start where Messenger *comes to the court and inquires for* Œdipus *down to the death of* Jocasta, as told by a Second Messenger. (*Pp. 44-56*).

The great booming lines of Sophocles call for augmented voice, vigorous physique and dynamic power. No weakling could read these lines with requisite power. Full lines, group grace and vigorous action make the pantomime in these scenes noteworthy. If you would have a beautiful voice, train in the classics. If you would acquire beauty in strength, be proficient in the classics.

244. "Paolo and Francesca," Stephen Phillips

Paolo, the handsome brother of Giovanni, the tyrant, desires to leave the home of Giovanni. But Giovanni wishes his young brother to remain home and guard the master's bride, Francesca. Old Angela, the blind nurse, tells Giovanni he is to be betrayed by one who unwillingly comes awooing. Paolo is frightened of his love for Francesca. Giovanni and Paolo discuss their love and trust, and later the meeting of Paolo and Francesca takes place.

Act II, Scene 1 (pp. 10-13). Take entire scene.

The struggle of Paolo to be loyal to his brother, as well as to his own conscience, makes this scene rich with acting strength. And the discovery that his brother Paolo is the one whom Giovanni must fear gives his part real dramatic zest. Giovanni may be tyrannical but not brutal in this scene.

245. *"Richelieu," Edward Bulwer-Lytton*

The aged Cardinal has been set upon by assassins, but escapes, and goes to Court, just as Mauprat has been sent to the Bastille. Richelieu breaks upon the scheming of Baradas, and advances to the King.

Act IV, Scene 1 (pp. 124-125). Begin where FRANÇOIS *exits and* RICHELIEU *speaks: "Room, my Lords, room. The Minister of France can need no intercession with the King!" To end of scene.*

This scene differs greatly from the one in "Old English" wherein the old fighter bluffs his way through an important and critical board meeting. Richelieu is in deadly earnest and fights for his own power and life, believing in his destiny. Righteous anger vies with protected tyranny.

246. *"Richelieu," Edward Bulwer-Lytton*

Act IV, Scene 2 (pp. 125 ff). Begin scene with entrance of JULIE.

JULIE: *"Heaven I thank thee,*
It cannot be, or this all-powerful man
Would not stand idly thus,"

down to entrance of BARADAS *and* DE BERINGHEN.

The great man has to admit that his dismissal from power has already been consummated—his defeat is complete. But in that hour of governmental defeat he stands triumphant with his ecclesiastical prestige. Glorified defiance in the presence of uncertain villainy.

247. "She Stoops to Conquer," Oliver Goldsmith

Young Marlow and Hastings are led by the mischievous Tony to his own home, where reside the Hardcastles. The men think they are at an inn rather than in the home they were seeking. Miss Hardcastle and Miss Neville agree to play a prank upon the men. Miss Hardcastle acts as the maid. Tony comes in very much spattered and informs Hastings that his suit with Miss Neville is progressing.

Act V, Scene 2 (pp. 665-670). Start with the entrance of MRS. HARDCASTLE *and carry through to end of play.*

The "aside" may be very good drama, as may soliloquy. The rendition must be made to fit the occasion, rather than to display any personal talent. This rollicking play approaches broad comedy but must not reach the fringe of commonness. Manners are a good part of this play.

248. "The Sunken Bell," Gerhardt Hauptmann

The good wife Magda comes into her home, bringing flowers to her two boys. She is waiting to hear the great bell that her husband, Heinrich, has cast for the village. He has been away all night, working for the great holiday. A neighbor comes to the happy home and tells Magda of the foreboding evil experienced by the people in the village. No flag had yet been hung in the church on the hill. The neighbor had heard that the wagon and the bell had broken down. Magda is frightened and asks Neighbor to care for her children while she leaves to learn more details. The crowd bring in Heinrich, more dead than alive.

Act II (pp. 157-161), down to HEINRICH'S *speech: "'Twas for the valley, not the mountain top."*

The contrast of the trusting wife and the doubting Neighbor works to a crescendo of unrest until the Bellman Heinrich is borne in upon a litter. The distracted wife is the more grieved at his attitude toward death. Tragedy in the events to come are more potent than the futility of Heinrich's present.

249. "Tartuffe," Molière

Into the happy home of Orgon and Elmire has come the perfidious Tartuffe. By his pious representations, Tartuffe has completely won over the gullible Orgon and has the promise of Orgon's daughter in marriage. But Mariane, the daughter, loves Valere and is being aided by Elmire's companion, Dorine. The real affection of Tartuffe is for Elmire. Damis, the son, suspecting the intentions of Tartuffe, hides in a closet, to spy upon him. Scenes in this play indicate the introduction of a new character, rather than change of location.

Act III, Scenes 2, 3, 4, 5, 6 (pp. 135-154).

This play was written to expose the weaknesses of men and hold them up to ridicule. Molière's attack on religious hypocrisy is world known. Written in 1664, its complete production was not given until five years later. Tartuffe does not appear until the third act, but he is well introduced before we see him. Dorine is neither servant nor relative, but a character type now defunct. Especial care must be given to her delineation. Tartuffe starts out as hypocrite and exposes himself as such. [Rev. Davidson in "Rain" (Maugham) is a greatly different type and more to be pitied.] Note the long speeches, but how well they talk.

250. "Virginius," James Sheridan Knowles

The first meeting of Appius and Virginia. Virginia enters with her nurse and her uncle Numitorius, and talks on one side of scene as Appius and his attendants enter. A good scene to practice for old, conventional aside speeches and for the management of two groups talking independently.

Act II, Scene 4 (pp. 25-26). PLEBEIAN: *"Grant me a minute's pause, I shall begin," to end of the act.*

A great deal of thought and action must be read between the lines in most of the classic plays. Knowles knew little of theater, but wrote for such men as Macready, Kemble, and Kean. Great power of eye and magnetic manner. Pantomime of suggestion, as well as that of portrayal. Appius calls for such power seldom seen in popular actors of to-day. "Naturalness" is the vogue of present-day acting, as the heavy tread fitted those of the first part of the nineteenth century.

251. "William Tell," Friedrich Schiller

The tyrannies of Gessler are becoming unbearable and the citizens are growing more rebellious. As a test of subservience to the King and Gessler, a cap is put upon a pole for the peasants to bow to as they pass. The people avoid the place, not wishing to recognize the sign, though the place was usually very popular. The famous apple-shooting scene takes place.

Act III, Scene 3 (pp. 171-184).

A patriotic scene of more than ordinary interest. Class distinction is evident in the group, the people, the soldiers, and the aristocrat. Contention with rich and poor, the oppressor and the oppressed, love of country and love of children—these elements of dramatic action are portrayed in masterly manner.

PANTOMIMES FROM THE PRECEDING PLAYS

252. "Cyrano de Bergerac"

The scene is laid in Ragueneau's cook shop, in 1640. Each soldier and cadet carries his sword; velvet and lace abound. This particular shop is a popular rendezvous of gay Paris. Meat, ducks, geese, and peacocks occupy left part of shop, as they hang from iron bars. An immense fireplace, in the back, is filled with sizzling roasts. On the counter at the left are vases of natural flowers.

On the right, near the front, is a door. A stairway on the back leads to a little room, in which you may look and see a table set for two. The gallery leads to other small rooms.

The round-ring chandelier is laden with heavy candles.

The ovens glow under the staircase and all the copper kettles glisten and shine.

Huge cooks bustle in and out in early morning preparations. Small apprentices go and come as occasion demands. White caps and clean aprons are evident. Many of the caps have guinea and chicken feathers adorning them.

One cook is putting various kinds of pastry in the glass cases and on the wooden shelves.

Four or five tables are scattered conveniently in the fore part of the shop and chairs are set for customers. Two tables are covered with dainty cakes and pastries.

Ragueneau, the fat, chubby little cook, has a desk in the rear, on which are many papers.

He prefers being known as a poet.

In this scene, the cadets are assembled, and are making good use of the various pastry tables. All the men have taken wine and are calling for Cyrano to tell his story about the taking of the bridge.

Cyrano, heavily plumed and booted, loves this cosmopolitan place and has just had rendezvous with the beautiful Roxane. She has asked him to especially look after a handsome arrival in Paris, one Christian.

Le Bret, good friend of Cyrano, is joking him about his love for Roxane, when the handsome Christian enters. The newcomer goes to a table somewhat apart, as the others do not recognize him, though he is dressed as all other cadets. A large soldier goes over to Christian and asks Cyrano to tell the story of his bravery for the benefit of the new recruit. Cyrano and Le Bret are conversing aside. All the cadets join in the request which Cyrano ignores.

Each of the cadets tells Christian to avoid one subject above all others: Cyrano's nose. Christian looks over at Cyrano and smiles at his ungainly nose. The others caution him again. One cadet takes the handkerchief from Christian's pocket and tucks it out of sight with a warning gesture.

Once again the men ask for the great story. As Cyrano comes down, the cadets draw up their stools, but clearly in view of all is Christian. He thinks this will be an excellent place to prove his bravery. Surely, so little a man could do no harm. Christian sits astride a heavy chair; hat cocked back on his head. A small package, with his name on it, rests beside him.

Cyrano starts to tell his story, describing the night scenery of fleecy clouds, sinking moon and ultimate darkness, until one could see no further than—

Christian breaks in and indicates his nose.

The men all rise slowly, some back away, leaving center of room clearly to Cyrano. Cyrano stops and looks at newcomer contemptuously. Asks a cadet who Christian is and cadet can only say he is a newcomer, arriving this morning. His name is—the cadet gets the package and shows name to Cyrano. The man of Roxane's affection! One whom he had promised to protect. Cyrano pales, and then, in husky voice, looks at crowd and resumes.

The men are amazed, when the stranger again comments by pulling his nose. The men again rise and are dumbfounded when Cyrano does not draw his deadly sword. Christian is smiling, rocking the heavy chair to and fro.

Once more, Cyrano, with constrained anger, begins. Christian pulls out his kerchief and blows his nose vigorously. Unable to stand more, Cyrano wheels upon the crowd and they scatter pell-mell. He orders them out,

Brevet and all. They go out expecting Christian to be cut to mincemeat. The last cadet closes the door slowly.

Cyrano and Christian remain, face to face, and look at each other for several seconds. Cyrano picks up the parcel and asks Christian if that be his name. Christian defiantly answers "Yes." So this is the young man of her affections!

Cyrano takes his hand off his sword and opens his arms. Christian rises and hesitates, but Cyrano insists and holds out his arms. One of the cadets peeks in, others appear at different exits, doubting their eyes. One laughs heartily and points to his nose. Cyrano, drops his arms from Christian, walks slowly toward the offender as he draws his long, keen blade. Again, there is a silence as of death, when—

CURTAIN

253. *The Girl of the Golden West*

The scene is laid in the Girl's cabin, late at night. The road agent, Ramerrez, known to the Girl as Johnson, has fallen in love with the Girl. When he learns she owns the Polka, he refuses to rob her saloon. His love is sincere and the Girl is happy with his presence.

Woukle, the attendant squaw, sees Johnson kiss the Girl, and leaves in disgust. The storm is increasing on the outside though the lovers are unaware. The fire burns cheerfully and plays fitfully on the bright red blankets hanging in front of the Girl's bunk and on the rough floor. The Girl snuggles closely to Johnson and they are content in their new found bliss. Johnson looks into her eyes and realizes he cannot go further with his love and decides to leave immediately. The Girl does not understand, but his sincere manner assures her, and he promises not to be gone long. He gets his hat and coat and opens the door. It is snowing.

The Girl gets up and closes the doors, goes to the

window and pulls back the curtain, wipes the frost from the windowpane, tries to peer out. Johnson goes up to her—he must leave Cloudy to-night. She won't hear of it. He can stay in her bed, she always sleeps on the floor in front of the fire on snowy nights, and it won't put her out at all.

Two shots are heard, in quick succession, as if coming from the foot of the mountain. Both look up. Johnson is most apprehensive. Goes to door and listens. More shots are heard, some of them closer. The Girl is preparing her bed in front of fire. Throws pillow on the big fur rug. Johnson puts his overcoat on and tells her he must go—if any one should come, they wouldn't understand. She goes near him, pulling him into a chair. She sits on the floor and leans against him. He tells her again of his undying love, but keeps looking furtively toward the door. The Girl drowses and he apologizes, kisses her good-night and they rise. She goes over to her bed and pulls some quilts from it, then throws them on the big fur rug. Johnson puts his coat and hat on the bed.

She puts a lighted candle on the hearth, blows out the lamps on the mantel, the stand and bureau. She climbs up on the table, turns down the hanging lamp, steps to floor, notices that she has turned it too low, glances at Johnson, making sure that he does not see her, gets up on table again, turns the wick higher, then goes into the wardrobe, where she makes her toilet for the night.

Johnson starts to go to bed, turns quickly, listens, then goes toward the bed—pauses—runs to the door and listens. His face is full of resolve. He is ready to meet any emergency. He goes behind the curtains of his bed.

A brief pause, with the night wind growing louder. The Girl comes out of her wardrobe, sits on floor and takes off her slippers and puts on moccasins, then rises and comes down to the fire, arranges the rugs and pillow, says a brief prayer, lies down and tucks herself in.

She remains there a minute as the fireglow lights up her face. She raises up on her arm, looks up at the curtains, sighs and lies down to sleep.

Suddenly a voice is heard to call and some one knocks on the door. The Girl rises and gets the candle on the table. Johnson throws open the bunk curtains and pulls his revolvers from his pockets.

The Girl goes to the window, Johnson urges caution, but remains near bed so as not to be seen. The knocking increases. She wants to let them in but he points to her night clothing. The knocking is louder, she motions Johnson back behind the curtains, as Jack Rance, the sheriff, calls. She knows Jack is very jealous of her.

She opens the door and the men enter—Rance first. He is wearing a luxurious fur overcoat, his trousers tucked into his high-heeled boots; he goes to the table, takes off his gloves and warms his hands over the candle. Sonora, wearing a buffalo overcoat, cap and ear muffs and high boots, comes down to the fireplace. Ashby, the government agent, follows with a lighted lantern. He has on two overcoats. Nick comes down to the Girl, then crosses to the fire. He has pieces of blanket tied around his legs and feet. Rance turns up the wick of the hanging lamp. All are snow covered. Sonora, going to fireplace, rubs his hands and stamps his feet.

The Girl asks them what is the matter. Rance looking around suspiciously, points to her thin attire, and the Girl indignantly picks up a rug from the floor, wraps it around her knees and sits. The wind rises and falls, crying in the cañons.

Rance produces a handbill and shows the picture of Ramerrez, with a reward of five thousand dollars on his head. She gives it little heed.

Nick spies Johnson's cigar, recognizes it as one of the rare Havanas which the Girl had given Johnson at the Polka. The Girl's eyes follow Nick's glance. Unseen by Rance, there is a glance between Nick and the Girl.

Nick puts the telltale cigar in his pocket, looking about to make sure that he is not seen.

Rance comes to Girl and sits on table. He shows her the handbill once more, and the Girl looks at it more carefully. She is still unconvinced, though the picture is a close likeness. Rance pulls out a picture taken from the notorious Nina Micheltorena and puts it by the side of the handbill picture. He indicates that the two are one and the same. The men verify his accusation. Rance shoves the picture of Johnson in front of the Girl and turns it over. She reads "To Nina with Love." To make the thrust more cutting, Rance produces a picture of the popular Nina and puts it between the two pictures of Ramerrez.

The Girl rises and laughs bitterly. She turns to Ashby and apologizes for vouching for Johnson. She picks up the Micheltorena picture and would tear it in two, but Rance intercedes and puts both pictures in his pocket. He leaves the handbill as a souvenir of her dance with Johnson. She shows she is tired and sleepy and Sonora suggests they all leave. Pretending unconcern, she bids them all good-night. Ashby follows Sonora, then Rance, and last, Nick, out of the door. Nick asks her if he should stay, but she thanks him, and he goes out.

She bolts the door and stands with her back against it, her eyes blazing.

Johnson appears from behind the curtains of the bed. He goes toward her but she stops him. He comes closer and tries to explain. She looks out into distant space. A sudden revulsion of feeling, as she wipes her mouth. Again he tries to explain, but she points to the handbill. He walks over to the table, looks at the reward notice, turns to her, and nods his head in admittance. He would say more to her, that he loved and intended to play straight from the moment he kissed her. It is the kiss she can't forgive—Nina Micheltorena! She doesn't care if they kill him.

He takes out a pistol, but not much caring whether he lives or dies, looks at his pistol, then puts it back in his holster and goes out empty handed—his head bowed.

She goes to the door and closes it, walks to the table, looks at the handbill and tears it into bits. Her resentment toward him rises with each thought of his duplicity.

A shot rings out, close to the door. With a bravado toss of the head, she is glad they have got him. Johnson falls against the door outside. They have shot him—heaven forgive her, she does love him! She rushes to the door, opens it, and he staggers in. Her arms are around him to help him. He leans against the wall. The Girl closes the door. Johnson is holding his right side. He motions her not to lock the door; he is going out again. As he swings around, lurches and nearly falls, the Girl pushes him into a chair. He tries to rise. The Girl holds him close to her and kisses him. She loves him despite all.

There is a rap on the window. Rance is peering through but he cannot see Johnson. The Girl looks around for a hiding place; seeing the loft, she gets a chair and stands on it, pulls the ladder down, and urges Johnson to hide. At first he refuses, but hearing a rap on the door, he gets up. His handkerchief is pressed to his side. He staggers and she helps him. Another rap at the door. She gives Johnson a push and with an effort he climbs the ladder. She urges him up, telling him she loves him.

He reaches the loft, collapses, falling on his knees. He lies on the floor of the loft. She cautions him to be quiet. He draws the handkerchief out of sight. The Girl is now at the door, sure that Johnson is unseen.

She opens the door and Jack Rance appears. He slams the door behind him. She wants to know what he is after. Rance cocks his revolver and looks about the room. He is certain that Johnson is there. She denies having seen him, but Rance stops her and listens. The wind is howling. After a slight pause, Rance comes down to the table, he uncocks his revolver and puts it in his holster. The Girl is leaning against the bureau. He takes off his hat, shakes the water from it and drops it on the table. His eyes never leave her face. He goes to fireplace, shaking his coat and looking about. She tells him to go ahead and search the place, but never to speak to her again, since he doubts her word. He can search and leave.

Rance starts to put on his coat, but changes his mind. Throws his coat down on the floor and advances toward her. She looks at him, but he comes close to her, puts his arms about her and kisses her. She struggles to escape from him and picking up the bottle from the table, raises to strike him, then sinks to the floor, sobbing. Rance stands looking at her, his vanity is badly hurt. Takes up his hat and starts to put it on. His coat is on his left arm. The Girl rubs her hands on her dress and comes reluctantly toward him. He hopes she will forgive him, and offers his hand to her in friendship.

As he holds out his hand, a drop of blood from the loft falls on it. Slowly, after a pause, he holds out his hand for the Girl to see. Pulls out his handkerchief and wipes off his hand. Looks at blood. She says it was a scratch but Jack denies that. As he holds out his hand again, more blood falls on it. Rance looks toward the loft. Pulls out his pistol and puts his handkerchief in his pocket. The Girl grabs his hand, he brushes her aside and draws down the ladder. She tries to stop him, but Rance has found his man.

Rance orders Johnson down. Johnson moves to ladder and stops. Rance gives another imperative command, revolver in hand, leveled at his rival. Step by step Johnson comes down the ladder, his eyes fastened on Rance. His hands are held in the air, but slowly fall as he reaches the bottom steps, and with unseeing eyes, he lurches to the chair behind the table, falls forward, his head resting on the table, unconscious, in the half shadow. Rance puts his revolver in his holster.

The Girl pleads with Rance for Johnson, but Rance laughs derisively. She picks up her own pistol and points it directly at Rance. He laughs at first, but sobers with the earnestness of her look. Having got his undivided attention, she tosses her pistol back in the drawer. She moves quickly to him and tells him she will play him a game of straight poker. If she wins Johnson is hers, but if he wins he takes Johnson and her too. He is good enough gambler to take the chance!

He looks for a chair, gets one and brings it to the table. He pulls off the table cover and throws it on the floor. She asks him for his word of honor and offers her hand on the bargain. He shakes her hand, but when she starts to withdraw it, he holds it. He would pull her to him again, but she draws away from him. She tells him to fix the lamp. Rance, his eyes still on her, does not find it at first, then looks up, sees it and turns the wick. She goes into the shadow of the wardrobe.

Rance takes a deck of cards from his pocket and sits at table shuffling them. The Girl comes from the wardrobe, blows out the candle, and tosses Rance a new deck. He looks at her, bows and takes his cards off the table. She sits opposite him and takes her cards. He shuffles and asks her if she is ready. She tells him to go on. She cuts and he deals. The best two out of three will win! He glances at his cards, she at hers. Rance produces King high; the Girl does likewise. Rance shows a Jack next, and she produces a Queen. One for her! Now she shuffles and deals. They look at cards. He has a pair of aces. She shows her cards—nothing. They are even. After he has dealt the next hand he reaches across, places his hand over hers and the cards. He thinks he is the winner. He spreads his cards out before him, still holding her hand and looking at her. Then, he looks at his cards, she is looking at his cards too. When he sees them he smiles, sure of his victory. The Girl collapses with a shudder. He leans forward, very calmly, as he pushes cards in front of her. He throws his cards face down on the table, as she tells him she is fainting. She asks him to get her some water. He looks around, finds the bottle, but where is the glass? As he turns away toward the cupboard, she puts her cards in the bosom of her dress and draws five other cards from her stocking. Tells him to Hurry! Hurry! He drops the bottle, turns and leans forward as if to possess her, his arm around her shoulder. He is triumphant in supposed victory, thinking she was fainting because she had lost.

The Girl rises, laying down her hand on the table. A glorious light is in her eyes as she looks at Rance. Three aces and a pair!

He looks at her. There is a slight pause. He bows, bitterly but with politeness. Always the gambler, he picks up his hat and coat and leaves the room, slowly.

The Girl drops the cards to table, after Rance has gone, and takes Johnson in her arms.

CURTAIN

254. *The King's Henchman*

A Devonshire forest at Halloween. It is in the days of the early Anglo-Saxon. The moon penetrates a foggy clearing. Æthelwold, handsome and fearless in war, timid in love, enters and calls for Maccus, who stumbles in. Maccus is a clumsy clown type of early English period. They are lost. They look around to find what hospitality this particular spot may offer. They have but little food to eat, bread, cheese and ale, which Maccus unravels from a cumbersome wallet. Æthelwold is tired and would lie down. He munches his crust in the moonlight as Maccus looks at the empty wallet. Maccus thinks it best to look about for their party. Cautioned not to go far, he leaves.

Æthelwold, on the moss, is soon asleep. A faint light is seen moving in the mist. Soon Ælfrida, a beautiful young girl of seventeen, enters. She is followed by a heavy waiting servant, Ase, who carries a torch. They have reached the place where they are to try the magic spell of Halloween. Ase indicates this is best place for a girl to see a lover and starts to go, when Ælfrida, frightened, calls her back. Reassuring her, Ase gives her the torch and stumbles out.

The girl must be alone to work the charm. She looks at the moon, counts a magic number, looks over her left shoulder as she sings her song and awaits the vision of her lover-to-be. The fog momentarily lifts and the moonbeams fall flush upon Æthelwold. Ælfrida, at first, wants to scream, believing she saw an apparition. She passes her hands over her face and looks again. A breathing man! She almost drops the torch in preparation for flight, but curiosity, and the possibility of the charm's efficacy, hold her spellbound. She looks around for Ase, but sees no sign of the departed nurse. The young girl carries the torch over to Æthelwold to better see his face. He *is* handsome. She leans over him—touches him and waits. Growing more bold Ælfrida kisses the sleeping man on his brow. He talks in his sleep and sends her scurrying to the edge of the clearing. Her long skirts swish past and he sits up, heavy-eyed, sword ready. He challenges the trembling apparition and she comes into the open, ready for flight. He rises slowly and she is too frightened to move. He touches her garment and then her cheek. Could such beauty be real? He does not hurt her, but is very tender. He, too, trembles at the beauty before him. He drops his sword and she lets the torch slide from her hands and rest against the log. With growing assurance he steps close to her. It is love at first sight, each doubting the existence of the other. Emboldened, he takes her in his arms and she lifts her face to his. They stand in close embrace, for interminable seconds, and when they sit upon the moss, her head drops upon his breast. They fear to break the exquisite spell. She kisses him to reassure herself of his reality. Ase calls, and Ælfrida looks up, startled. She must be gone! The torch! The spell!

CURTAIN

255. *Lady Windermere's Fan*

Lady Windermere, dressed for a party, has come to the luxurious bachelor apartments of Lord Darlington. By her manner, we know the experience is her first. She is anxiously awaiting the arrival of either of two men, her husband, to whom she had addressed a letter, telling him she was leaving because of the Erlynne woman, or Lord Darlington, who had offered his love but a short time since. She stands by the fireplace, slowly removes her cloak and impatiently tosses it onto the sofa. She taps her hand with the beautiful fan, gift of her husband, as she becomes more and more anxious. She walks across the room. Stops and peers out of the window at center, which opens back of a heavy curtain. She looks out upon the street, but sees only the fog and the blurred lights. She stands between the curtains in nervous doubt. In a moment, she goes over to sofa and sits, looking into the glow of the fire. With a sudden resolution, she drops her fan on the sofa and rises to put on her coat. She will return home perhaps— Starts, as the door at left slowly opens.

A mature lady, beautifully dressed, looks in cautiously, sees Lady Windermere and rushes toward her. Lady Windermere recoils at her approach. Mrs. Erlynne (the mother of Lady Windermere, whom she had deserted as a tiny babe, and has remained incognito to her always) pleads with her to leave immediately, that she is mistaken in her opinion of Lord Windermere. Lady Windermere wants to know how Mrs. Erlynne learned she was to be found in Lord Darlington's room. Mrs. Erlynne hesitates in telling. Lady Windermere makes it very plain that she does not, now, intend to leave. Takes her coat and throws it on the sofa, and sits down in defiance. In desperation Mrs. Erlynne draws out the letter she had found and shows it to Lady Windermere. Surprised and angry, the younger woman advances to Mrs. Erlynne, demanding that she be told how Mrs. Erlynne had come by the letter. Mrs. Erlynne pleads with her to leave before it is too late. The mother tears up the letter and puts it in the fireplace and tries to coax the younger woman to go. Lady Windermere sits and cries quietly; Mrs. Erlynne moves as if to embrace her but refrains, instead she picks up the coat and offers to help put it on. Lady Windermere begins to doubt less the sincerity of the other, and accepts the help with the coat. She accepts the sincerity of the intruder and that there has been a misunderstanding between them, that Lord Windermere is true to his wife.

They are about to leave, when men's voices are heard in the hallway. In desperation, Lady Windermere turns to Mrs. Erlynne and thinks it is a plot to trap her, but Mrs. Erlynne shoves her back to the curtain, telling her to leave through the windows, if possible. Mrs. Erlynne looks around and sees bedroom door at left and runs into that room, closing door carefully.

Five men enter. Lord Darlington, Lord Windermere, Lord Augustus, Cecil and Mr. Dumby. They must make themselves comfortable about the room. They have been turned out from the club at two o'clock. They help themselves to the brandy and Lord Darlington, excusing himself, sits at side table to write a hurried letter. All chide him about his love affairs. Dumby is lolling in a big chair, the heavy Augustus and Windermere sit at table center. Cecil is on the sofa. Dumby and Cecil are guying Lord Augustus for his affection for Mrs. Erlynne, when Windermere intercedes for him.

Cecil begins laughing and he asks Lord Augustus to come to him. As Augustus approaches, Cecil points to the fan on the sofa. Both men laugh heartily and begin to look around the room, toward the doorways.

Lord Windermere rises, and goes to Lord Darlington to bid him good-night. Cecil calls Lord Windermere to him and points ominously to the bedroom. Smiling, Lord Windermere comes to the sofa and sees the fan in Cecil's hand. Hardly able to believe his eyes, he seizes the fan and stands transfixed. He stares at it as if it were a charmed token of evil power. All the men look at him, as he imperatively calls Darlington. Lord Windermere wants an explanation and shows Darlington the fan. He is surprised and cannot explain how it came there.

Windermere starts to go toward the bedroom when Darlington steps in front of him and bars the way. The curtain moves and is seen by Lord Windermere. He strides toward the covered windows as the bedroom door vigorously opens and Mrs. Erlynne enters. They all turn at the sound, and are surprised to see her. She is the only one, seemingly, at ease. She comes over to Windermere and takes the fan from him, stating she must have taken it by mistake. Lord Darlington is both astonished and angry. Windermere looks at her in utter contempt. The others smile knowingly at Darlington and Mrs. Erlynne. Lord Windermere strides to the curtains, opens them! There is no one there!

CURTAIN

256. Richelieu

The scene is laid in the Gardens of the Louvre, in Paris, in the 1640's.

François, the faithful page of Richelieu, is searching for Mauprat. He wants the packet which Mauprat has, containing valuable state information and incriminating evidence against certain conspirators.

Mauprat, angered to a fighting mien, enters hurriedly, looking for the archconspirator, Baradas. He does not recognize François, who goes up to him immediately, and asks for the packet. But Mauprat is concerned solely with his search for Baradas. François implores Mauprat for the packet, as Baradas enters. Mauprat immediately draws and bids François to do likewise. François intercedes and asks Mauprat to leave Baradas to Richelieu. Brushing François aside, Mauprat challenges Baradas and makes at him. Baradas defends himself as François warns Mauprat of the approach of the King and his attendants.

The King is astonished to see fighting in his Gardens and inquires the meaning of such an affront. He asks if laws have died with Richelieu. He believes the Cardinal to be dead.

Baradas tells the King he fought in self-defense and tells the King his assailant is Mauprat. Baradas gives the command to have Mauprat seized and disarmed. The guards seize Mauprat. He makes a futile struggle with the guards as the young King looks on.

The gates open and Richelieu, pale, with eyes flashing, and in his Cardinal's robes, enters. He is followed by his faithful Capuchin, Joseph. Baradas is consternated, and the King amazed, that the dead should come to life. Louis dislikes the report of a mock death.

Mauprat breaks from the guards and kneels at the feet of Richelieu. Baradas and Orléans prompt the King in his demands upon Richelieu. Joseph stands near his master, despairing of any ultimate good. Richelieu puts his hand upon the head of Mauprat and accuses Baradas of treason. Richelieu pardons Mauprat, as one of the bravest soldiers in France. The King, urged on, countermands the pardon and tells the guards to do their duty. Richelieu once more intercedes and tells the King he has pardoned Mauprat. The King becomes angered and commands the guards to comply. They jerk Mauprat to his feet but Richelieu asks him to go, to spare them further humiliation. As Mauprat is leaving he tells François who has the dispatch. The guards and Mauprat leave as Richelieu stands in growing heat.

Richelieu breaks through the crowding conspirators and stands in regal splendor before the King. Louis asks the meaning of his being here when reported dead. Richelieu tells of the attempted assassination; he points out Baradas, Orléans and the others, but the King will listen no further and despite solicitations from Richelieu, sweeps out of the Gardens, followed by his train, all save Baradas.

Richelieu goes slowly up to Baradas and offers his hand in congratulations. Baradas trembles as he takes the Cardinal's hand, as Richelieu names Baradas as his successor. Baradas sees the sarcasm of the gesture and leaves in a great huff. Richelieu stands, watching the conspirator off, then turns with head toward heaven, and slowly walks in the opposite direction, the faithful Joseph close at hand.

CURTAIN

SCENES FROM SHAKESPEARE

The greatest genius of the dramatic world is William Shakespeare. This statement is so universally accepted that it is worth any student's attention.

In the sixty-one scenes which follow, there has been no attempt to pick out the best acting scene of each play, though this has been done more consistently than at first seemed possible. In finding the scenes to present the greatest number of acting problems, it is not at all odd that they should generally contain the greatest element of drama, action. Accompanying these actions, we are conscious of emotional motivation or presence. But few of Shakespeare's best scenes depended upon conversation. Though most of the great speeches are said in the quietness of soliloquy, they are the direct expression of some great dramatic situation. When we find Shakespeare giving his pearls of wisdom, we find him preparing an audience for didactic reception. Polonius' advice to Laertes, Hamlet's instruction to the players, and Portia's mercy speech are examples of such preparation. The soliloquies were consistently emotional outbursts.

Actors who would present Shakespeare adequately and intelligently, must have trained bodies for emotional expression and beautiful diction for vocal interpretation.

The text used is the William G. Clark and W. Aldis Wright Globe Edition, with Gollancz notes, as published by the Stokes Company of New York in 1911. We are not here concerned with questions of scholarship involved in the text, but more with the desire to present scenes from a good, complete edition in a single inexpensive volume.

For purpose of ready reference, the alphabetical order of play titles has been used. They are marked comedy (C), tragedy (T), or drama (D) in a general classification. The main purpose for the study and presentation of each scene is briefly noted.

It is hoped that the mere reading of these scenes will whet the appetite to read and understand Shakespeare in his entirety. More great actors and actresses have come from the ranks of Shakespearean rôles than from any other source.

One is not dramatically educated if he does not know Shakespeare.

257. "All's Well That Ends Well" (C)

Act IV, Scene 1 (pp. 330-331). Florence.

Broad comedy, wherein a French Lord seizes the loquacious Parolles, has him blindfolded by the men who come from ambush. The jargon spoken by the soldiers affords good fun, following the outspoken wishes of the would-be soldier. Confronted by danger, Parolles would willingly sell information of his camp to obtain liberty or mercy. Mock seriousness and pseudo-fear.

258. *"Antony and Cleopatra"* (*T*)

Act II, Scene 3 (pp. 1143-1144). Rome.

Antony bids "goodnight" to Cæsar and Octavia, telling Octavia that his future conduct will be better. To appear at ease in Rome and yearn for love in Alexandria befalls the lot of many men—but with Antony this conflict parallels the soothsayer's prediction of Cæsar's ultimate dominance. Yearning underlying diplomacy.

259. *"Antony and Cleopatra"* (*T*)

Act II, Scene 5 (pp. 1144-1146). Alexandria.

Cleopatra hears of Antony's marriage. From the joy of ecstatic love to the pangs of hysteric jealousy. In this scene, we see Cleopatra in the height of passion, a veritable tigress of unbridled fury. The hapless Messenger and the solicitous Charmian but contrast her rage. A great display of violent jealousy.

260. *"Antony and Cleopatra"* (*T*)

Act III, Scene 3 (p. 1151). Alexandria.

The Messenger has returned from Rome, having seen Octavia. The vanity of Cleopatra is paid by the experienced Messenger, who has learned from his last report to Cleopatra. One sees as she wishes, and servants readily comply. By the questions of his mistress, the Messenger describes Octavia, and leaves the Egyptian queen in a happier mood. Vanity appeased with simple flattery.

261. *"As You Like It"* (*C*)

Act III, Scene 3 (pp. 264-266). The Forest of Arden. Start where ROSALIND *and* ORLANDO *talk together, as exit* JAQUES. ROSALIND: *"I will speak to him" to the end of scene.*

A happy bit of fun with the lovesick Orlando talking unknowingly to the girl of his affections. Another type of vanity, in that Rosalind joys in the love she is hearing expressed by the man who tells for his own gratification. Orlando's misery is his chief source of enjoyment. Contrasting loves with but one common desire.

262. "Comedy of Errors" (C)

Act I, Scene 2 (pp. 114-116). Ephesus. Mistaking of the DROMIOS *by* ANTIPHOLUS *of Syracuse.*

Antipholus knows he has given Dromio some money, but Dromio of Ephesus appears, instead of Dromio of Syracuse. The twin motif was very common to Elizabethan drama and is one of the best comedy vehicles for mistaken identity. (Twin sister and brother in "Twelfth Night.") In this scene, each is disconcerted by actions of the other. Humor through incongruity and discomfort of others. Stress of situation laid upon the servant.

263. "Comedy of Errors" (C)

Act IV, Scene 1 (pp. 123-125). Ephesus.

Antipholus of Ephesus is being harassed by Angelo and an officer for a payment for a chain. Antipholus is certain Dromio has taken the money for same, as Dromio of Syracuse enters. Another scene of comedy wherein we laugh at discomfiture of others, with stress of situation laid upon the master.

264. "Coriolanus" (T)

Act III, Scene 1 (pp. 827-832). A street in Rome.

Coriolanus escapes the violence of the mob. He is met by Brutus and Sicinius and others. He is reprimanded for disapproving of the giving of corn to the commoners. The defiance of the mob by Coriolanus and the augmenting of the crowd by Brutus and Sicinius, the fighting against odds, the pleading of Menenius for fair play—these are elements of real drama and give ample practice for proper timing, exit and group entrance. Tyranny and militant patriotism.

265. "Cymbeline" (C)

Act II, Scenes 2 and 3 (pp. 1184-1186). Britain, Imogen's apartments.

Posthumus, husband of Imogen, has been exiled by Cymbeline. Despite the wishes of Cloten and the King, Imogen remains true to her spouse.

As Imogen sleeps, Iachimo comes from a trunk and intimately watches the beautiful wife. He takes a bracelet from her wrist and observes a five-pointed mole upon her breast; evidence enough to convince a doubting listener. A book turned down, adds further to his designs. Later Cloten is spurned in his suit and is told by Imogen that her husband's meanest garment is dearer to her. Cloten leaves to revenge.

Constancy besieged by all the wiles of scheming designers. Imogen is one of the truest and sweetest women in all literature.

266. "Hamlet" (T)

Act III, Scene 2 (pp. 1028-1032). Denmark.

Hamlet has just spoken his great soliloquy "To be or not to be" in scene previous. In this, he instructs the players with one of greatest speeches in literature—one to be memorized and understood by every person presuming public appearance. Hamlet asks Horatio to observe the King while the dumb show is being presented. The King and Queen with their train enter: the players present their rehearsed pantomime, that of a King having poison poured in his ear and the widow accepting the love of the murderer. The genius of this greatest of plays is found in this scene. What conflict of emotions! Love, revenge, remorse, hate, pity, fear, anger, each struggling for supremacy.

267. "Hamlet" (T)

Act III, Scene 4 (pp. 1033-1036).

Polonius prepares the Queen for the coming of her son, and hides behind the curtain. In a quarrel with his mother, Polonius, stirring behind the curtain, is killed by Hamlet who thought he had killed the King. The mother must bear the scathing denunciation of her revengeful son. The Ghost appears and urges clemency for the Mother Queen. Powerful fate sweeps all souls to their destinies. Quintessence of the Greek drama reliving in Elizabethan form.

268. "Julius Cæsar" (T)

Act III, Scene 1 (pp. 961-963). Rome. Beginning of scene to entrance of TREBONIUS.

The conspirators and friends of Cæsar have met, on the ides of March. They press upon him for various favors, ever getting closer. Cæsar asks them to go with him to the Capitol and leave the street. Trebonius leads Antony from the scene and the conspirators, led by Casca, kill the great leader.

Group scene for study of stage rhythm, leading to a great climax, wherein the principals draw down our dislike, though we cannot help but sympathize with Brutus.

269. "Julius Cæsar" (T)

Act IV, Scene 3 (pp. 973-974). Brutus's tent. Start when BRUTUS *is alone.*

The famous quarrel scene between Brutus and Cassius has just ended. Both Brutus and his faithful Lucius struggle against sleep. Alone, Brutus would read but is interrupted by the Ghost of Cæsar, who warns Brutus of the fields of Philippi.

The awakening of Lucius, and of the two guards, gives this scene a beautiful reality. The drowsy Brutus awakes to a consciousness of a fearful anxiety. "Brutus" has been ruined many times, by this short scene. He is never the coward.

270. "The First Part of Henry the Fourth" (C.D.)

Act II, Scene 2 (pp. 478-479). England.

Falstaff robs some travelers and is, in turn, robbed by Prince Hal and Poins. This scene gives a fair idea of the famous Falstaff, pseudo-warrior and happy heavy-weight. Buffoonery and seriousness both contend in this group scene. Falstaff was one of the characters Queen Elizabeth most enjoyed. Happy, healthy humor must dominate.

271. "The Second Part of Henry the Fourth" (C.D.)

Act II, Scene 1 (pp. 511-513). England.

In this play we have Snare and Fang, of the law, Shallow and Silence, country justices, and such recruits as Mouldy, Shadow, Wart, Feeble and Bullcalf. And the biggest rogue, good-fellow and ne'er-do-well is Falstaff. Falstaff owes money to the landlady and comes upon the scene with his mate-in-mischief, Bardolph.

Good homespun comedy of rascal freedom. Boisterous but artistic; buffoonery but obedient to laws of good comedy.

272. "Henry the Fifth" (C.D.)

Act V, Scene 2 (pp. 573-577). England.

Prince Hal has now become King Henry the Fifth. He is in France to meet the Princess Katharine. A great pageant scene, wherein we see the meeting of the English and French notables. The wooing of Katharine, who speaks in broken English, is a pleasant bit of dramaturgy, in itself. One of the first attempts to portray French dialect in English literature.

Contrast of large groups to intimate dialogue.

273. *"The First Part of Henry the Sixth"* (*T*)

Act I, Scene 2 (*pp. 580-582*). *France, before Orléans.*

Joan of Arc (La Pucelle) is brought before Reignier. The French are beaten back in battle, with great loss. In desperation Reignier agrees to see Joan La Pucelle. To prove her valor, Charles bids her to combat. With her blessed sword she overcomes Charles and he is convinced. The Dauphin, Charles, agrees with Joan, to hold Orléans at all costs.

The militant saint convinces by physical power and spiritual dominance; a combination demanding more than a passing study for proper technic. She is always the lady.

274. *"The Second Part of Henry the Sixth"* (*T*)

Act IV, Scene 7 (*pp. 641-642*).

The rebellious Jack Cade is chief interest of the play. With his rabble army, he defied authority until he became a danger to British peace. Falstaff has served purpose through three plays, and Henry now has other worries. With the British love of pageantry and the growing interest in national power, with the great Armada a matter of history, England is eager for martial scenes and patriotic exhibitions. Cade served such a purpose.

The fickle mob sways from one leader to another. Popularity dependent upon paid privileges soon fails and reacts against the unwise leader. Group ensemble with focus of interest passing to different sources.

275. *"The Third Part of Henry the Sixth"* (*T*)

Act V, Scene 5 (*pp. 683-684*). *Battlefield in England.*

The last play with King Henry (he appears as corpse in "Richard the Third") and the ascendency of Edward. Gloucester stabs Henry, who knows, at last, the part Gloucester has played in his life.

Again we have the historical pageant play, enjoyed by

the Anglo-Saxon. This war scene is typical of so much of the Elizabethan drama. The murder of the young Prince would not pass muster to-day, but those battle times lent different views. We note the tenderness Shakespeare always showed toward his women; in this scene, no harm must come to Queen Margaret. Ambition, with malice and avarice, defy integrity and filial devotion.

276. "Henry the Eighth" (T)

Act I, Scene 2 (pp. 735-738). England.

The great Wolsey and his servant, Cromwell, are names to conjure with in English history. The problems of government are at present not so deeply concerned with France. Local affairs take more attention. Cranmer and the loyal Wolsey weigh heavy upon Henry's ambitions. His wife and queen, Katherine, must be divorced so as to prepare for Ann Bullen. The affairs of State have always been intimately interwoven with the reign of Church.

Katherine enters the Council chamber to plead for the people in redress for excessive taxation. A surveyor is shown in and in a very excellent speech of logical presentation, falsely charges Buckingham with treason.

Malice and revenge reaching willing ears, triumph over honesty and loyalty. One of the best speeches in classic literature.

277. "Henry the Eighth" (T)

Act III, Scene 2 (pp. 754-757).

The loyal Wolsey is rebuked by the King and is left alone. He looks at letter given him by the King and discovers that it is his letter to the Pope. He knows his power is soon to be diminished.

Norfolk and Suffolk, with others, enter and tell the Cardinal he is to render up his seal and confine himself until further orders. The grand old fighter repudiates each charge against him, as we learn the many errors he committed for the good of his King. His parting with Cromwell is one of the great scenes of literature.

A great man crushed by the power of his own loyalty. Bitter disappointment in life's illusions. Anguish of soul for ingratitude, rather than the burden of his sins.

278. "The Life and Death of King John" (T)

Act IV, Scene 1 (pp. 423-425). England.

The hapless King John offers a character for stage portrayal too eccentric to appeal to most actors. France has sent ambassadors demanding that John abdicate his throne and possessions. The Queen mother advises John in all his deeds, though is seldom thanked by her son.

Arthur, Duke of Bretagne and nephew of King John, is possible deterrent to John's peace and power, and is a prisoner in a castle. In this scene, Hubert has been sent to bind the unsuspecting Arthur, by order of the King. The young Frenchman talks glibly to his awaiting executioner, expressing a wish that Hubert had been his father. Each word but tends to weaken the kindly Hubert. By signal, attendants arrive and would bind Arthur. His fortitude denies them the obligation, and the executioners gladly retire. As the iron cools, Hubert finally resolves to save Arthur and plans for his escape

Loyalty to sovereign, conflicting with love of the young prince; an agony of choice, with the present affection dominating.

279. "King Lear" (T)

Act I, Scene 4 (pp. 1059-1062). Britain.

In this play, we have the importunate King, his three daughters, each unlike the other, the noble Kent and the wise Fool.

In this scene, we see the loyal Kent disguised, ready to befriend his testy King. The King accepts him on probation. The Fool entertains in best court fashion until the arrival of Goneril. She promptly shows her disrespect for her father and the angered King leaves to go for his "respecting" daughter, Regan.

A character challenging the best of actors—Lear has defeated many of the ambitious. Impatient, touchy, and radical, but demanding loyalty and respect.

280. *"King Lear"* (*T*)

Act III, Scene 2 (pp. 1072-1073).

One of the great scenes of the realistic Shakespeare. The raging Lear fits well into the seething unrest of the elements. The very fury of the storm carries Lear's denunciation of his two ungrateful daughters to torrential heights. Kent's arrival is a striking contrast in character. The turbulent Lear denouncing ingratitude—the loving Kent thinking in terms of protection for his tottering King.

A scene of consistency with character and environment.

281. *"King Richard the Second"* (*T*)

Act II, Scene 1 (pp. 444-447). Wales. From beginning to exeunt KING *and* QUEEN.

John of Gaunt renounces King Richard, and York pleads for his reprisal.

The dying Gaunt wishes to counsel the King, ere he dies. The royal couple arrive and listen to Gaunt's admonition. Though the speeches are long, they are crowded with thought. Plots and counterplots, charges and countercharges abound. Choice phrasing runs all through the lines.

A physically weakened character rises to a vehement denunciation.

282. *"King Richard the Third"* (*T*)

Act I, Scene 3 (pp. 692-696). England.

The powerful Margaret vents vindictive ire upon Gloucester, later Richard the Third.

Queen Elizabeth is lamenting the prospective rupture

with Gloucester and his following. The malformed Duke enters and immediately challenges all present as to their friendships. He meets his match in the vigorous Margaret, bitter in her accusations.

A large ensemble in which most are principals and receive individual attention at some time during scene.

283. "King Richard the Third"

Act V, Scene 3 (pp. 726-729). Take to exit of RICHARD *and* RATCLIFFE.

A succession of ghosts appear to Richard.

A good scene for staging, in the production of the weird vision of dead souls, as they appear to the very real, frightened Richard. Nine ghosts is enough for any evening, and the staging easily could lead to rank burlesque, instead of its somber, serious nature. Fearing no soldier, the misshapen Richard was easy prey to the supernatural.

284. "Love's Labour's Lost" (C)

Act I, Scene 1 (pp. 166-167). Navarre. Start where DULL *and* COSTARD *enter and give the letter to the* KING. *Take to the end of the scene.*

Costard and Dull, Armado and Moth furnish most of the fun in this, Shakespeare's first play. In this scene, the King reads a letter, which is furnished to the detriment of Costard, though little to his discomfiture.

Broad comedy with comic eccentrics, in contrast to the regal and polite.

285. "Macbeth" (T)

Act I, Scene 3 (pp. 980-982). Scotland. The well-known witch scene.

Banquo and Macbeth arrive upon the heath, after we are prepared by the three weird sisters for their coming. This is an excellent example of Shakespeare's manner of dramatic preparation. The Witches give their prophetic tellings and disappear. All the play is forecast in the remainder of this scene. How fast ambition grows! When Angus and Ross tell Macbeth that he is Thane of Cawdor, all preparation for a great play is complete. A play or scene is no greater than its foundation.

286. "Macbeth" (T)

Act II, Scene 1 (pp. 985-986).

The dagger soliloquy with its pantomime of fantastical illusion.

Night effects are ever best for the supernatural, and Shakespeare was not unmindful of any opportunity to use same to best advantage. Banquo and Fleance have just left Macbeth, when his thoughts bear him to such an impelling motivation as seeing a dagger.

Troubled conscience debating between resolution and deed.

287. "Macbeth" (T)

Act V, Scene 1 (pp. 1002-1003). Lady Macbeth's sleep-walking scene.

A mind, burdened with many secrets of horrible consequence, slowly breaking down into segments of greatest impressions. Her share in the murder of the King is the theme thread of all her rambling thoughts.

The doctor and nurse are important parts in the scene, but they must be entirely subsidiary to Lady Macbeth. Again, the atmosphere of the night.

Anguish, suspense, bravery, horror—all fight for recognition in her distracted mind. A galaxy of dramatic emotions encompassed in a few brief moments.

288. "Measure for Measure" (C)

Act II, Scene 4 (pp. 105-106). Vienna.

Isabella pleads with Angelo for her brother's freedom. This scene is an example of the balancing measure used by Shakespeare to offset the common touch he gave to his comedians. Isabella is one of the most virtuous of girls put into a very questionable setting. The Duke of the play is one of nature's noblemen.

Indignation and honesty rise to defeat power and temptation.

289. "The Merchant of Venice" (C)

Act II, Scene 2 (pp. 226-227). Venice. Beginning of scene to exit of GOBBO *and* LAUNCELOT GOBBO.

The blind father is treated none too kindly by his lively son, Gobbo, who is always ready for fun and mischief, and any means of avoiding work. The anxious Launcelot Gobbo finds his son and together they go apace.

Comedy of situation, aided by two eccentrics of Elizabethan mien. Innocent fun aids in developing the plot.

290. "The Merchant of Venice" (C)

Act II, Scene 7 (pp. 230-231). Belmont. The PRINCE OF MOROCCO *chooses.*

The three "choosing" scenes of this play offer rich opportunity in pantomime.

The gallant Moroccan ponders before each casket, and, with hopes of winning the beautiful Portia, chooses the golden container. Grieved and chagrined, he and his expectant train make a hasty exit.

Portia has already won our hearts and confided in Nerissa the man of her choice, though bound by the will of her father. Suspense is dominant in these casket scenes, as we have been properly prepared for such a setting. Bassanio chooses much later in the play (*Act III, Scene 2*).

291. "The Merchant of Venice" (C)

Act IV, Scene 1 (pp. 240-245). Venice.

A realistic court scene; challenges the realism of to-day's murder play. Wonderful character delineation, dramatic moments holding with intense interest; mercy, revenge, avarice, compassion, exultation, and bitter defeat all striving for importance. Shylock and Portia, the principals, with their race hatreds, the theatric scales and knife—all elements of one of the world's greatest dramatic scenes. The gamut of emotion exposition.

292. "A Midsummer-Night's Dream" (*C*)

Act I, Scene 2 (pp. 199-200). Athens. The favorite Player's Scene.

A rollicking comedy, wherein Quince gives Bottom and his companions their parts for the play of Pyramus and Thisbe.

Broad comedy at its best.

293. "A Midsummer-Night's Dream" (*C*)

Act II, Scene 2 (pp. 203-204). Woods near Athens.

The antics of Puck with the sleeping Lysander and Hermia.

In this scene Titania and her train of fairies, Oberon with his mischief, the tired lovers seeking rest in the cool shade, the capricious Puck, the coming of Demetrius and Helena—Helena to be loved by the waking Lysander; such stuff as dreams and love are made of, fill this fanciful scene and give it the genius of the glorious pastoral.

Dainty, airy, graceful motion in dramatic setting.

294. "Much Ado about Nothing" (*C*)

Act II, Scene 1 (pp. 141-143) Messina.

Start: Don Pedro: *"Look, here she comes," to the end of the scene.*

Benedick is telling Don Pedro what he thinks of Beatrice, when the lady and three others arrive. Benedick makes his exit conspicuous, to better tell Beatrice of his "affections" for her.

In this, we see a loving couple, Hero and Leonato,

agreeing to parental wish, and Benedick and Beatrice, who vehemently deny any interest in the subject of matrimony.

Contrast in the technic of making love.

295. "Othello" (T)

Act III, Scene 3 (pp. 1110-1113). Venice. From beginning of the act to point where IAGO *obtains the handkerchief from* AMELIA.

The crux of the drama is found in this scene, with major characters present. Cassio asks Desdemona's aid in reinstatement with Othello, and Iago fastens on him the means of arousing Othello's jealousy to Desdemona's doom.

The building up of an emotion to a bursting point—built upon a common property (in this case, a handkerchief).

296. "Pericles" (C)

Act II, Scene 4 (p. 1223). Antioch.

The Prince of Tyre, Pericles, solves the riddle of King Antiochus and claims the hand of the King's daughter. Pericles is exiled.

In this scene, we have the old Chorus in Gower, who is interrupted by the dumb show—Pericles and his train—continue his story as the show passes on. The old English as spoken by Gower is interesting as a study in word forms.

297. "Romeo and Juliet" (T)

Act II, Scene 2 (pp. 892-894). The famous Balcony scene.

The beauty of language, as well as the romantic setting involved, make this an intriguing bit for every actor and actress.

The rhyming lines in Shakespeare invariably told the audience the scene was finished—such rhymes took the place of curtains.

Romantic love in appropriate setting—our interest is equal in both characters.

298. "Romeo and Juliet" (*T*)

Act V, Scene 2 (pp. 915-919). The Capulet tomb.

Death of Romeo and Juliet. To make death seem real, to accumulate logical incidents that intensify sorrow, the partial atonement of these deaths in the ending of the feud —these are grand moments for noble drama. The tragedy of the lovers' deaths must not be overshadowed by the jointure of peace consummated between the Montagues and the Capulets.

299. "The Taming of the Shrew" (*C*)

Act II, Scene 1 (pp. 290-291). Padua. Start: PETRUCHIO: *"Good morrow, Kate, for that's your name, I hear," and end scene with,* PETRUCHIO: *"I must and will have Katherine to my wife."*

A lively love scene, boisterous in outward manners, but Petruchio is always the gentleman. Vigorous lines in action, each positive in speech. Stage balance is well presented in this scene.

300. "The Tempest" (*C*)

Act II, Scene 2 (pp. 15-17). An uninhabited island.

On the enchanted island, Caliban and Ariel converse. The invisible Ariel causes trouble with his ethereal body and active tongue. As Caliban plots against his master with Stefano and Trinculo, Ariel leads all astray in their opinions of each other.

Eccentrics in unnatural setting—the grotesque made to appear natural.

301. "Timon of Athens" (*T*)

Act II, Scene 2 (pp. 927-930). Athens.

The great friend, Timon, suddenly pressed for funds, calls upon his friends and is deserted in his great time of need. Those whom he befriended most are the first to desert him.

Assurance in the faith of man slowly broken as each avenue of succor fails him. Love slowly changed to bitterness.

302. "Titus Andronicus" (T)

Act II, Scene 3 (pp. 859-862). Forest near Rome.

Aaron hides his gold in the forest and Tamora finds him. In this scene Bassianus is killed and Lavina is abducted, Quintus and Chiron fall into a pit. And this is the least murderous scene of the bloody play. Its chief value—a typical, gory play of Elizabethan fire and old style acting.

303. "Troilus and Cressida" (C)

Act I, Scene 2 (pp. 773-774). Troy. Start: PANDARUS: *"Here, here, here is an excellent place," to the end of the scene.*

This play is written about the greatest story in all literature. In this scene, we have the elaborate pageant of characters as they parade past the observer. Each passer-by represents his type as recorded in the story and art legends of Helen of Troy.

304. "Twelfth Night" (C)

Act I, Scene 3 (pp. 344-345). Illyria. SIR TOBY, MARIA, *and* AGUECHEEK *discuss* LADY OLIVIA.

Two rollicking characters are Toby and Sir Andrew Aguecheek, types which held the boards for over two centuries, and not entirely gone. Word abuses and puns were more frequent then than at present.

Fun for fun's sake, with situation consistent.

305. "Twelfth Night" (C)

Act II, Scene 5 (pp. 353-356). MALVOLIO *discovers his sudden affection for his mistress,* OLIVIA.

In Malvolio we have one of drama's best conceits, and the three mischiefs play one of drama's most delightful pranks.

Comedy of character abetted by comedy of situation.

306. "The Two Gentlemen of Verona" (*C*)

Act II, Scene 4 (*pp. 35-36*). *Milan.*

The two gentlemen, Valentine and Proteus, discover they love the same lady.

A situation scene, wherein each lover adds zest to the ardor of his rival. Climatic in the intellectual rather than in the physical.

307. "The Winter's Tale" (*C*)

Act IV, Scene 3 (*pp. 388-389*). *Bohemia. Start with* POLIXENES: *"Oh, father, you'll know more of that hereafter." To his speech, "As thou art tender to it."*

A jolly beggar picks the pocket of a helping clown. This scene used to call for hearty laughter; we now but smile on such. Thieving to amuse us must reach into greater figures for to-day's audiences. We are no longer petty with our laughter.

A clever business scene.

SUGGESTIONS AND QUESTIONS

1. What is meant by the terms "modern" and "classic" as applied to drama? Whom do we consider as the first of the moderns, in point of time? importance?
2. Compare the following characters: Old English, Old Man Minick, Peter Grimm, and Dick in "Yellow Sands." Also compare Mila ("The Daughter of Jorio"), Du Barry, Gioconda, Mrs. Erlynne in "Lady Windermere's Fan," and Mrs. Warren in Shaw's play.
3. What is meant by a "situation" play? Name five situation scenes from the plays in this chapter.
4. Discuss five scenes of this group in which character is more important than situation or plot.

5. Discuss three scenes in which "suspense" is dominant dramatic element.
6. Which characters furnish the best comedy: Hein ("The Concert"), Cyrano de Bergerac, François Villon ("If I Were King"), Peale ("It Pays to Advertise"), Pike ("Man from Home"), Aubrey ("The Show Off"), or Finley ("Three Wise Fools").
7. Analyze the carriage and walk of any five characters from scenes in this group of plays.
8. Explain the difference between "dramatic" and "theatric" and verify from Belasco plays.
9. Which is the best acting scene, the prologue of "Escape" or the first act in "The Great Divide." Develop fully.
10. Explain "sentimentalism," and give possible relation to following: Daniel Gilchrist ("The Fool"), John Ferguson, and Wolsey ("Henry the Eighth").
11. What are major differences between modern and classic plays? Develop by appropriate examples.
12. How do these dramatists develop character in their plays: Shakespeare, Ibsen, and O'Neill?
13. Whose women offer greater interest to present-day audiences—Shakespeare's or Ibsen's? Why?
14. What chiefly determines the fact that men predominate in numbers in most of the great plays?
15. Apart from sex relations, what important parts do women have in great drama? Verify.
16. Is vice dramatized more than virtue? If so, what is the reason? Would you change this? Does this affect technic of acting? How?
17. Do scenes suggested from plays in this chapter prove or disprove that the elements of drama are: action, contention, suspense, characterization, and dialogue? Which are the most essential? Prove conclusion by appropriate examples.

CHAPTER XIII

COMMEDIA DELL'ARTE

FOR centuries, improvisations were the chief source of comedy for European audiences. The art has almost disappeared from our boards. Certainly, great acting can result from spontaneity, especially when the actors are trained. Occasionally, we see real *commédia* in the smaller towns of Italy and Austria, and even in Mexico. But in England and the United States, the art is almost dead. Ireland partially revived the art at the Abbey Theatre, where the actors go about the stage as they please, with no determined stage directions. The director fixes the stage deportment from the responses of his actors. Real *commédia* calls for impromptu conversation, as well as acting. The actors are given a situation from some one in the audience, and act and talk until the audience is satisfied or disgusted. To take a situation, evolve real comedy, and bring it to a successful conclusion, was the height of acting and was royally rewarded. Out of such stuff came Harlequin and Hanswurst, Clown and Pantaloon, Scapin and Scaramouche. These types subsequently became traditional, but they started in pure improvisations.

Great benefit can be derived in class room dramatics by reviving this quick-thinking art. Thirty situations follow, which are but suggestive as to its scope and possibilities.

The audience calls out the situation, after the actors have taken the stage. The audience determines when the actors should conclude.

Situations for Commédia dell'Arte

1. Two men and a woman take the stage. Director or audience calls out, "You receive your lover, tell him your husband has gone for a week, sit on his lap, as husband unexpectedly opens door. Follow through." (For the benefit of those who have never seen the real *commédia,* this situation can last two minutes, or it may extend a half hour. Proper *dénouement* is important. The husband may be jealous and direct his remarks entirely to the lover, while the wife tries to interpose—the husband may get a gun and debate with lover and wife which one he should kill, finally being convinced he should shoot himself—the lover may turn on his mistress and denounce her as a shameless woman, try to convince husband he has saved his honor and knew the husband would return and learn real nature of wife—the husband may take the situation as a joke, assign all bills and documents to the lover as he bids surprised couple adieu—the lover may admit his love, challenge the husband to a duel—or, *ad infinitum!* None knows what the other will do or say next, and "me mother wit" is severely taxed. When the husband enters, depends upon actions and conversation of lovers. Inasmuch as audience determines and adjudicates *commédia dell'arte,* it has another virtue, that of combining interests of actor and audience in an integral unit!

2. Two elopers. They have just come from stairway, apparently safe. They take one embrace, each grabs a suitcase as father enters front door. (Talking is done all through pantomime and talking with action is carried on until a successful conclusion is reached.)

3. Cashier is given thousand dollars to put in bank. She is held up by her brother, immediately after treasurer leaves.

4. Two young ladies are in river swimming, a tramp comes to tree and lies down for siesta. His feet, un-

knowingly rest on girls' clothes. (Don't take this literally or too realistically—representation is quite sufficient. The tramp *could* be gallant.)

5. Judge is passing sentence on criminal. Broken-down woman runs up to judge, hands him picture, points to criminal, and faints. Follow through.

6. Three girls are dining. Winter. Coffee tastes peculiar. One of guests finds small bottle on floor, marked "arsenic." All look at hostess. Follow through.

7. Girl has two callers. Each man is determined to be last present. Mother enters. Follow through.

8. The serenade. A spurned lover has climbed to the balcony of his beloved. He has just tapped on the window when the town constable passes. Follow through.

9. Husband and wife are golfing as Sweet Young Thing comes up with caddie. The last drive has torn the trousers of the flirtatious husband. The caddie reports the issue to the friendly wife. Follow through.

10. The Johnny Boy is proposing, as they sit on the park bench. He is winning, chiefly by his display of wealth, present and potential. The process-server hovers over him, within the protection of a nearby lilac bush. Follow through.

11. The renowned artist is about to play at the home musicale of Mrs. Newly Rich. Miss Fluffy Clothes, the daughter, dashes in the room, dragging her newly acquired admirer. They are collegiate. The artist's presence is a mere incident. Follow through.

12. Two old cronies are fishing. One has fallen asleep and the mustachioed fellow is reading Izaak Walton. The sleeper gets a bite, Mustachio pulls up fish and puts it in his own basket, casts quickly as game warden coughs. Follow through.

13. Isobel has put on stockings and dress of elder sister Janice. Janice goes into bedroom. A family quarrel, with blows, is imminent. Mother enters as little brother escorts Isobel's caller into parlor beyond. Little

brother informs the household of the evening arrival. Follow through.

14. Father hangs a picture, with mother as guide and director. Brother and sister come in to further direct. Mrs. Snoop talks through the window. Follow through.

15. Father is coming home very wobbly. The family of four have a hurried consultation as the earner of bread ambles up the pathway. Son hurries out; returns to living room with ginger ale bottles for each of family. Father is greeted, a moment later, by a supposedly drunken orgy. Follow through.

16. The lawyer for the Old Woman's Rest has called the twenty inmates into the office-parlor. Aunt Het, recently dead, has left a will. They all comment among themselves as to her worth. Lawyer reads will—each is given a small fortune. Follow through.

17. They have come to be married. Both are over sixty. Minister is reluctant at first, but, hearing their story, consents to a ceremony. He has misplaced his Bible and wife can't find it. A dictionary is brought as substitute, using only sober words. Follow through.

18. Detective has come suddenly on four Negroes in Peglar's Pool Hall. They are discussing the races. Detective tells them they are under arrest, shows a piece of paper, and hurriedly puts it back in pocket. Lines men up and begins searching. Bugs is nervous and tries to hide something. The Dick is looking for diamonds. Bugs is trying to get rid of some loaded dice, not knowing detective's mission. Follow through.

19. Annette is entertaining Jimmy at her first meal. Young Bobby flavors all of Jimmy's edibles variously with salt, pepper, paprika, sugar or vinegar while Annette is receiving Jimmy in the hallway. Mother comes in and joins them at their repast, as Bobby leaves for play. Follow through.

20. An entomologist is obliged to fill a hand of bridge. He sees a very rare specimen of "cootie" on the hostess'

shoulder ribbon. He is dummy. Game progresses to his deal, and he has not yet gotten his find. Follow through.

21. A gallant of Spain has placed a burning love letter in the fan of his English hoped-for. He places fan in usual resting place of his beauty, awaiting her return from the dance. The folded fan is inconspicuous, but the Countess finds it and toys with it. The Countess affects Juan of Spain. As girl comes up, Countess opens fan and letter falls out. Follow through.

22. Toby Pickwick goes to his room in the hotel. It is moderately late. Turns on lights, puts coat and hat in closet, comes into room and looks for suitcase. Finds one near bed containing lady's clothes. Goes to telephone as—his divorced wife enters from the bath. Follow through.

23. A couple stand before a lawyer, a mutual friend. They can't stand each other because he always wants butter on his toast and butter makes her sick. Two weeks of wedded life is sufficient for each! He won't give up his butter. Lawyer suggests that the wife go to her mother's place in the country, as the mother enters to make out her will. Follow through.

24. Father tells son their "fortune" is a thing of the past. The son's marriage could be only possible panacea. Marriage to whom? Father points out approaching demoiselle and urges son to save the family. As father goes out, a very eccentric, though young, old-maid enters conservatory. Son is game, and proceeds. Working fast, he surprises maid who is about to succumb as father returns. The wrong girl! Miss Eccentric is merely a serving maid! Follow through.

25. A masquerade is in progress. A couple is on the veranda, each trying to guess the other's identity. The third party, Mephistopheles, joins them and wishes to take away the lady. Robin Hood is reluctant. As Mephistopheles kisses shoulder of his Guinevere, Robin Hood resents. Follow through.

26. Piers is courting his country cousin. The geese pass by as Hans, the husband, is whistling in yard. Piers is clapped under a clothes basket, as Hans sits on it to take off shoes. Follow through.

27. A handsome youth is receiving a wallet of bank notes for a document. Solicitor is eager. Youth's father enters. Questions presence of solicitor. Sees signature on document. A forgery. Follow through.

28. Pygmalion has fashioned his statue in most modernistic manner. His statue is his very life. Wife comes to studio and does not understand the oddity nor the husband. In adulation and hope Pygmalion wishes that the statue could live. It does! Follow through.

29. Old Gentleman reports to the police that he has been robbed of his purse. Names prospective culprits. Two are sent for, across street. They are questioned. Purse is found by one of accused, in Old Gent's umbrella. Follow through.

30. Prima donna is standing before audience and pianist is waiting. Blackmailer comes to side stage and smiles malignantly. Singer turns and sees her Nemesis. Follow through.

The above thirty situations are but indicative of the genius of the *commédia.* To get two or more people on the stage or in a room and have them make all conversation and respond to each other in each new situation, is the essence of "naturalness" in acting. The Romans were most adept in this and can be studied with profit, though little remains of the actual work done. Improvisations were not recorded. Their newness and unawareness is chief value for developing actor's confidence, quick thinking, and unaffected responses. The trained actor is easily detected in such presentations, and the amateur is often surprised with his own invention. The audience should be judge as to the merit or demerit of each enactment.

Any study which leads to spontaneity and freedom in

an art, within the bounds of beauty, law and reason, can do naught but improve the artist and ennoble the art.

Review and Questions

1. Name the chief characters of *commèdia dell'arte* and the functions of each.
2. What mental faculties are developed by improvising? What is chief talent necessary for a good actor?
3. How can *commèdia* encourage acting spontaneity?
4. What virtues are there in *commèdia* which benefit the audience?
5. Write three brief plot situations and develop at least half a dozen conclusions for each.
6. Write a plot situation and put three different sets of characters to same brief plot. Note variations of unfoldment and climax. What principle of drama is shown by this?
7. Which of the situations in this chapter of *commèdia* offers the best comedy situations? Why?
8. Who are good improvisers on American stage to-day? Why do we see so little of this art? Would it aid acting in America?
9. What are possible dangers from overindulgence of improvising on the stage?
10. As one becomes adept in *commèdia dell'arte,* which usually dominates: gesture or words? Develop.

INDEX OF CHARACTERS

The numbers refer to pantomime numbers.

Index of Characters

Index of Characters

Index of Characters

INDEX OF EMOTIONS

Italicized figures refer to pages; other figures refer to pantomimes.

NOTE: It will be obvious that there has been no attempt to catalogue all the emotions which are contained in the pantomimes of this volume. There is sufficient reference to emotions to aid in their recognition and portrayal. It is evident that anger, crying, laughter, surprise, and suspense all vary in as many ways as there are emotions. Such examples have been designated as will manifest these variations. Many emotions are but gradations of greater or more elemental expressions.

Index of Emotions

Index of Emotions

Index of Emotions

INDEX OF PANTOMIMES

The numbers refer to pantomime numbers.

Index of Pantomimes

Index of Pantomimes

INDEX OF SUBJECTS

NOTE: *Indexes of Character, Emotions, and Index to Pantomimes Supplement This Index.*

Index of Subjects

Index of Subjects